INDIA'S STRATEGIES FOR INFORMATION WAR & CYBER DETERRENCE

INDIA'S STRATEGIES FOR INFORMATION WAR & CYBER DETERRENCE

ASHOK PATHAK

Vitasta
LET KNOWLEDGE SPREAD

Vivekananda International Foundation

Published by
Renu Kaul Verma
Vitasta Publishing Pvt Ltd
2/15, Ansari Road, Daryaganj
New Delhi-110 002
info@vitastapublishing.com

ISBN 978-93-86473-87-5

First Edition 2020
Second Reprint 2022

MRP ₹995

Cover and layout by Somesh Kumar Mishra
Printed by Chaman Enterprises

Dedicated to my Parents

With gratitude to Vivekananda International Foundation and the selfless scholars who work for national security

The goal of Information War is to achieve political objectives through skillful use of knowledge; if this fails then escalate the conflict in a manner so as to achieve a better and sustained state of peace with minimum casualty to own people and property as also to those of the adversary.

Contents

Foreword

THE NATURE of warfare has been evolving constantly in the light of the emergence of new technologies. Advances in ICT, sensors technologies, cloud computing, big data analytics, artificial intelligence, machine learning, blockchains, drones, and cyber security have revolutionized the way wars of future will be fought. Social media has emerged as a major arena for spreading disinformation and controlling narratives. Today's warfare is defined as 'Information Warfare' (IW). The term itself is imprecise and it includes many dimensions of warfare such as psychological, space, cyber, and economic warfare and the revolution in military affairs. The non-military dimensions of warfare are as important as the military dimension. Different countries have different views on what constitutes IW. In India, we have yet to evolve suitable IW doctrines and strategies.

Brigadier Ashok Pathak (Retired), in his book *India's Strategies for Information War and Cyber Deterrence,* deconstructs the concept of information warfare and examines its application in the Indian context. The book tries to identify what India's strategies should be to meet the challenge of information warfare. The author notes that information warfare is a 'continuous struggle within and between the nations at political, economic, perception, cyberspace, and military levels to gain the position of advantage'. It involves the 'dynamics of international trade, foreign policy manoeuvres, shifting international alliances'. Preparing for information warfare will require a comprehensive 'all-of-society' approach. The author emphasizes that to meet the IW challenge; the nations will have to draw strength from their self-belief, internal harmony, resilience of the people, as well as the economic strength and decision-making capability of its leadership. A holistic approach will be needed to make effective strategy for fighting the information war. The book has a number of useful suggestions for the Indian policy makers.

Major countries have been discussing and developing the concept of IW for several decades. We need a similar debate in India. India is a late starter. Brigadier Pathak, who is himself an Army veteran with vast experience in the Corps of Signals in the Indian Army, is well qualified to write about IW strategies for India. The VIF is happy to publish this book, which will hopefully generate a healthy debate on the subject.

December 2019 **Dr Arvind Gupta**
New Delhi Director, VIF

Preface

IN 1991, the use of a new phrase 'Information War' (IW) turned 'viral' (as per the social media lexicon). The war in Iraq (1991) was called as the First IW. The phrase stood for a new form of war linked with the stunning victory of the US-led coalition forces over Iraq. Every other military term or activity either got influenced or got encompassed in the IW glossary. Those who took serious note of this phenomenon included matured nations such as Russia and China.

Then the World Trade Center (WTC) attack happened in 2001 on 9 September. The Second Iraq War of 2003 followed. For some reasons the '2003' war with Iraq was not called the Second IW. After quick capitulation of the Iraqi war machine and Saddam's execution, American involvement in Iraq, Syria, and Afghanistan cast a lengthy shadow in time spanning almost a decade. By 2005 or so, Americans stopped using IW in their military discussions and writings. However, some of the central concepts such as interoperability, synergy, combined arms, and multiservices teams, and so on got embedded in the new doctrines brought out by the US Department of Defence.

Meanwhile, military literature emanating from major military powers especially the US (US War College, Department of Defence, RAND organization), China, Russia, as also India was full of various descriptions and prescriptions on IW. There is no consensus on the details though every source of this literature agrees that the environment, dynamics, and dialectics of conflicts within and between nations have gone through irreversible change. Even after three decades of its emergence, we realize that IW is still evolving. Nevertheless, there is one common thread in this evolution. IW is much more than war as we knew so far. It is not confined to the battlefields known to the armed forces of nations. It is a continuous struggle within and in between the nations at political, economic, perception, cyberspace, and military levels to gain position of advantage as per the chosen goal. It is waged through the dynamics of international trade, foreign policy manoeuvres, shifting international alliances, state-sponsored terrorism, and proxy wars. It draws strength from the internal strength of the nations which includes the self-belief, internal harmony, well-being and resilience of the people, resoluteness and decision-making capability of leadership, and economic might. Nations continuously manoeuvre to get a better position of perceived advantage so that they can pursue their growth trajectory as per their perceived values and goals. In a state of equilibrium, the struggle generally is devoid of physical destruction and violence. However, once the equilibrium is disturbed, the escalation commences to more direct conflicts which may lead to physical destruction and violence. The goals, and hence the pathways for different countries are based on the way a country perceives herself and the adversary. This also establishes international relations and respective foreign policies.

Russians, Chinese, Israelis have different views on the subject of IW. It is not 'one-size-fits-all' case. It does mean different things to different nations. It is not a standard design as in the case of Gillette razors across the globe. It is more like fashion apparel for teenagers on the lines of Zara or Hennes & Mauritz (H&M). Very high level of customization and very fast rate of obsolescence. How do we design the customized model for India? This is the central theme of this study.

The theme may appear well defined but the domains of activities and knowledge that affect the theme are many and diverse. Hence, the readers need to be patient since some of the subjects may initially appear to be irrelevant—because generally a 'military-oriented' reader does not expect discussion on leadership, economy, political decision making, international relations in the context of IW. Nevertheless, the global information environment and the networked world bring all these disciplines within the ambit of conflicts amongst nations including in the IW spectrum.

Since the subject emerged as a result of a major war fought by the US-led coalition forces, the first part of the study deals with close scrutiny of the evolution and proliferation of IW among some select militarily active nations. Thus evolution of IW through an American experience, building up and operationalization post Iraq wars, proliferation of IW ideas in other nations and in India form the first four issues of part one.

The driving force behind IW has been dramatic advances in information and communication technologies, Internet. Consequently, cyberspace became the most critical arena for continuous conflicts amongst states as also societies. Thus, cyber war became an integral part of any conflict involving nations or non-state actors. Hence, the second part of the study deals with the knowledge and technologies relevant to modern wars or IW. We discuss cyber war, information security, artificial intelligence, communication, and big data in the context of IW. I have made a very conscious effort to avoid technical jargons and technicalities without diluting the essence of the subject. Considering the range and depth of technologies as also managerial practices essential for IW, a separate study is required to address the subject. To facilitate discussion on a common platform, important words and phrases have been defined and explained in the glossary at the end. Similarly, for the benefit of the readers, important references containing critical facts or data are given in the relevant text itself. Besides, endnotes also contain the references for the study. A large number of abbreviations have been used. Though the conventional practice of giving the expanded version of the abbreviated word or phrase has been followed, a list of abbreviations and their expanded forms are given—after the glossary—in order of their occurrence just to cater for some omissions and help the readers.

IW has also been referred to as 'third wave war'. These are wars in the information age distinct from those in the agricultural and industrial age societies. Hence, it became essential to have a look at relevant theories of the first and the second wave wars—practiced by the agricultural and industrial age societies. Thereafter, check the epistemology of IW to derive relevant conclusions on the differences between the earlier wars and the third wave wars. Thus, the third part of the study deals with important theories of first and second wave wars and critically examines the epistemology of third wave war (IW).

During the study, I noticed that in the unfolding of events in different countries that were scanned, political and military leaderships played very important roles. Similar situations, with similar clues were addressed differently by different sets of leaders. Generally, the value systems, geopolitical ambitions and posturing, as also prevailing culture made huge differences in leadership decisions both politically and militarily. Thus, the nature and speed of decision making affected the performances of nations in peace and war. Hence, before coming to the final issue of India's strategies diplomacy, coercive powers of some select nations, performance of India's political and military leadership was addressed.

Finally, coming to the aspects of India's strategy. Considering a wide range of understanding (or at times lack of understanding) of what is meant by 'strategy', there is a need to elaborate the approach adopted in this book. There is a tendency to go by the dictionary meaning of the word, which defines strategy as 'a plan of action designed to achieve a long-term or overall aim'. Another approach is to provide a military touch to the word whereby strategy means 'the art of planning and directing overall military operations and movements in a war or battle'. Both these dictionary meanings or definitions do not meet our requirement. These descriptions do not answer the question 'why'. Thus, why do you want that long-term aim to be achieved? What tells you to have that 'aim'? In case of the second description in the context of war the most relevant question in IW is why are you fighting that war? What end state are you looking for as a nation? Because war has always been a national affair and not limited to military manoeuvres.

Why does a nation go to war? The literature and events during the past several decades clearly link wars among nations due to their respective perceptions of threat to their ideology or their value system. The core ideology as also reaction to particular situations emanate from a nation's self-image—what their people think of their global positions or geopolitical posture. It may also be the perspective of prominent leadership in position of authority. Ideally, the leader's perspective or vision should be shared by the people at large—at least in democracies. It is this self-image that decides how nations act in a given situation. This also is the starting point of strategy—the core ideology and the purpose of existence shared by the widest range of people forming that nation (ideally). Everything else follows. While developing strategies, identifying the core is the most important and critical job. Once the core is identified, the remaining components are vision, mission, goals, objectives, policies, and rules. The core is fixed as long as the nation exists. The degree of flexibility increases as we move away from core to vision and so on. The most flexible components are the rules. Rules must never force change in policy or goals or vision.

In the context of IW, perceptions within and outside the national boundaries are subject to constant sharing of information at societal and individual levels. In the global information sphere, control over the flow and form of this information has become impossible.

If through this work, we are able to contribute in building up an edifice of India's national security then the credit goes to some of the most dedicated and intellectually endowed people who guided me through this project. I am extremely grateful to General Gautam Banerjee of VIF who encouraged me to undertake this project. He elaborated to me the critical need to formulate an approach map specific to India's needs. My sincere thanks to Shri Arvind Gupta, Director VIF who patiently heard me during my numerous presentations and made me present the case to the research guidance team of the VIF. It is his patience and nudge which got me on a meaningful course. The research team made my task challenging and enjoyable as I discovered new ideas. General Sawhney of the VIF has been generous in his support and encouragement during the course of this study. I am grateful to General D Kumar, Chairman Task force for preparing the guidelines of structuring India's Cyber Power. His deep understanding of the subject and clarity of approach enabled me to continue in the right direction. He found time to read and analyse my drafts twice and gave me very insightful and valuable guidance.

During my study I approached a number of organizations and experts—Army Training Command (Shimla), Signal Officer in Chief, Army War College, Jawaharlal Nehru University (JNU), Bharat Karnad (of India Policy Group) and General Prakash Katoch for idea engineering as also for being the sounding board to test my study. I am grateful to General Prakash Katoch who spared time for going through the questionnaire and then spent more than an hour giving his expert advice on the issues that I raised. His thoughts have been included in the study. I realized that the subject must be very keenly studied and debated in the non-military academic institutes also. I tried my best to interact with academicians whom I knew. Here also my success rate was very low. Dr Nisha Kant Ojha was very kind in contributing to the study through discussions and feedbacks. His contribution was very valuable since he is actively involved in consulting and training activities with Diplomatic Mission as a Principal Advisor (Information & Technology), India. He is also Eminent Faculty with Para Military Forces in India in the field of Cyber Security & Counter Terrorism. His hands-on experience on working with the Russians (Ural Federal University) and the Chinese as part of India's ITU representative has been very valuable.

Introduction to Information War

Need, Relevance of Issues and their Linkages with Developing Strategies

Warfare is the domain of the entire nation. Restricting it to matters military can lead to serious threat to the existence of the nation

Introduction

ALMOST THREE DECADES after the phrase IW came up on the RADAR of Indian think tanks and military organizations, any effort to add something to the existing knowledge on the subject will look redundant. But, there are some compelling reasons. First, the IW concept—gifted by the Americans to the rest of the world—was based on an irrational and highly lopsided model. Nevertheless, it spread too fast and too wide. Obviously, by the time the dust settled on the battlefield, the originators themselves realized the fallacy of this theory. The Americans dropped the term in their military literature post 2005. Second reason, which needs to encourage studies like this is the fact that we as a nation have unwittingly got entrapped in the mental frame of 'disciplined followers'. 'If it is from the West the idea must be great'. 'If the idea or achievement is unique to India it is a reflection of a closed mind trapped in some bizarre glorification of the "great" ancient history of India.' For a very large section of our elite, Indian history starts from 1947 when the British gave this country everything good that we have today. This elite also thinks that India has always been a fragmented society integrated into a geographical entity by the British!

Thirdly, in the specific case of IW, our current thought process and action plans reflect the models which the Americans moved away from almost a decade ago. We talk of battlefield transparency (Westmoreland coined it in 1969 during the Vietnam War) whereas the real life situation clearly indicates enhanced 'fog of war' in the information age characterized by information overload. We think that technology has changed the combat ecosystem; the Americans have realized that leadership, cognitive abilities of troops, loneliness, psychological effects on the soldiers are as relevant today as these were during the last great wars. We think that we won all our wars except the one in 1962 since we killed more enemy soldiers, captured more territory, and destroyed more tanks/guns etc. Contrary to this thought process our ancient sages as also the current thinking on victory and defeat in wars is not based on the above calculus. It was very evident to Kautilya—as the current military thinkers have realized—that complete victory in any war is illusory. The measure of a successful war is the type and length of peaceful coexistence of the warring factions after the war is over. Thus, the journey is from peace to war and better state of peace. Hence, good leaders avoid war as far as possible. But, when they fight they make sure that culmination of war achieves better state of peace. In all this, the nature of war has not changed a bit. Yes, we have new tools and means to achieve the same goals.

Fourthly, the most widespread and regressive tendency in our approach is to yearn for same types of force structures, weapon mixes, tactics and objectives pursued by the Americans. In the bargain, we tend to forget the basic differences in being 'India' and aping America or at times China. India cannot be and should not be either a clone of America or China.

Fifthly, in our enthusiasm to look at modern military technologies (mostly of American and Western origin) with awe and admiration, we tend to believe that military technology ensures (almost) victory in war in spite of substantial data to the contrary. There are numerous cases where armies with vastly superior military technologies have lost—and lost badly.

Finally, there is a widespread belief that increasing defence spending (many authors quote some percentage of GDP) and adopting other transactional approaches pertaining to military personnel ensures national security.

This belief holds in spite of glaring evidence refuting this hypothesis. Nations with disproportionately large military budgets and most highly paid and powerful Armed Forces placed their national security in jeopardy due to reckless use of military power. The most dangerous situations emanate from excessive control of the military or arms lobbies over the national leadership.

Hence, this humble effort to initiate a debate to think in the Indian context, based on Indian value systems, oriented towards achieving our lofty goals centred around the well-being of an average Indian citizen.

Thus the aim of this study is: *To develop India's strategies for IW in the overall envelop of national security.*

Though IW as we know it today is derived from the American experience and related writings, our emphasis will be to see those experiences and writings through the prism of Indian realities both in terms of strategic context and national security environment.

The approach in addressing the core issues of developing strategies as also drawing the rubric of modern warfare is very different to generic discussions on IW. It is quite possible that readers who are accustomed to discuss IW as affairs specific to the Armed Forces with moral support of the nation may find some parts of the study difficult to link together. To remove this difficulty, it will be relevant to draw a brief rubric of war for the purpose of this study and then outline the process adopted for developing strategies.

War is an affair of the entire nation (not only of the Armed Forces) between two countries or groups of countries under very close gaze of international organizations established for maintaining peace (hence there will be acute pressure for avoidance and hence quick termination). This international pressure is inversely proportional to the political and economic might of the nation as also the strength of character of the national leadership. Countries like Vietnam and Israel may not be economic or military biggies but they have great capability to ignore international pressure when their national security or pride is at stake. For China, the US, and Russia, international pressure is just a phrase.

The reasons or trigger for overt war could be disturbance of regional or global balance of power or offensive expression of radical value systems (religious belief/confusion that governments are illegitimate if they do not follow a particular faith or system) or domination of political/economic systems. It can also trigger from a superpower's aspirations and resultant ambition to dominate the affairs of the world. Thus the full spectrum of war includes the existing stage of equilibrium, political, economic and foreign policy related measures to gain a better stage failing which overt war (mostly undeclared) along with all other means perceived to be effective to achieve the set goals, termination of conflict, negotiations, and efforts to sustain the revised state. Now a brief discussion on the process for developing strategies that we have adopted.

Strategy at National Level

The dictionary meaning of strategy as we have seen earlier, 'a plan of action designed to achieve a long-term or overall aim,' or 'the art of planning and directing overall military operations and movements in a war or battle,' will not serve our purpose. This definition does not answer the question, 'why'. Why have that aim? or Why start the war? Also in some discussion, it is suggested that first formulate the policy and then plan strategy to achieve the policy. This approach is inherently wrong since policy cannot be formulated in a vacuum. Academically speaking policy comes much later—after the vision, mission, goals, objective—then the policy to achieve these and rules for the functional level. We may look at the academic frameworks that are taught in business schools.

Strategy in the context of corporate environment is taught in business schools. This includes these definitions/explanations:

- Mintzberg's five Ps (Plan, Ploy, Pattern, Position, and Perspective) based strategic approach.
- The general definition of strategy as art and science of formulating, implementing, and evaluating cross-functional decisions that enable an organization to achieve its objective.
- Michael Porter's approach of strategy as 'positioning' or his generic strategies of cost leadership, focus, and differentiation.

None of these fit our purpose since IW as we have seen is not a routine business. It is much bigger in scope and impact. Harvard Business Review (HBR) magazine *On Strategy* in one of their papers describes strategy as a function of ideology, vision, and lofty goals. This approach is broad based and can serve as a model for our purpose because national strategies are not just some means and policies for resource allocation or for growth or any of the popular headline numbers. Strategies for a nation encompass a much bigger domain in terms of time, space, complexity, quantum, and type of efforts that are required.

There are some elementary, though academic, aspects that are relevant here:

- The starting point of strategy as per the above paper is core ideology. Ideology has two distinct components. First, the enduring core values, and the second is core purpose, which defines existential being of an organization; in our case 'being' of the nation.
- The vision and goals emanate from the core values and core purpose. While the core (values and purpose) remains

unchanged so long as the nation exists as an independent entity everything else can be changed to adapt to the changing environment.

How are core values and core purpose relevant in the context of IW? This form of war is about the capability and efficiency of taking decisions with available information. The decisions that a decision maker or set of decision makers in the country take depend on their value systems, what they think of their nation, their belief in their people and faith in their capabilities. The process of decision-making starts with a goal or objective.

The decision makers then go through the value chain of collecting data, converting the data into information and intelligence, selecting a course of action, implementing it and using the outcome to affect course correction in next decision cycle in the same domain. At each of the above activities the personality attribute emanating from the value systems and beliefs of the decision makers come into play. Look at the two sets of cases with regard to decision making at national level.

What prompted Israel to stand on her own and defeat the Arab nations decisively every time these nations threatened Israel's territorial integrity? What prompted China to challenge the might of nuclear powered US forces in 1951 in Korea within one year of establishment of People's Republic of China? Remember China had no nuclear weapons in 1951. What has been the root cause for Vietnam standing up to the might of French, US and the Chinese forces in the face of huge asymmetry in terms of number? What made Sony of Japan decide way back in 1950 to declare in their vision statement that they will develop products which will be the best in the world? Please recollect that Japan was a defeated and nearly destroyed nation in 1945. Within a couple of decades, the Japanese products—of not only Sony but also scores of other Japanese companies—were ruling the global market. Toyota, Honda and the like beat the likes of Ford Motors and a number of German carmakers in the Western markets besides at the global level. Japan did not protect her industries. They could not. It was not because of interest rates or cheap capital. It was because of the core values dear to the Japanese people.

On the other end of the spectrum why is it that almost all the Arab nations are struggling to be counted both militarily as also economically in spite of abundance of natural resources and a very bright past? Most of the Latin American countries continuously commit economic blunders. Mexico, bordering with the richest nation in the world, is famous for all the wrong parameters. Pakistan, bordering India, has not been able to embrace democracy in spite of living alongside the world's largest democracy.

In case of India also, the list of paradoxes is long. How is it that a country that produced some of the greatest warriors and that has a five-thousand-year-old world-renowned epic, Bhagwat Gita espousing the need to fight for a just cause without fear or ambiguity, has been found to be a soft state to be pushed around by internal and external forces inimical to her security? Why are many of our decisions when faced with external, internal or a deadly combination of these two threats governed by timid behaviour or weakness? Why is it that in spite of being a nation of entrepreneurs in the not too distant past we have floundered in economic policies and performance for more than five decades after independence whereas many nations that became independent around that time went past us by a long distance? Before we think of IW all this needs to change and change drastically.

Thus the starting point of IW in our context and even in the context of any nation is to know and share the unchangeable core comprising of the value system and the purpose of existence of the nation. Everything else is secondary to this edifice. How do we find the core? Jim Collins in his famous book *Good to Great* says, 'you do not find the core you discover it.' We can look at a brief example.

In 2016, I was participating in a strategy formulation meeting in a private university in Greater Noida (in North India). Obviously, the top echelon of the university—promoter, vice chancellor, and all the deans—were present. The question being discussed was, 'what should be our vision?' Somebody read out the vision statements of a few globally acclaimed educational institutions—Harvard, Stanford, MIT etc. I was little surprised since I had read the vision statement of the university displayed in very bold letters at the main entrance of the admission block. It was also on the website of the university. I asked the conference coordinator, 'Are we changing our vision?' I got a surprised look from every one. They asked me, 'What is our vision?' I said, 'It is displayed at the entrance.' I then read out the vision statement, which I had on my laptop.

The above case highlights some facts. There are two basic criteria for ideology and vision. First, you do not copy somebody else's ideology. It will not help. Second, if those responsible to operationalize the vision do not remember what the vision is (in spite of very bold and beautiful displays all over), it is as good as not having a vision.

This study involves suggestions to identify the core and setting the sights for a future based on the existing strengths and weaknesses. The latter (road map for achieving envisioned future driven by shared values and purpose for existence of nation) is based on seven pillars. These include people and the leadership, political economy, knowledge base technology and industrial infrastructure, internal security environment, Armed Forces, adaption to ICT, and lastly international relations.

With the above plot, the first two chapters scan the external environment which includes evolution and operationalization as also comparison with earlier theories, current knowledge base etc. Third and fourth chapters focus on the internal environment specific to India. The final chapter lays out the strategic aspects including brief discussion on values and vision followed by SWOT framework and approach map on the seven pillars mentioned above.

At the outset, I am extremely grateful to the eminent scholars who contributed their time and energy in reviewing the draft. When the initial draft of the study was being reviewed by the scholars at VIF, a number of reviewers raised questions pertaining to the relevance of some of the issues included in the study. These, relevance-related questions were related to inclusion of discussion on first and second wave wars, comprehensive national power, leadership, political decision making and political economy. A related comment by the reviewers pertained to linking up the discussion at several places with developing strategy.

Coming to the relevance part of this study, the relevance of each issue discussed in the five chapters is given below:-

Chapters 1 deals with the external environment scan for the purpose of identifying opportunities and threats:-

- Evolution of IW through an American Experience. Part of external environment scan for developing strategies as explained in the introduction.
- Building up and Operationalization Post Iraq Wars. Continuation of external environment scan for the purpose of implementation of strategies.
- Impact on China, Russia, Israel, Pakistan. Also part of external environment scan; links up implementation of concepts by different nations in accordance with their value system and self-beliefs.
- Analysis of Epistemology. The objective here to look at the events and theories critically to remove the theory blindness effect. In other words, there are many concepts propagated in the new theories, which are not supported by facts.
- Comparison with the first and second wave wars. This part waters down the newness in the IW concepts and theories. Even the Americans have now realized that the nature of war as also its purpose have remained unchanged. The only change has been in the means.
- Comparison with the concept of CNP. The need for including this part was to underscore that war is the domain

of the nation and not only a military matter. The entire might of the nation comes into play in a conflict—or it must come into play in an appropriate manner. The theory of CNP supports this view. However, the CNP theory is based on resources and numbers. Application of these numbers to real-life situation does not support the theory. Hence the need to include the art of using the resources or elements of CNP. This is where people and leadership count.

Chapter 2, Technology Base, Knowledge and IW discusses issues that are part of external environment scan pertaining to knowledge and technology:-

- AI, Communication and Big Data
- Cyberspace
- IW Defence
- Cyber Deterrent
- Cellular technologies and impact of 5G.

Chapter 3, Current IW Theories and Impact on India addresses the internal environment scan for bringing out strengths and weaknesses:-

- Literature review of think tank organizations and books/ articles written by Indian scholars on the subject to gauge the current trend and likely trajectory for India's IW doctrine.
- Some of India's Major Military Conflicts through the Prism of IW Theories. Part of internal environment scan to assess the behavioural and implementation aspects in military conflicts.
- Paradigm Shift in Myanmar, Uri and Balakot events in the backdrop of some major wars India fought in the past. This section is included to highlight the major changes in our approach to national security—in the context of IW—over the last five years.

Chapter 4, Netwar-Political and Economic War in Indian Context is in continuation of internal environment scan. The relevance of this chapter came under maximum scrutiny during the review. Queries like, 'Why include "leadership" in IW?' The query is very relevant since IW is considered to be all technology. That is what the American literature post the first Iraq War told us. Then the next question—'Why include "politics" in IW? After all, Armed Forces are apolitical. Also the political leaders in the past took those decisions and behaved in that matter due to prevailing national and international situation.' The third objection was on inclusion of 'political economics' in the study.

The inherent weakness in the draft was that these disparate issues were not linked to the main flow of the study. This was done based on the valuable guidance. A brief link up may be in order here. First leadership. The phrase Information War is quite misleading. It suggests that outcome of war depends on information. This is an incorrect assumption. Organizations and nations lose battles and wars in spite of equal amount of information available to both sides. The crux is what you do with that information and how fast. This is where leadership becomes the all-important factor. Different leaders react or act differently under the same stimulus provided by the information system and environment.

General Thapar in 1962 and Field Marshal Manekshaw in 1971 had got the same orders—to commence war when their troops were not prepared. Both the chiefs responded differently that made the difference between defeat in 1962 and victory in 1971. More such examples when we come to the issue proper. Since leadership as a subject is very widely referred to and rarely understood, a small brief on the modern concepts of leadership is in Appendix A. Now the question of including the political decision making in IW. We all agree that wars are fought to achieve a political end. IW is no different. Hence, the military commanders must know what political ends are being achieved. They must be party to formulation of political goals so that they can derive military goals. Besides, in case of series of suboptimal political decisions and poor political executions, the Armed Forces bear the brunt of such misadventures. Operation Blue Star (Golden Temple Amritsar 1984) and Operation Pawan (IPKF operations in Sri Lanka 1987-1990) are just two cases in point. As regards inclusion of economy, we need to remember that the IW not only needs top class technologies and knowledge base for the military, it needs to support infrastructure of very high order to cope up with the dynamism of war in the information age. This requires balanced economy. Kautilya's treatise on statecraft that includes military affairs also is named *Arthashastra*—which roughly translates into knowledge of economy.

Since very little has been written on IW which is India specific, this is an attempt to generate appropriate debate especially among the non-military societies including academic institutions, think tank organizations and others entrusted and interested in national security. This will help us to formulate and more importantly internalize our own theories and concepts to address our current and near future threats.

What this book is not:-

- It is not a thesis or a report. Hence, the style is exploratory, in the form of discussions. At the same time, it is not a collection of personal opinions and experiences.
- It is not about telling the Armed Forces how to fight modern wars or IW in particular. The Indian Armed Forces have acquitted themselves very well in most of the wars under the circumstances they were launched. But the moot issue is that 'IW' or even 'war' is not an Armed Forces subject. Nations fight wars including IW; the Armed Forces are but a component. In the context of IW, the Armed Forces come in for a short length of conflict spectrum characterized by its intensity and 'must win in shortest possible time frame' condition.

It may not be out of place here—at the cost of pre-empting the findings that the discussion on strategic framework will be based on the following pillars:-

- **People and the Leaders:** India has been a vibrant democracy since 1947. Peace and war must be centred around her people, their sense of belonging to this unique nation, their pride and ambitions as a nation and equally important their well-being and happiness. The expression of all these must ideally come through their leaders whom the people in a democracy elect to represent them. Thus the awareness of people, their psychological robustness to elect the right type of leaders, their productivity, creativity, and innovative skills constitute the most important pillar. These strengths will insulate us from the continuous netwar, perception management techniques, and subversion. It also prepares us for 'political war'—one of the components of IW.
- **Vibrant Economy:** Indian economy needs to move from factor-driven approach to efficiency-driven systems by 2024 and then to innovation-driven growth by 2030 in synch with the fourth industrial revolution that establishes the constant requirement of constructive disruption, ability to manage fast-paced changes and be resilient and agile in short economic cycles. The way GDP is growing is more important than how much it is growing. An inclusive, distributive, and innovative growth cycle will keep the economy in synch with the other pillars. A robust and vibrant economy as mentioned above provides resilience against economic war by the adversary.
- **Dynamic Knowledge and Technology:** From a net importer and consumer of new knowledge and technology we need to move to an era where we receive and internalize new knowledge, create new concepts, knowledge, and technology to be exported to the world at large. Higher rates of investments in this field is one of the inputs. More relevant than the quantum of investment is the way the investment is used.

- **Robust Internal Security:** Border Management, policing, judicial systems, governance, and administration constitute this apparatus. This apparatus must be people friendly, efficient, and effective. Failure of these agencies drags the Indian Armed Forces into tasks that are not ideal for them. Also, when people find the Armed Forces pitted against them for a long duration of time their faith in the most respected organization in the country for ensuring national security erodes. Besides the Armed Forces lose critical resources of time, capital, and energy on this task, which can be ideally performed by agencies established for this role.
- **Armed Forces:** Motivated Armed Forces that are efficient, effective, and capable of synergistic concentration of effort and hence impact at the selected targets in time and space are essential in IW environment. These forces must be able to interoperate and collaborate with each other (Army, Navy and Air Force) as also other organizations as per the operational requirement. They must possess demonstrated capabilities to win military conflicts as also operations other than war in shortest possible time with minimal casualties to own forces as also minimal collateral damage to the enemy. Thus, precision application of effort with focused logistics, capability to operate in small combined arms or multi-service teams and very high degree of cognitive ability to gain battlespace awareness within the adversary's OODA loop would be essential elements of Armed Forces. Given the preponderance of embedded systems in the IW, environment indigenization is an essential and critical requirement. We need to develop the weapon systems for the way we want to fight the war.
- **ICT Adaption:** The overarching importance of ICT is established by its duality of use. ICTs provide most precious domain for governance in a vibrant democracy, facilitate creation and distribution of wealth, sustain the banking

systems, track and neutralize internal threats and so on. This virtual domain is also the dominant part of the battlespace in IW. It is at the heart of network centric war, which helps in concentrating the effort at the point of decision without physical movements of forces. India must go all out to create a high speed, nationwide, secure, and agile cyberspace for military as also non-military use.

- **International Relations**: Modern world is intimately interconnected. These linkages are through cyberspace as also through common threat perceptions, trade interests, societal linkages, historical backgrounds, cultural similarities, and so on. This interconnected global environment needs to be harnessed for economic growth through trade, forming part of supply chain for high value products and services, joint cyber war operations both defensive as also offensive, counter terrorism and securing major sea routes critical for our international trade. Hence international alliances, coalitions, and treaties form an important pillar for IW. We should also be aware that the world comprises of nations and societies, which have evolved through substantially different pathways. Henry Kissinger writes in *World Order*, about four prominent ways in which different regions or civilizations in the World perceive international relations. First, the Westphalian approach followed by the Europeans who believe in the multiplicity of political systems of sovereign states and allow interactions based on balance of power (generally this is the dominant concept followed globally). Second, the US approach of democracy and freedom for the world where the US is for mankind. This also implies that the US as the sole superpower reserves the right to intervene in any region or any country if as per the US perception that region is out of synch with the concept of 'democracy and freedom'. Third, the radical Islamic approach with different shades all converging on Islam. This approach legislates that the only way to govern humans is through Islam—which is beyond national boundaries. The concept of democracy and sovereign governments is illegal and to be removed by just war. Lastly, the Asian complexity with China considering the Chinese emperor as the ruler ordained by the heavens to rule all under the sky. All others are inferior to the Chinese kingdom. As per Kissinger, the Indian approach transcends temporal affairs of the world order. Their concept addresses the universe as one which gets destroyed and created in cycles comprising of millions of years. Thus, in spite of centuries of foreign rule in India, the core culture and the belief systems came out unscathed. They looked at the aggressors in detached equanimity. The temporal (ideal) state was governed by Kautilya's treatise in Arthashastra. Kautilya is much more pragmatic—in fact aggressive—in that people are at the centre of a kingdom. The king has to dedicate all his energies and wisdom to the well-being and security of his people. War is a legitimate and important activity of the state and must be fought when victory is most probable. Kautilya talks of espionage, assassinations and all other means to subjugate the adversary. Thus the Indian view is unique in striking a balance between the belief of '*vasudhaiva kutumbakam*' (all existing on earth are one family) and the importance of each nation as a sovereign entity. As technology brings these disparate ideological approaches together in the modern comity of nations the deep-rooted fault lines do appear in various forms.

★★★

Evolution of IW through an American Experience

Political and military debacles in Vietnam provided the trigger, and spectacular victory in the First Iraq War gave the marketing slogan for information war

IW Concepts in the Present Form

As mentioned earlier, this chapter is part of external environment scan and analysis for the purpose of developing strategies. Dominant activities and originators' literature (primarily American) provide the objective data for analysis.

The current literature—emanating from the US think tank organizations and eminent writers—on IW dates back to 1980s. By 1990, the US concepts on IW were firmly established. The Gulf War of 1991 was named as the First Information War. The epistemology of the subject is closely linked with conflicts involving Israel or US. If the military conflicts form the basis of concept development, then we need to go further back in history to 1969.

In October 1969 General William C Westmoreland (US Army), impressed by the effects of precision guided ammunition on the Vietnamese positions (Vietnam War 1955-1975) said, 'On the battlefield of tomorrow enemy forces will be located, tracked, and targeted almost simultaneously through the use of data links, computer evaluated evaluation, and automated fire control.' This statement was recognition of use of Intelligence, Surveillance, and Reconnaissance (ISR) technologies along with the automated decision support systems. Subsequent military writers referred to this environment as 'digitized battlefield'. The US forces were credited to have mastered the art of dominating the digitized battlefield with their superior technologies. Incidentally, very few precision-guided weapons were used in the Vietnam War. Bulk of the bombs dropped by B52s were conventional bombs.

Nevertheless, in spite of this mastery, the US lost the Vietnam War within six years of Westmoreland's observations on the digitized battlefield! An interesting incident depicting how a technically inferior (or less endowed) force copes with a technological superior force has been described in a management book (*Competing for the Future* by Gary Hamel, CK Prahalad). Years after the culmination of the Vietnam War, a retired US senior veteran met his Vietnamese counterpart and asked him, 'How were you able to move your troops and logistics across the intricate river network when our air force had destroyed all the bridges on the rivers using precision-guided ammunition?' 'You destroyed the wrong ones. The real bridges across which we moved were about six inches below water level,' replied the Vietnamese officer. It is important to register this fact while preparing for competitions and conflicts in the information age.

There is another interesting information. About 14 percent of casualty to the US troops in Vietnam War was due to friendly fire—the blue on blue fire (Ventre). So much for the precision targeting! We will see the novelty of fighting in such situations—conceptualized and discussed in great details in contemporary military literature as 'asymmetric warfare'. Though this concept of 'asymmetric war' itself is vague. There has always been more than one factor of asymmetry in all the wars!

Coming back to the development of the American theory of IW, four years after the Vietnamese War, in a different continent, the Syrian and Israeli forces clashed on the Golan Heights. An American General (Don Starry) studied the outcome of this war. He brought out the concept of 'deep battle'. The Israeli Forces had engaged the massively superior Syrian Forces at the head (point of contact), mast (the reinforcements and the build-up forces), and the tail (logistics). The Israelis had used their ground forces in complete unison with the Israeli Air Force and their surveillance elements. The results of General Don Starry's studies were embodied in US Army Field Manual 100-5 under the heading AirLand Battle. This was in 1982.

The AirLand Battle doctrine consisted of an entire package, which included revised force structure, new weapon systems (F 16 fighter aircraft, patriot missile system) and so on. Forces on ground (Army), in the air (Air Force), the surveillance systems, communications, and logistics were grouped together as one cohesive unit. (Toffler *War and Anti War*). We also need to consider some more data before we are completely taken in by the 'AirLand Battle' theory.

First, the US Armed forces were smarting under the ignominy of defeat in the Vietnam War. True to the American character, the nation and the Armed Forces were under massive restructuring and rethinking. New strategies and doctrines were being discussed and tried. Israeli military victory on the Golan Heights was spectacular by all standards. The US think tank scaled it up to the American standards. New doctrine, supported by new weapon system, new force structure, better inter-service synergy, seamless interoperability between army, air force, logistics, space-based system, air defence and so on.

Secondly, US are the largest exporter of arms and ammunition on the planet. Her defence expenditure is more than that of the ten next countries put together. For obvious reasons her military doctrines, concepts, technologies, and weapon systems need to be the best in the world. The process starts with the concepts and doctrines. Once the lesser countries buy these (concepts and doctrines), the next stage is for the commensurate technologies and weapon systems.

If we remove the grandiose scale of American analysis of Israel-Syria conflict on the Golan Heights, a different picture may emerge. Let us re-visit the battle with the eyes of a non-American observer. Around 1400 Syrian tanks attacked the Israeli positions on the Golan Heights held by two weak Israeli brigades. It was a surprise attack. As expected the Israeli brigades lost bulk of armour (battle tanks) and substantial ground. But unlike most of the lesser-known Armed Forces, the Israeli brigade commanders held on. They did not run away. Damaged tanks were quickly repaired in the combat zone and pressed into battle. They delayed the Syrian advance till the Israeli reserves arrived.

The reserve formation did not take up defensive positions to beef up dwindling defences. They also did not attack the head of the

Syrian column. Instead they contained the head, attacked the middle and the rear echelons. This requires guts, innovative thinking, and an unyielding spirit to fight, and above all self-belief that, 'yes we can do it'.

The Syrians were surprised and lost balance. The head of the Syrian column withdrew to restore the situation. The Israelis kept up the tempo. The withdrawal turned into retreat and full-blown flight from battle.

Lessons learnt from this engagement could also be in terms of resolute leadership, will to fight, excellent logistics support by way of in situ repairs, seize and maintain initiative, etc. Another question which begs our attention is, 'Did Israeli defence forces ever lose to any Egyptian, Syrian forces in spite of huge "asymmetry" in numbers?' Secondly, if we consider synergistic application of short-term and long-term interdiction along with air superiority exploited by speed of operation and deep surveillance of the battlefield, the result will be very much similar to AirLand Battle. To that extent, the Indian forces in Bangladesh fought AirLand and Sea battle to force a decision in eighteen days. This is less than half the time the US forces took to defeat Iraqi forces!

However, there are two major differences. First, we do not make grandiose declaration of victory. Second, which is more critical is that we forget the lessons learnt (of synergy and interoperability) very quickly. Hence, by the time Kargil was thrust on us, the Indian Armed Forces were relearning the lessons again.

The First Iraq War 1991
(The First Information War as per Alan D Campaign)

By 1993, the AirLand Battle concept was revised. This led to formulation of field manual 100-6 heralding an era of Information Warfare. It was around this time that Alvin and Heidi Toffler had come up with their bestseller *War and Anti War*. Since military and strategic writers in the US consider Gulf War of 1991 the First IW, it may be relevant to analyse its relevant aspects.

Iraqi forces had captured bulk of Kuwait threatening Saudi Arabia—and as a consequence threatened global oil market. The UN Security Council approved military intervention by coalition forces under US leadership. At this time IW doctrine was still in the making—emerging as it was from the AirLand Battle. The massive American arms industry was in the process of modernizing their Air Warning and Control Systems (AWACS). The Joint Surveillance and Target Attack RADAR System (JSTARS) was in the final stages of induction for accomplishing target acquisition and tracking role for the ground forces. The E2C Hawk Eyes for similar role for the marine forces was recently inducted.

As the US forces commenced their operation Desert Shield (the First Gulf War) the AWACS, JSTARS, and the E2Cs were also launched into operations. The AWACS were supporting the US Air Force for which it was designed. However, besides picking up air targets (which were very few since the Iraqi Air Force was very quickly destroyed and were unable to challenge the might of US Air Force), the AWACS also picked up ground targets which they transmitted to their respective Air Commands or Joint Force Command. This information was then downloaded into floppies, which were taken to the respective combat teams. Similarly, the ground targets detected by the JSTARS were disseminated to division and corps headquarters from where the data was sent in floppies in military trucks to the ground forces that were in position to neutralize these targets.

This arrangement, in spite of huge capital invested in the systems (AWACS, and JSTARS) proved to be futile. By the time the concerned ground troops could identify the target after reading the floppies, the targets had moved from the location. This is where the American military research institutions, students in their prestigious engineering colleges got down to work and set up data links in the aerial platforms and ground receiving stations for the ground forces, so that as the AWACs, JSTARS, and even E2C flew over the target area, the captured data was directly beamed to respective ground stations, which were accessed by all the ground stations. These stations passed on target information to relevant ground forces for immediate destruction. In addition, the US research and innovation teams configured air-to-air links between the three platforms.

In terms of strategy, this indicated three very basic aspects in use of ISR in active conventional operations. First, the information or the intelligence must reach the troops designated to engage the target (shooter) directly and at the earliest. Second, for optimization of aerial platform it must be able to gather inputs for the ground as well as the air targets and should be able to pass the relevant input to the concerned shooters in the form they understand the information. Lastly, the most important aspect is inter-operability among the systems of three services (army, air force, and the navy) that brings in the desired synergy in the combat zone. Hereafter the combat teams and other elements of ground forces got real time data from the JSTAR or the AWAC or E2C—whichever platform was flying over the target area. The impact on the war fighting capability of US Forces and the allies was dramatic. No Iraqi target in the theatre was safe.

The war took just forty-two days. Of these thirty-eight days were spent in airstrikes. In spite of greater strength of ground and air troops, Iraq lost the war very comprehensively. This war brought into focus the element of interoperability and real time availability of information to troops in action. During this war, the American media brought the war into the living rooms of people around the globe through CNN. The world was mesmerized by precision targeting of Iraqi military installations. Though a very large number of 'dumb' bombs also fell all over the Iraqi territory killing people in hospitals and their homes, these were not shown by the CNN. The smart cruise missiles and attacks on Scud launchers were shown with all the multimedia and graphic effects. Precision targeting of information became as important as precision targeting by weapons. This new mode used by the media was named as 'spin doctoring' the information.

The set of lessons from the first gulf war (Desert Shield and Desert Storm) highlights the role of ISR, interoperability, and deft handling of media. The allied forces and especially the air force commanders wanted everyone to believe that the modern air force with its range, speed, lethality, and precision has made ground operations redundant. The early hypotheses formed on the basis of the First Iraq War or the First Information War on this account were proved wrong. The lessons of Dunkirk were relearnt in Kosovo in 1999.

The Iraq War of 1991 is an ideal proof of the dictum, 'nothing succeeds like success.' It also created a bandwagon effect. Overnight new theories were made and everyone started accepting it. Daniel Kahneman in his book, *Thinking Fast and Slow* talks of 'theory blindness' effect. The sudden emergence of the theory of Information War did create the 'theory blindness' effect. All around countries spent time and energy in justifying the theory advanced by such a successful war fought by the only superpower on the planet. No one stopped to question the findings. No one questioned the other aspects of war.

We can look at the entire episode from a different angle—divorced from technology and any new theory. First and foremost, how about questioning and analysing the role of information system in deciding on the commencement of war. The most important decision in any war as far as the political leadership is concerned is the choice of the option of 'war'. Did the Americans exercise their information system and superior knowledge base to achieve the same results without having to fight the war? The second most important decision for the political leadership pertains to termination point of the war. The least insignificant part of the decision as regards to political leadership is in between the start and end of war because this 'middle' domain is within the jurisdiction of Armed Forces fighting the war.

Let us look at the least significant part first since this is the part which is discussed most in all the literature which came up in the wake of 1991 Iraq War. Since war is a two-sided affair, there is a need to look at the other side also. The war fighting capability of Iraqi Armed Forces is an important aspect here. They were equipped with fairly modern Soviet as also US weapons. The men who used these systems were technologically primitive compared to the tech-savvy coalition troops. Secondly, the only major war the Iraqi Armed Forces had fought earlier was against Iran and learnt all the wrong lessons especially while applying those lessons while fighting some of the most modern Armed Forces. Thirdly, Iraqis lacked the tenacity and innovativeness of Vietnamese or Israeli forces. It was not difficult to neutralize the electronic equipment of coalition forces by using area weapons, which could trigger high voltage electromagnetic pulse. Once the Iraqi forces realized the ISR superiority of coalition forces, they could have dispersed and used techniques to deceive these surveillance systems as was done by the Vietnamese. But Iraqis did none of these.

The defeat of Iraqi forces was as much a function of their low morale, poor war fighting capability, ineffective leadership as it was due to all the superiorities of US and coalition forces. Another factor, which is glossed over while eulogizing the success of the 'first information war' is the fact that 23 percent of casualties in the US forces during this war was due to friendly fires (P 59 Daniel Ventre's *Information Warfare*). This must appear shocking considering the theory that the First Gulf War was won due to information dominance. In terms of developing strategies there are many other reasons for US victory. These are:-

- Interoperability of communication systems of the three services—army, air, and the navy. The interoperability transcended beyond the technical systems to culture of these forces.
- Synergy in application of various types of forces in time and space was remarkable. Using differently capable air crafts—electronic surveillance, jammers, anti-radiation missile fitted aircraft and ground attack aircraft—in synchronization with

the overall objectives paid rich dividends.
- Innovation during the war to make the systems more capable improved the capability of the allied forces.
- Deft handling of media ensured that the people at home and the world at large remained supportive of the US cause.
- Tech-savvy US troops used the high technology weapon system to the limit of their exploitation.
- The sheer speed of the allied operation surprised the Iraqi forces.

Conflict Termination and New End State Post 1991 Gulf War

Once Saddam Hussein read the writing on the wall, he surrendered to the allied dictate by withdrawing from Kuwait without any preconditions. He also agreed to inspections by the international team anywhere in Iraq for weapons of mass destruction. Thus, he removed the cause for continuation of the war in 1991. At this juncture, the political leadership in the US was to take the second most important decision—that of termination of war. A good conflict termination would have ensured better end state for the victorious state, sustained period of peace and hence end of miseries of war and violence. How did things turn out after this war?

The First Information War in Iraq resuscitated the Al Qaeda. The dying terrorist organizations got a fresh lease of life! In 1993 they executed the first bomb blast in World Trade Center which killed six Americans and wounded around a thousand. This signalled the Al Qaeda operations in mainland US. This was a precursor to 9/11. Eight years later the Al Qaeda launched the biggest terrorist attack on US where more than 3000 people died. This was September 2001. US forces launched the second offensive in Iraq in 2003 within twelve years of achieving the most spectacular victory in the First Information War! This time the UN and the European allies of NATO were not on board. Majority of Americans did not vote for Second Iraq War. Saddam Hussein had consolidated his position as the undisputed leader of the Ba'ath Party ruling Iraq. Thus while during the First War in Iraq the US was fighting a demonized Saddam Hussein, during the Second Iraq War Saddam Hussein was a hero for his people.

A number of scholars and most of the European nations felt that Saddam was able to maintain a fine balance among the various warring factions in Iraq. They also felt that after Saddam Iraq would become a difficult region to handle. Notwithstanding the lack of UN support and reservations by the European allies, within twelve years of winning the 1991 Iraq War, the US forces had to launch Second Iraq War. This fact depicts poor conflict termination. At another level, it also raises serious questions on the necessity of the First Gulf War. Could that War (1991) be won without fighting? That would have actually vindicated the American information system.

Kosovo

Where does Kosovo fit in the epistemology of IW, as it is known today? There are a number of similarities. First, the coalition forces which addressed the issue in 1999 were the same–NATO. So also the leader of the coalition–the US. The issues involved were ethnic within the erstwhile nation of Yugoslavia. It was not a new issue. Simmering internecine violence had been in the works for more than a century. There was also an eccentric leader to deal with–Milosevic. The Muslims in Kosovo and the Albanian Christians were the two major groups at loggerheads. Milosevic on the Albanian side exploited the sentiments of centuries-old animosity between the groups for his political triumph.

Once negotiations between the American interlocutors and Milosevic failed, NATO decided to apply the recently learnt lessons of First Information War in Iraq. Massive air attacks were planned. It was believed that Milosevic would not be able to withstand the lethal, precise air attacks for even four days. Second, the spin doctoring of media was planned to get the world opinion on the side of the allied forces. This failed. First, the air attacks failed to impress Milosevic. Second, there were very daring and independent reporters right in Kosovo who reported what they saw and felt.

After almost forty days of air attacks, which proved to be insufficient to impress Milosevic, the NATO forces threatened Milosevic with ground action. Milosevic surrendered immediately!

If we go back into history of the region, some more relevant facts and similarities emerge. Kosovo as also the Serbian and Albanian people were part of the communist regime in erstwhile Yugoslavia. It was in 1989 that the Serbs celebrated an event, which had occurred 600 years ago–the battle of Kosovo Polje where their famous and revered Prince Lazar had fought and died. The celebrations in 1989—orchestrated and led by Milosevic—had religious overtones. The old hatred between the Serbs and the Turks was resurrected. The Albanian Muslims and Christian Serbs in Yugoslavia found themselves in a tense situation.

NATO had interest in the region since the communist empire of erstwhile USSR crumbled under Gorbachev. The Eastern European countries—Yugoslavia being one of these—found their new alliance in Western Europe. The US and the NATO did not want widespread violence in the region. 1989 when the first signs of ethnic trouble emerged to 1999 when full-blown civil war raged in the region was the period where NATO under the US should have so planned their moves that unnecessary internecine killings could have been avoided. The fact that the Albanians and the Serbs went at each other's throats and NATO was forced to use air strikes in the region and later sent ground troops to fight, signalled the first stage of failure. For developing strategies, what we learn from Kosovo is that templating is dangerous when it comes to applying the lessons learnt in earlier conflicts. Most importantly at political level, the early signs of inter-societal conflicts must be handled swiftly and wisely. There are problems which do not get resolved on their own. Procrastination in taking timely and appropriate decision lets the problem grow much bigger than anticipated.

Second Iraq War

The start of Second Iraq War within twelve years of the culmination of the much publicized spectacular victory of 1991 Iraq War raises two questions. First: Was the First Iraq War terminated at the right time and with right assurances? The second question is: What all means and knowledge resources were utilized by the Americans and the British Forces—who fought the Second Iraq War together—to win the war without fighting it? In light of these two questions and what we now know as the answers, it is quite obvious that the Second Iraq War was a disaster right from the beginning.

The objectives of Second Iraq War included elimination of weapons of mass destruction (this was more of President Bush's perception than actual intelligence obtained through CIA and UN inspectors), eliminating Al-Qaeda, and preventing terrorism from spreading to the rest of the world. It did not take much time for the US forces to defeat Iraqi military in the second war. Prior to launching the air strike the US Armed Forces had sent e-mails through Iraq's secured military network, as part of their cyber war activity, to all the Iraqi workstations to line up their tanks and leave in civilian clothes so that the US Air Strikes would not harm them. A large number of Iraqi 'fighters' obeyed!

Nevertheless, in spite of comprehensive military victory by the US forces none of the war objectives were achieved. The weapons of mass destruction were not discovered in Iraq because none existed. Instead of eliminating Al-Qaeda the war helped dramatic growth of Al-Qaeda and its transformation into ISIS. The new incarnation of Al-Qaeda in the form of ISIS was found to be much more violent, popular, and determined. It spread its tentacles beyond Iraq to Syria, Pakistan, Lebanon, and other Arab countries. Elements of ISIS even reached India.

This is where the situation became difficult to handle. The presence of US forces in Iraq became an irritant not only for the Iraqi population but also for the American people. US were losing her soldiers to terrorist attacks in Iraq on regular basis. More than 4000

US soldiers were killed between 2003 and 2008. For a superpower this is huge loss of trained personnel. The civilian casualties in Iraq were in millions. More than three-fourth of the Iraqi population was displaced. Some three million Iraqi people fled to Syria and other Muslim countries in the region. About 50,000 entered US. The US and the allies spent more than three trillion dollars on this war. This is twice the amount spent by the US and the allies during the Korean War from 1950 to 1954.

Instead of eliminating terrorism, it gave a new lease of life to terrorism in the region. Finally, President Obama pulled out the US forces from Iraq in 2011 leaving the region highly unstable and ripe for sustained insurgency.

Within two years, the Islamic State of Iraq and The Levant (ISIL) and then Islamic State of Iraq and Syria (ISIS) were born. The series of events also transformed the way Americans and the Europeans looked at terrorism. The NATO and the US Forces were pushed into war in Afghanistan against Taliban. The Second Iraq War—in spite of all the technologies and military strength possessed by the US—cannot be termed as a successful operation.

Coming back to the concepts of IW formulated by the US Department of Defence way back in 1994 and 1996 on successful completion of the First Gulf War we need to look at a bigger question. How does IW concept answer the fundamental questions concerning war between two nations or between state and its citizens in the knowledge era? Why should a 'third wave' nation go to war? What are the factors in the knowledge system which can insulate a nation against war or continued violence internal as well as external? What are the other means and mechanisms which can effectively prevent physical destruction of resources and loss of human lives? If 'information' and 'knowledge' are the new resources for which the third wave societies compete then why should there be violence and killing of innocent people?

The evolution of IW concepts and doctrines appear to be based on the assumption that the concerned players are already at war. The theories and concepts are based on immediate operational victories in conventional short-duration wars. Some of the most important questions relating to 'before' and 'after' the war were ignored.

Knowledge societies need to know how to avoid war in the first place. Alternatively, once wars become inevitable how to prevent recurrence of war for at least next 50 to 100 years. In other words, IW should be more for maintaining equilibrium and peace.

Nevertheless, we may still look at the operational aspects of IW as evolved by the American experience. This will help us to pick up the salient features in terms of leadership, organizational structure/ culture, and operational concepts independent of expensive technologies generally not available with less-endowed countries.

★★★

Building up and Operationalization Post Iraq Wars

Operationalization of theory into actual conduct of battles and wars requires internalization and reflection

Just after the conclusion of the First Iraq War, a number of definitions of IW appeared in the military literature emanating from US think tanks as also from the official publications from the US Armed Forces. It appeared in the US Army Training and Doctrine Command (TRADOC) pamphlet 525-5 of August 1994, US Department of Defence Manual 100-6 of August 1996, RAND authors–John Arquilla and David Ronfeldt wrote numerous papers on the subject between 1999 and 2001. Martin C Libicki again of RAND contributed to the debate on the subject. The major takeaways from all these range from operations in the strict military domain to areas where the military has very limited or no jurisdiction. Thus at one end the focus is on combined arms operations to enable the commander's decision cycle and oppose that of the adversary supported by all available information systems. An extension of this approach is to include the military information environment linked with the global information environment. At the other end of the spectrum, it is defined in terms of components such as ideological, political, economic, and command and control warfare. In this, the military comes into picture only during the last part—command and control warfare. The ideological war is primarily perception management of the adversary and perhaps own population, political war is to influence the decision making of political leadership and economic war is to damage the economic system of the adversary.

Martin C Libicki writing for the National Defence University Institute for National Strategic Studies (US), *What is Information Warfare*? in August 1995 gives out seven categories of IW. These include command and control warfare, which attacks command and control systems to separate command from forces. Secondly, intelligence based warfare aimed at collection, exploitation, and protection of information by systems to support attack on other warfare forms. Thirdly, electronic warfare, which is communication combat in the realm of physical transfer of information (radio electronic) and the abstract format of information (cryptographic). Fourthly, it is psychological warfare—combat against the human mind. Fifthly, hacker warfare, which involves combat at all levels over global information infrastructure. Sixth category is economic information warfare, which involves control of economics via control of information by blockade or by imperialistic control. The seventh component is cyber warfare, a futuristic abstract form of terrorism; fully simulated combat and reality control are combined in this warfare category applicable in the far term. Libicki in his paper quoted above does not feel that IW is anything new. As per him multiple functions of modern warfare are being attributed to this new form called as IW. He goes to the extent of suggesting the announcement of third wave as per Toffler in his *War and Anti War* more of an illusion. Libicki felt that IW, as a different technique of fighting war, does not exist. 'Defining IW is akin to blind men trying to figure out the shape of an elephant by touching various parts. To them IW appears like a "tree" or a "rope" or a "rock" depending upon which part of the elephant they touch. May be the rope, rock and the tree exist but there is no elephant!'

The above description of different conceptual frameworks illustrates the fact that there is no unanimity of concepts or ideas on Information Warfare.

The central theme of all these discussions hinges on the criticality of information systems/information environment and the fact that military has much smaller role in the entire spectrum of IW. Netwar, political war and economic war do not give much scope to the military to operate. Even the cyber war needs major contribution from the non-military domains of the nation.

It may be prudent to note here that the euphoria (on IW) started in 1993, peaked in 2004 and by 2015, it ebbed away. The US Department of Defence dropped IW from its official vocabulary. Instead, they now talk of Information Operations. At the same time, IW is embedded at functional level in the US Armed Forces.

We will look at those issues in some detail but before that some basic questions need to be raised. Have the new technologies in information systems changed the way nations engage in war? Are the reasons for which they go to war any different now than what they were in 'industrial age'? Has IW reduced the extent of physical destruction, loss of life, and societal trauma since it is based on precision targeting?

The answer to these questions would lie in deeper analysis of the epistemology and close scrutiny of the new forms or categories of warfare postulated by the IW concepts that emanate from the literature on the subject. We will first take the widest range of components of IW appearing in US literature. The major components of IW include Net war, political war, economic war, psychological operations, electronic warfare, military deception, operation security, information assurance and computer network attacks. How do we describe or understand these components and who are the main leads in each of these?

Netwar

The available literature on the subject very broadly describes this as an ongoing activity in the global arena using the global information environment with the primary focus on shaping the perceptions of target nations, people, and societies. It is the political leadership at the national level that decides what the world at large and selected nations in particular must perceive of their country in the context of global positioning and national security. Obviously before we expect others to perceive us in a specific way, we must be clear as to who we are.

Netwar uses all the components of global information environment to convey their messages to the target audience. Internal activities and reaction to global cues are tailored to ensure that the desired perception is strengthened. This is where synergy comes in as the single most factor in all the IW operations. Military has a role here in terms of offensive, proactive, or active defence approaches to external threats including proxy wars.

However short, swift, and decisive military actions pay rich dividends. While looking at netwar we need to be aware of the clash of deep-rooted self and world views people have and how these come into severe conflict when technology brings these contradictory views in intimate contact. Though it is inevitable that these close contacts bring in changes but the type of changes and societal reactions are unpredictable and at times bring in turmoil amongst the societies and nations.

Political War

Libicki and RAND papers define this in terms of affecting the decisions of political leadership. However, the American elections in 2016 indicate that the political war expands to facilitate enthroning or dethroning a particular type of political leadership or leader. At another level, this may also be directed at diluting the positioning of a particular type of political culture in the target nation. Thus, the Russian involvement in influencing the American elections in 2016 may be directed at undermining the strength and credibility of American democracy. A quid pro quo to what the American did to USSR in 1991 during Gorbachev's regime. There are enough cues to identify this kind of activities to influence the Indian political landscape.

It is easy to see the linkages between political war and netwar. Through people-to-people contacts using social media and subtle help from mainstream media and overt activities, political systems can be supported or discredited. This provides the best and most non-violent way of subjugating the will of the adversary in behaving the way the aggressor wishes the target nation to behave. Remember the impact China had on India while annexing Tibet and Aksai Chin. Also, in 1967 China was able to get a hold on Jelep La–in East Sikkim, under Indian occupation (till then) without fighting.

On the other side of the border, Pakistan continued to soften the Indian response to her activities in the Kashmir valley. The ruse of cultural ties, Pakistani artists performing in India, and cricket matches kept the soft approach on while Pakistani establishment continued her activities in Jammu and Kashmir (J&K) with active support from the political party in power in J&K.

Economic War

The American literature identifies economic war as blockades, sanctions, sabotaging economic or financial systems. But, in the Indian context this all may not be very relevant. Our emphasis in the context of fighting a successful economic war would involve developing the human capital for higher productivity, innovation, creativity to provide us respectable positioning in the international pecking order. This will also give us economic resilience and agility. The arena here is the entire range of economic activities ranging from agriculture, manufacturing, services, technologies, and managerial skills that are used to harness technology for creating national wealth in a transparent manner and ensure judicious distribution.

International trade provides a lucrative route for economic war. Going back to theories of mercantilism, absolute and comparative advantages in international trade, the developed nations can use various tools such as conditional loans, quotas, imposing high tariff based on working condition of workers in the target country or on some environmental issues etc. to keep the developing nations at the lower levels of value chains in the bilateral and multilateral trades. In international trade, politics and economy come into play—most time as opposing forces. It is politics, which generally wins. This makes international trade a fertile ground to wage political as well as economic war.

In case of India, economic warfare will also entail pragmatic alliances and trade agreements, our stand in the WTO, and keeping our sea route safe and under constant surveillance. Thus in the military domain, the Indian Navy and strategic arm of the Indian Air Force and the Army will have their respective roles.

Psychological Operations

Psychology deals with the human mind, repeated response to a given situation (personality), human behaviour, and disposition. In our case, the focus would be to manipulate desired changes in the behaviour of the target group of people, nation, society, by concerted use of various components of information systems. It would involve engaging with media. At times, there may be a necessity to control the media but given the presence of social media and abundance of techniques for communication, control of media can at best be effective for a very short duration. Most times controlling the media becomes counter-productive since controlled media loses credibility. Selective scaling of facts, providing information, which supports own operations and withholding information, which can be detrimental to own approach can be some of the methods for skilful engagement with the media. Careful wording of information can achieve desired impact on the target group. Launching propaganda operations also helps psychological operations. During intense conflicts misinformation, intoxication, banning adversary's propaganda can be of great help. However, any propaganda, which is based on lies, is short-lived and results in loss of credibility. For a longer time-horizon, thoughts, opinions, beliefs, and emotions can be built up in the target society or even at the international level. Once initial success is achieved in these activities, then own operations become that much easier. In the First Gulf War (1991), it was very easy for the US to muster up international support against Iraq. However, for the Second Iraq War (2003), the US media was not able to convince her own people to support invasion of Iraq! The concept of embedded media used in the First Gulf War proved to be too crude to succeed in the Second Iraq War.

Implementation of psychological operations (psyops) presumes deep knowledge of theories of communication and information, psychology of individual, and their behaviours and cultures. It is almost impossible to predict the direct or indirect impact of selected psyops on the target. Second important aspect is that psyops were prevalent much before the digital age.

The success or failure of psyops depends on the perception of the target audience. It is here that the psyops get linked with perception management. While psyops are for comparatively smaller time duration as part of military operations, perception management is a continuous process as part of Netwar. We need to recognize and understand the limitation military organizations have while conducting psychological operations on their own. Militaries world over are not trained and equipped to wage psychological operations in target countries, since all their activities are viewed with suspicion if not supported politically by all concerned.

The Indian Army tried psychological operations in Sri Lanka (*Assignment Jaffna* by Sardeshpande); the results as per the author and the commanding general in that operation were next to zero. In Kashmir, psychological operations by the Indian Army have not shown any tangible results in the light of overall resolution of the problem or changing the attitude of the people.

Electronic Warfare

The goal of EW is to control electromagnetic spectrum. It involves any military action using directed electromagnetic energy to control the EM spectrum and to attack the enemy. There are three subdivisions:

- Electronic Attack: Electronic Countermeasures (ECM). Aimed at neutralizing the enemy's capability to use electronic systems such as radio, RADAR, radiating communication links in cellular networks, computer networks. It involves jamming, use of LASER and particle beam weapons, high power microwave beams to destroy enemy equipment. These measures also include non-nuclear Electromagnetic Pulse (EMP), High Energy Radio Frequencies (HERF), and number of other such area weapons. (Please see glossary). ECM also involves electronic deception by sending manipulated information on the enemy networks.
- Electronic Protection: Electronic Counter-Countermeasures (ECCM). This deals with the systems design, which is resistant to jamming by any kind of attack. Communication security and cryptography are other methods of electronic protection.
- Electronic Surveillance/reconnaissance: Search, intercept, identify, and locate sources of electromagnetic energy in order to recognize immediate threats (ESM). The surveillance of communication system is Signals Intelligence (Sigint), whereas obtaining electronic signatures of non-communication systems such as RADAR is Electronics Intelligence (Elint).

Military Deception

This involves measures designed to deceive the enemy. The overall goal of deception is to make the enemy believe or act in a manner that helps friendly forces and places the adversary at a disadvantage.

We can use the same channel that the adversary uses for information collection and analysis. Military deception aims at desired behaviour of the adversary. Hence, for successful deception we need to know the way the enemy thinks and takes decisions, the information collection networks and processes for decision making, information dissemination systems through which the decisions are conveyed for execution, physical activities that are undertaken by the enemy for executing a given decision.

The upstream information flow needs to be used to feed information for the deception. This flow is from the sensors, receptors, troops in contact to the decision makers. The downstream information channels need to be used to gauge the impact of deception plans.

For deception to be effective, a large number of information and activities need to be orchestrated in consonance. The fact that all these activities are designed to deceive the enemy is known to very few (to ensure security of deception plan). This will create a dilemma among own troops who are likely to be misled. Nevertheless, this level of disruption will have to be accepted since if own troops are privy to the deception plan their actions will give away the plan or will caution the enemy.

Operation Security

All activities and processes that prevent the enemy to access critical information, which can help him in discerning our plans and intentions, are grouped under OPSEC. The process has five distinct actions:-

- Identify critical information
- Analysis of threats through intelligence, counter intelligence and open source intelligence
- Analysis of vulnerabilities
- Analysis of risks arising from the vulnerabilities
- Application of appropriate OPSEC measures

A major constraint in formulating OPSEC plan is the dynamic

nature of critical information. Some of the information may not be critical immediately but will become so at a certain stage in the operations. Besides, a large number of unclassified information if picked up by the enemy can help him in visualizing our operational plans.

Besides, security of information always has costs attached in terms of delays, difficulties, and additional resources. In order to achieve uniformity of plans it will be prudent to list out some of the information critical during a given phase of information.

Information Assurance

This involves protection of information and information systems by ensuring their availability, integrity, capacity, confidentiality, and their non-repudiation. Three major stages in the process include protection, detection, and reaction. It includes computer security and information security.

Computer Network Attacks

These are operations intended to disrupt, prohibit access to deteriorate, destroy, and steal information contained in computers, carried out by computer networks or targeting computers and networks. An electronic attack such as use of electronic magnetic force does not fall under CNA but is part of electronic attack.

Concepts, which have not changed:

- Decision Cycle Loop
- Information Systems
- Force Capability and
- Principles of War in IW

The Decision Cycle: Observe-Orient-Decide-Act

Information War is a misnomer. Victory or defeat in war is not that much a function of information. It depends on setting the correct vision/goal/objective. This to be followed by identifying and collecting the relevant, accurate, timely and adequate data which is then converted to information, intelligence, courses of action and selecting a given course of action. A constant factor of all warfare—past, present and even future—is the accuracy and speed of taking decisions as per the chain described above.

In the context of IW, the generally accepted hypothesis is that if the information system is superior the process of taking decision too will be better. It may be pertinent to analyse these aspects. First, the decision-making process is described as the Observe Orient Decide and Act (OODA) cycle. How does it work? Firstly, the decision has to be in a context. The context will define the ecosystem. The ecosystem will have to be observed to pick up clues.

Hence the first part of decision cycle will be 'observe'. Once the clues are picked up from the decision cycle ecosystem the observation narrows down to a sharper focus. This is the 'orient' phase. From the narrow focus observation and orientation emerge a set of alternatives to choose from. As the decision maker choses an alternative, she or he is prepared to bear the opportunity costs of alternatives, which are to be forgone. While accepting the opportunity cost, the assessment process for evaluating the opportunity cost must be fairly accurate. The opportunity cost cannot be higher than the payoff the decision maker is seeking from the chosen alternative. All this happens in the 'decide' phase.

Once the decision is taken, the same must be activated. This is the 'act' phase. This happens through the command and control apparatus, which is primarily communication system. After activating the decision, the output and the outcome must be evaluated. Here output and outcome are entirely different entities. Immediate output must never be confused with long-term expected outcome. We may win a battle at the cost of losing a war. We can win a war at the cost of losing overall goal of waging the war. In the worst case, the decision maker can initiate a long war and realize much later that the war could have been averted. In such a case, eventual victory in the long war will not be worth the effort and miseries very common in war.

Thus, IW is as much about preventing war as it is for winning battles and wars. It will be very educative to analyse the 'victories' in various successful information wars in the light of this higher goal of achieving political objectives without fighting a war. This decision cycle exists in an information environment and its efficacy is based on the information system supporting the decision cycle. Hence, the next obvious question is, What comprises an information system?

Information System

The modern tools of information system have evolved a digitized and scientific understanding of knowledge. It starts with data, which for our purpose can be facts, concepts, instructions collected in a formalized manner, which can be transmitted and are suitable for communication, interpretation by humans or automated systems. Data can even be in the form of electronic signals (bits) in particular format as per the protocol of the communication system. Data in itself does not make much sense. Though it is a very useful possession in the context of 'data war'.

Thus, the next level is processing the data collected from the relevant environment so that it makes sense for a given situation. This becomes useful information. Conversion of information into intelligence would mean comparison and interpretation of information, which should eliminate deception/manipulation by the adversary and should generate various decision alternatives/courses of action.

Thus, the information system comprises of sensors, which provide data, processors for filtering and arranging data into information, receptors who use the data. These can be decision makers or the decision support systems or automated weapon platforms. Databases for orderly and retrievable storage of data should be regularly updated and properly secured from corruption and theft.

From databases, the next components are 'transmitters' which provide the connectivity. The quality of transmitters depends on the information carrying capacity defined in terms of speed (kilobits per second, megabits per second, gigabits per second, terabits per second, etc.). The information system needs to have rules that define the system operation and structure.

The last and most important component of information system is synergy that ensures that the system functions better than the sum total of individual components. Thus, in essence, the information system is a synergized integration of doctrines, procedures, organizational structure, personal equipment, facilities, and communications that are designed to support a commander's exercise of command and control across the complete range of military operations. This system collects, processes, analyses, stores and disseminates information as per the operational requirements. Can information system in itself win a conflict or war? If this were so, then countries would not need Armed Forces and people who operationalize the information system to their advantage. As we have seen earlier, there is a growing realization that the cognitive abilities of the people in the information environment make a huge difference to the value drawn from the system. Thus, the obvious question to the answer is, What comprises information environment?

Information Environment

An 'environment' is a universal set in which 'system' fits in as a subset. Thus, system is part of a relevant environment. When we define a system, we look at tangible entities or principles, processes, rules, and people. In the context of tangible entities, system conveys a set of entities that work together to create a product or effect. These entities are networked and sum total of their individual performance is always less than the synergistic use in a network. In case of intangibles, system comprises principles, concepts, processes, rules, and people who perform in synergy to create an impact or achieve a goal. Here again the synergistic impact is much higher than effects in isolation. Thus, systems approach is based on synergy.

The environment comprises discrete systems. All the systems in an environment are not connected but the environment sets the rules of the game and creates methods for achieving synergy. An information environment comprises of all the relevant technologies, entities, processes, people, and rules. Thus global information environment will comprise of all the technologies that facilitate availability, processing, transmission, storage, and manipulation of information. The entities here will be all the available sensors, computation machines, network architectures, software, people, and rules across the globe. A military information environment will be that part of the global information environment that is used by the militaries of the world. Coming to specific military information environment of a nation, the availability factors shrinks to what is available with the military of that country.

Force Capability and Enablers to Exploit Information System

Two monographs published by the US Army War College—both written by General Gordon Sullivan, *War in the Information Age* (Sullivan and Colonel James M Dubik) on 6 June 1994, and *The Army in the Information Age* (General Sullivan and Lieutenant Colonel Anthony M Corolles) on 31 March 1995—provide very clear insight into the conceptual direction in the US on the type of force capabilities, principles of war in the Information age as these prevailed during that time. We need to remember that what the Americans thought in 1995 may not be the same as what they think today. The reasons that we are referring to the American writings of 1994 and 1995 are:-

- Bulk of our theories and writings are still tied to the early American concepts of post Iraq War of 1991 and the famous writings of Tofflers.
- Our war doctrines reflect the same old concepts of early nineties.

General Sullivan had been in the US Army for more than forty years by the time he wrote these monographs as a retired officer. He had taken part in most of the wars the Americans fought from early fifties to early nineties. In view of his rank, he has had exposure to the apex level discussions in the US Armed Forces.

Even in mid-nineties Sullivan felt that the nature of war has remained unchanged. Leadership, offensive spirit, and self-belief as an organization make the difference between victory and defeat. Some of the critical components of force capabilities that can be gleaned from the two monographs are as under:-

- **Optimize Information System Capability:** This is an innocuous looking capability, which is exceptionally difficult to acquire. First part of the capability is information-based operation. This entails capture of right information in right time frame and move it to the right component of the force in right time frame and the relevant force or weapon platform acts within the decision cycle loop of the adversary to engage/neutralize the right objective. The range of information system gives the commander the means to sense a widely dispersed battlefield. The precision guidance of weapons at long ranges gives him the capability to strike at much longer ranges. The volume of fire coupled with accuracy enables commander to ensure desired lethality or destruction. Again, the sensing capability provides him the means to assess the damage he has caused.
- **Generate Speed in Space and Time to Achieve Momentum and Surprise:** The optimization mentioned above ensures that the ICT enabled force generates speed and surprise both in terms of speed and lethality. Sullivan mentions two types of surprise. First, the physical component of surprise—the enemy has no capability to protect his forces even when he comes to know of offensive forces. Second, the surprise achieved by speed, which translates into the enemy's inability to react since he does not have enough time.
- **Precision Attacks with Adequate Lethality:** Control of battlefield would entail keeping the initiative with own forces and making the enemy react as per own plans. Overwhelming lethality in the modern warfare may not be the right

approach though the Americans have followed this strategy in Vietnam, Iraq, and even in Afghanistan. The results have not been very flattering. Ideally, the lethality needs to be at its lowest. Instead, if the control can be exercised by psychology operations, perception management, and non-lethal weapon system the resultant outcome would be more suitable to avoid a long-drawn war of attrition leading to worse end state than what existed in the beginning of the conflict.

- **Cost-effective Results:** This entails precision targeting with speed and required destructive or disruptive effect. As regards the quantum of casualties, there is a need to minimize casualties on both sides.
- **High Degree of Agility:** This capability is a function of mobility, logistics, dynamism of force structure, and adaptability to combat situation in terms of weapon mix and range of application. The concerned forces need to train very hard to attain this capability. Most nations prepare their best and most elitist troops for this capability. It is not technology which makes this possible but the extreme cognitive preparation, adaptability, and exceptionally high degree of commitment, motivation, which help achieve this capability. The technologies that support this capability are stealth, movement, sensors, precision targeting, and secure communications.
- **Adapt to the Changing Battlefield Environment**: This would involve flexible force composition as per the changing conflict situation. In order to be effective the force composition should be on tri service basis and even capable of including paramilitary and non-military groups for specific tasks. It is important to note that information warfare is not the exclusive domain of the military. Substantial part of the conflict spectrum belongs to non-military domain. In terms of modularity of force structure and its psychological preparation, the Indian

Special Forces are the closest to the ideal requirement.

- **Simultaneity of Operations:** Modern information systems, the precision weapons with long ranges, highly efficient and rapid logistics buildup provides a unique opportunity to the commanders to address the tactical, operational, and strategic objectives simultaneously. This will immobilize the adversary in terms of employment of reserves as also create decision dilemma.
- **Switch to Operations other than War with Relative Ease:** This as of now is more relevant to the American forces that have coalition arrangements with NATO and other armies in the world. In Indian context, there is a need to develop such coalition especially for the purpose of defensive and offensive cyber war. During the past couple of years, the Indian Armed forces have been involved in joint operational exercises with other Armed Forces—notably of US, Japan and at times even the Chinese Army.

Principles of War and Implication

The principles of war need to be independent of the means of waging and conducting war. These are somewhat like the core ideology of vision statement, which endures environmental changes and remains the same over hundreds of years though the approach to realizing the vision may change. The generally accepted principles of war—before the advent of the information age, included selection and maintenance of aim, offensive action, application of combat superiority at the point of decision, economy of force, manoeuvre to gain position of advantage, and unity of command. In the context of Information War, the principles of war hinge around the information system capabilities and their exploitation. These include the following:-

- **Sever the link between the troops and the leaders at the earliest:** This apparently flows from the Iraq war where for the first thirty-eight days of the war the coalition forces' air forces destroyed the Iraqi air defence radars and other communications emanating from their headquarters. Having done this, the ground forces took just four days to neutralize Iraqi resistance, which resulted in capitulation of Saddam Hussein's regime. In essence, it involves destroying the command and control network of the adversary. If we scrutinize the wars in pre IW era, the enemy's decision-making processes or grounds which facilitated decision making (observation, communication etc.) were always the prime and first targets. To that extent there is limited novelty in this principle except that command and control nodes have become so much more effective and enabled in the information environment that their destruction is an absolute prerequisite for progress of own operations.

- **Degrade enemy's sensor and intelligence capability:** This again is part of the command and control warfare where the enemy is decapitated by making him blind and incapable of disseminating his command his forces. Similar approach was followed in earlier wars.
- **Maximize acquisition of knowledge and ensure smooth dissemination without any choke point:** This aspect has gained tremendous importance due to the disproportionately high advantages of modern information systems in planning and conduct of operations. Nevertheless, given the dramatic improvement in sensor technologies and data transmission technologies, the decision makers are prone to be overloaded with information. Though, there are automated systems for quick decision-making based on artificial intelligence and neural networks, these automated systems may not match the cognitive ability required for strategic decisions. At times there are likely to be failures of automated systems in the operational domains also. Casualties to own troops by friendly fires in Vietnam wars and both the Gulf Wars range

from 14 to 24 percentages. This is a very high percentage and hence human intervention in decision-making before the trigger is pulled remains very important.

- **Operate within a tight decision loop even if it entails taking justifiable risks:** Own decision loop has to be shorter than that of the adversary. This pertains to shorter OODA cycle. However, there is one major paradox here. Collection of timely, accurate, contextual information and making it available to the decision maker in the form it is required is considered to be the key to decision making in the tight OODA cycle. However, there are innumerable cases where the decision makers make grossly poor and damaging decisions in spite of all the other technical capabilities of a good information system. Hence, a tight decision loop is more a function of cognitive efficiency and capability of the decision maker who can see through the maze of data and information and arrive at the correct decision in the context of organizational objectives or strategic intent. We will see more of this issue later.
- **Centralize policy, decentralize execution:** Centralize policy facilitates maintenance of organizational aim and goals. In other words, since this policy emanates from the core ideology and the vision there is no scope of flexibility at the lower echelons. However, approach to achieving the aim or the strategic intent will change as per the changing operational environment. Hence, the execution must be left to well-trained and committed leaders at the relevant levels of the hierarchy.
- **Information systems should be interoperable, allow horizontal and vertical flow of information:** Extremely important to ensure synergy in execution. Here interoperability is the most important factor. This involves proper selection of connectivity protocols, harmonizing the communication doctrines and common practices. If required appropriate gateways can be installed at the requisite points where the

information flows from one service to the other.

- **Pre-empt escalation to the higher levels of conflict:** This would allow keeping the initiative in all phases of the operation. It will involve seeing the future first and reaching there before the adversary. Though this is an important principle enunciated by the American strategists, they have seldom followed it either in Vietnam or in the Gulf wars.

In 1991, major militaries in the world were watching the events in Kuwait and Iraq. The NATO, led by the Americans, were involved with Iraq and Kuwait. Japan, Saudi Arabia, and Germany bore the financial burden. China, Russia, and also India monitored the performance of coalition forces in the Middle East deserts.

China and Russia were impressed and overawed by the sheer technological prowess, the financial muscle required to create and sustain such a force. At the same time, they were quick to conclude that something new has happened in military affairs. It was perhaps the blitzkrieg of ideas and new papers on the subject emanating from the US media, that the idea of a new war form—information war—was so easily sold to China and Russia. It may be interesting to scan the proliferation of these concepts to some of the countries relevant to India's security.

★★★

Impact on China, Russia, Israel, Pakistan

Political and military debacles in Vietnam provided the trigger, and spectacular victory in the First Iraq War gave the marketing slogan for information war

As part of external environment scan it may be relevant to study the impact of Iraq wars and hence the IW concepts on some other major military powers. In view of immediate relevance to India, we may look at IW concepts developed in Russia, China, Pakistan and Israel.

Discussions in this section establishes the fact that although none of the nations mentioned above questioned the basic tenets of IW as propagated after the Gulf War, the level and the form of adaption have been a function of their respective:-

- Geopolitical aspirations
- Threat perception
- Politico-Military dynamics
- Demonstrated capability to adapt and manage change
- Resources available in terms of technology, human capital, national power, and economic health

Hence, the relevance of this section when it comes to adapting the available knowledge on the subject to the Indian aspirations and conditions. Some parts in this section may appear to be digressing from the main theme of the study but lateral views help to correct the perspective and hence sharpen the focus on the main objective. This is where the parts on the historical evolution and behaviour of political leadership fits in.

Russia

Authoritarian and at times very ruthless leaders traditionally have governed Russia, with scant regard for democracy and rights of her citizens. Post Bolshevik revolution there has been limited participation of people in governance through the communist party. Erstwhile USSR or even present day Russia has been a great military power for centuries. No country has been able to subjugate the Russians through military might, be it Napoleon or Hitler. Russia fought both the great wars alongside the western countries. During the First World War, she was with France and during the Second World War, Russia was part of the Allied forces. However, Russians have always been wary of the Western European countries and the Americans. The rivalry came to the fore after the Second World War heralding almost four decades of cold war.

Balkanization of erstwhile USSR into Russia and other smaller nations had been a highly traumatic event for the Russians. It marked culmination of social, economic, and political crises. After 1991, the Russian revival was seen to be accelerating under President Putin. Russian intervention in Ukraine and their cyber-attacks on Estonia, Georgia are an indication of traditional Russian nationalism. Putin's role in the American elections of 2016 and their involvement in Syria will revive the Russians' pre-eminent importance in global affairs as a counter to American monopoly.

Russia has not demonstrated any major capability in innovation and flexibility in adopting macro-economic strategies, and micro economic efficiencies. She has always been an economic underdog in the global comity of nations. The rich natural resources especially oil and natural gas perhaps made the Russians complacent and inefficient. Nevertheless, her progress in military technologies has been impressive.

During the Cold War period, Russia competed with the Western powers in conventional and nuclear weapons. The West was always wary of the Russian 'numbers' in ships, aircraft, tanks, guns, soldiers,and also nuclear warheads. Russian weapon technology seldom came close to that of the West. After the breakup of USSR in 1990, the Russians found themselves way behind the Americans in weapon technology especially after witnessing the First Iraq War. This prompted the Russians to focus on the cyber war technologies, which are cheap and can be very destructive in conjunction with conventional weapons (termed as kinetic weapons by the Americans and of course by most of the Indian writers!). They have operationalized large number of ideas and technologies especially in the cyber war domain.

Russian reaction to the First Iraq War 1991—heralding a new war form—is similar to that of the Chinese. They realized that Russian technology is not so advanced as that of the US and the NATO allies. Besides, Russia does not have the economic muscle to invest in such high technology weapon systems that can match the NATO and the US. Nevertheless, it was very obvious to the Russians that to match the Western capability, Russia needs to change the way their military had been preparing against the NATO forces and to maintain some credible military alternative to the West.

As per the Russian approach, information operations are broken into two components, information-technical and information-psychological and not into so many elements as the US Armed Forces do. Information-technical includes all technical aspects dealing with the network, network attack weapons, cyber weapons, and so on. As regards Information-psychological, the Russians were more concerned, and also had better in-depth understanding of this domain compared to the West. In 1990, Russian society had gone through a disruptive phase. The nation was still coping against the psychological and social shock from disintegration of the great Soviet Union. They were wary of the Western temptation engulfing the Russian society. Besides, they discovered a form of ideological invasion by the West in the form of intellectual information warfare.

The Russian academicians were fairly advanced in understanding the role of propaganda, which produces subconscious association of ideas and assists in manipulation of minds. This affects reasoning, behaviour, values, emotions, beliefs, decisions, and actions. Thus, reducing the resistance capabilities of the enemy.

Even the Kosovo war in 1999, was seen in this context by the Russians which as per them was a virtual war, the first 'no contact' war. As per the Russians, what made the West win in Kosovo was their superior information technologies and control over the international media. Here also the Russians found themselves quite inadequate against the Western forces. Tight control/or intense influence of the media by the West was identified as a key component in waging successful psychological operations.

The Russian military experts while analysing the first Chechen conflict accept that their Information War in this conflict was a failure. One of the reasons for this failure as per them was that the Russian media were not under state control and were often financed by Chechens. Thus, the entire media favoured Chechen rebels. Besides, Russia's Defence Ministry did not provide journalists with official information that the Russian public needed.

As General of the Army Makhmut Gareyev noted, 'No army can operate successfully if...it is being morally beaten down by its own compatriots and the media.' For the second conflict, information centres were established in two republics that are neighbours to Chechnya, the republics of Dagestan and North Ossetia. Journalists were supplied with videos and briefing material and escorted to specific locations by Russia's official representatives. In this way, the information centres were able to better control information produced about the conflict. The reader should not buy this line without questioning the credibility of media which is 'fed' by the Armed Forces. Remember the difference in credibility of American media in 1991 and 2003! Also, the Russian understanding of use of media by the NATO in Kosovo may not be very accurate.

At the start of the second conflict in Chechnya in 1999 more than 150 control points and radio-electronic facilities operating in the interests of the illegal armed formations were found. By the end of September, seventy-seven of them had been destroyed by fire engagement, including twenty-two of the thirty-eight radio broadcasting stations. The power was cut off from eighteen radio-electronic facilities. Some 90 percent of the base stations (to include re-transmitters) for radio relay, cellular, and other types of communications were either seized or put out of commission.

These two conflicts in Chechnya bring out the synergy between components of IW addressing the psychological warfare aspects and those involved in conduct of physical destruction. This also highlights the Russian propensity to use cyberspace (which for them includes the Internet and the media) in conjunction with weapons, which can cause physical destruction of the selected targets. This war form was named as hybrid war in the IW taxonomy.

The Russian IW capabilities are built around psychological

warfare or psychological operations. Thus in consonance with this prioritization, the building blocks of IW, as per the Russian concept, are social control, social manoeuvring, information manipulation, disinformation, fabrication of information, lobbying, blackmail, and extortion of desired information. At operational level, their approach in waging psychological operations revolves around the following:-

- Create new and imaginary threats so that the target audience becomes indecisive and is distracted from the main goal.
- Flood the target with large volume of contradictory information so the processing systems of the target get overloaded.
- Magnify the major weakness of the adversary to a disproportionately high level so the target audience's decision-making processes are paralyzed.
- Create enormous amount of chaff so that the adversary's sensors are exhausted.
- Mislead the enemy through deception plans.
- Create rift amongst the allies through process of division.
- Subdue the main threat to the enemy so that the adversary becomes complacent.
- Russian concepts of psychological operations also include provocation so that the enemy is made to commit costly errors.
- In their doctrine, the Russians reserve the right to wage conventional war against IW threats.

Russians also focus on netwar, which involves intelligence agencies, intellectuals, scientists, journalists, and activists to disseminate information for the target audience or general global audience to shape the thinking and decision-making processes of current or potential adversaries. In essence, the Russian concepts emanate from the question of survival of the Russian civilization, which is conservative in the post-liberalized era. Conservatism is the chosen word by the Russians for excessive centralized control and hierarchy-driven fixated society.

Their concept of information security too is based on state of protection of national interest in the information sphere to maintain balance among the interest of the individual, society, and the state. In the military, the psychological operations are directed against the morale of the soldier and to compromise their patriotism.

Notwithstanding all the emphasis on psychological warfare, the Russian propaganda has not been able to impress the Western audience so far. The Western media is seen to be free, open to diverse ideas and views, and also supported by massive affluence of Western societies. Hence as per the dictum, 'what you see sells', the Western media is much more credible.

Russian IW capability in the technical domain is focused on software weapons, which include virus that can break through information security, programmable microchips, Trojan Horses, remote attack tools, hacking, Electromagnetic Pulse (EMP), anti-satellite weapons, and automated control system. As per the NATO assessment, Russians are very advanced in Information Warfare technologies, processes, and doctrines. There have been a number of cases where the Russians have been charged with triggering cyber attacks against the neighbouring states, which were part of the erstwhile USSR. Prominent among these attacks are against Estonia in 2007, Georgia in 2008, Chechnya, Ukraine, Crimea. Some of these attacks were hybrid in nature where the Russians used conventional weapons in conjunction with the non-lethal cyber weapons. A close scrutiny of all these attacks reveals that:-

- The methods used were not very advanced and sophisticated.
- The end result was not what was desired. The target country came out stronger from the attacks.
- Russian reputation in the region did suffer a setback.

Russian Cyber Operations to Influence American Elections 2016. (Report prepared by CIA, FBI, and the NSA)

The three agencies in the US, which were tasked to examine the extent of Russian involvement in influencing the American presidential elections in 2016 were unanimous in their finding that the Russians did influence the American elections successfully. As per these agencies, the attempt was audacious, direct, synchronized by Russian diplomatic activities during those times. The primary objective of Russian involvement was to attack the credibility of American democracy. A gist of the report is given in Appendix B.

China

Chinese history as a nation dates back to 4000 years (1700 BC). On this account, she is one of the most ancient nations in the world along with India. A number of foreign powers have ruled China in the past. This includes Mongolia and Japan. Modern communist China came into being on 1 October 1949 along with a part of China – Taiwan – becoming Republic of China and the Mainland China came to be known as People's Republic of China. Taiwan is under the American protection and hence a reason for Sino-American conflict.

Like Russia, Mainland China has been governed by a single party for the past seven decades. There is no scope for multi-party democracy in China in the foreseeable future. However, in spite of single party communist rule, China has been able to re-invent herself at least thrice during the past seven decades. To start with, the Chinese leadership had the courage and determination to engage the American forces on the Korean War from 1951 to 1954. This resulted in bifurcation of Korea into North and South Korea. North Korea has been under the influence of China and Russia.

With this China emerged as a serious contender to American influence in Korea. China as a nation has been very ambitious and has not hesitated in challenging Americans even when the nation was just born. In 1954, Chinese forces marched into Tibet and annexed an independent country. There was not much opposition from the UN or the neighbouring India. In 1962, China inflicted a humiliating military defeat on India and asserted herself as the unquestioned military power in Asia.

However, on the economic front the first two decades since 1949 had not been very good. Especially the period of Great Leap Forward under Mao was a disaster. It was in 1970 that China commenced opening up her economy. In 1979, she formalized trade relations with the US. Post 1980, China embarked upon a very rapid economic growth. By 2012, China was the second largest economy after US (though still far behind the US economy). She overtook Germany as the highest exporter in the world. China has the largest number of people connected to the Internet, though all the Chinese Internet users are heavily monitored and have restricted freedom to use the Internet. Chinese cyberspace has the capability of isolating itself from the global Internet as and when the need arises.

Thus China has shown tremendous capability to adapt to the economic challenges at a reasonably fast pace. The leadership has shown remarkable capability to take decisions and operationalize the decisions in a very short time. Since 2014, Chinese growth rate has slowed down and India has taken over as the fastest growing economy. In spite of the impressive rate at which China has grown and emerged as a global power, there are major shortcomings, which are likely to obstruct her march to global supremacy. First, though China boasts of largest number of Internet users in the country, the quality of content that flows and is generated in the Internet in China is very mediocre—mainly advertisement and government controlled information. Bulk of the technologies developed by China are through infringement of Intellectual Property Rights and stealing from West through cyber espionage. Of late, the Western countries including the United States have become very wary of China's cyber activities. The Chinese road map for embracing IW doctrines is primarily focused on her long-term goal to challenge American supremacy.

Post First Gulf War in 1991, the People's Liberation Army (PLA) transformed from a mechanized to an informationized force. The Chinese have drawn a distinction between Information Warfare (IW) and Information Operations (IO). As per them, IW occurs all the time, in peace and war. It is part of the ideological struggle. An IO only occurs in wartime. In 2002, the PLA's IW General Staff proponent, General Dai Qingmin, listed six forms of IW in the authoritative Chinese journal China Military Thought. These are operational security, deception, computer network attack, electronic warfare, intelligence, and physical destruction. These match with what the US Armed Forces pamphlet on IW.

Two of these forms stand out. These are electronic warfare and computer network warfare. China's concept of 'integrated network-electronic warfare (INEW),' similar in content to the US concept of network-centric warfare, refers to a series of combat operation actions with integrated use of EW and CNW measures on the informationized battlefield designed to disrupt the normal operation of the enemy's battlefield network information systems, and protect one's own. The objective of INEW is to seize battlefield information superiority. Dai, the Chinese IW military expert, had earlier defined information operations as, 'a series of operations within an information environment as the basic battlefield condition, with military information and an information system as the direct operational target, and with electronic warfare and a computer network war as the principal forms.'

As per him, there are three characteristics of information supremacy. First, it is an integrated combat posture that can greatly affect the war as a whole. Second, it allows freedom in the information dimension; is conducted in three areas (electromagnetic space, computer network space, decision-makers' cognition and belief system) and two levels (attack against information systems, attack against human's cognition and belief system). Third, it influences events in the information dimension so as to affect events in the physical dimension. China intends to use IW in one of three ways. Depending on the geopolitical situation confronting its leaders, it can be a tool of war or it can be a way to achieve victory without war or a means to enhance stability through the promotion of new military theories.

There is another Chinese view on the First Gulf War. As per Colonels Qiao Liang and Wang Xiangsui of PLA, the 1991 Gulf War has created more myth than reality. It was a war between highly unequal forces. The coalition forces used diplomacy, sanctions, psychological pressure, political isolation, and market-dynamics besides using modern technology. One of the lessons from this war as per these Chinese writers is emergence of unrestricted war where economic, religious, regulatory forces can be used to achieve victory. The Chinese added terrorism, creating chaos in the enemy country, ecological aggression, use of Internet to subvert the leadership and the people as new elements in this unrestricted war.

If all these components are included in the conflict spectrum, then there is no distinction between peace and war. Nations exist in perpetual conflict environment. The emphasis is on 'control' and not on killing. The Chinese called it soft power where people are not slaughtered. Also, the military is not the main force to fight this war. The entire nation is involved in this continuous undeclared war. Besides, this kind of conflict may not be between two nations. Other non-state groups such as drug peddlers, hackers, financial criminals, fundamentalists, traffickers, ideology-driven fanatics, etc. can wage wars against state. Alternatively, nations can use one or more of these groups to exploit social, political, judicial, administrative, financial, or ethnic weaknesses in the enemy state.

The Chinese are also aware of the tremendous costs of high technology weapons and appear to be wary of pursuing a policy of procuring or investing huge finances in weapon systems. They compared a B2 bomber, which (at thirteen to fifteen billion dollars) costs three times its equivalent weight in gold. As per them excessive expenditure on high technology weapon systems is an American trait not suitable to the Chinese. The Chinese Armed Forces and the people must learn to do more with less. Please note that the Chinese expenditure on import of weapon systems has been continuously decreasing compared to just the opposite trend for India's import (2010 to 2016).

The focus of Chinese as a nation is to force the enemy to make a cognitive error so that friendly forces get a diplomatic opportunity. Against a strong enemy such as US—strategic manoeuvre, speed, Computer Network attack and communication satellite attack should be employed to neutralize the combat zone superiority of the adversary. The term used by the Chinese to fight an asymmetric war with a stronger enemy is 'ShaShouJian' which means assassin's mace. It is that weapon which the assassin uses to neutralize a stronger prey.

There is also reference to the '24-Character Strategy'. A strategy enunciated in twenty-four characters of the Chinese language. As per this strategy, 'Calmly observe, secure the position, face the events with calm, hide our capabilities and wait for the right moment, try to maintain a low profile and never claim leadership.'

Chinese security establishments have found cyberspace a very potent domain to conduct information war. It was just after the First Gulf War that the Chinese commenced exploiting cyberspace to gain information and wage psychological, ideological, and espionage operations. However, in the beginning these operations were attributed to non-state actors and patriotic Chinese hackers. Since 2007, the Westerns nations and the US have attributed Chinese cyber offensive operations to groups actively supported by the Chinese military.

The Federal Bureau of Investigation (FBI) of US and the German intelligence have placed the blame at the Chinese government for all cyber espionage in European countries and the US. The primary objective of this cyber espionage is to steal sensitive information pertaining to military technologies of the West. Information pertaining to Government organizations, defence manufacturers, and supply chain partners were attacked and sensitive information was stolen. Besides, the Chinese also extract information from personnel of Western MNCs working in China. It was also reported that the Chinese have raised specialized information warfare units, which conduct EW, cyber, psychological, and perception management operations.

An interesting feature of Chinese strategy is the policy of active defence. China declares that her strategy is purely defensive. They do not have any offensive design against any nation. However, their defensive strategy is active or proactive in nature. In pursuance with this policy, China launches military or non-military operations against threats perceived by them. These operations are unrestricted. Bulk of the operations spectrum is non-violent, non-contact. Most of these operations are launched in cyberspace. It is only when the need arises that these operations become overt military operations.

In consonance with this policy, China has acted in Korea (1952), Tibet (1954), India (1962), Vietnam (1979). Even the current cyber operations are considered pre-emptive in nature. The Chinese government has exploited Edward Snowden's revelations to influence international perception. They quote Snowden to say that the US forces were the first to start threatening Chinese security. They have called American allegation as false and incorrect.

In synch with the Chinese grand strategy, the Chinese government has engaged with major international powers on streamlining the international cyber security and cyber behaviour norms. They took part in the Cyber Working Group with US and other Western nations including Russia. In May 2014, the Chinese suspended talks with the US in Cyber Working Group due to the quality of diplomatic relations. However, they formalized Cyber Security Agreement with Russia, which has been dubbed by media as Cyber Pact between China and Russia

American Reflections on Chinese Military Power Approach and Confrontations with the US

The American establishment finds China very opaque and secretive. As per the American Congress Report on People's Republic of China, they are not clear about the motivation Chinese have for such fast-paced modernization of their Armed Forces. To a third party, this doubt amongst the American leadership is quite intriguing. China in her own way is doing what the American have been doing for a long time. The Chinese can legitimately question the presence of US carrier groups in their backyard.

As per American perception, China wants to exploit knowledge created by others. They have around three thousand spy companies doing this job for the Chinese. Their students and residents in the US send information back to China. Bulk of this is economic intelligence. The US leadership also feels that China is not only extracting dual use technology from the US and advanced European countries but is also disseminating this information to countries inimical to the US interests (Iran, Sudan, Myanmar).

There have been open confrontations between the US and China in the past. In 1999, when the NATO forces bombed Chinese embassy in Belgrade (by mistake), the Chinese responded by Distributed Denial of Services (DDoS) attack on a large number of US websites. As per CIA, as China's foreign interest widens, Beijing will call upon her intelligence network to provide inputs to assess the intentions of states capable of harming China's interests. In the context of technology and information warfare, it is interesting to note the Chinese concept of gaining information. The CIA terms it as processing mosaic or grains of sand. This primarily involves:-

- Employing ethnic Chinese sources.
- Not utilizing elaborate intelligence tradecraft.
- Chinese rely more on amateurs as against employing intelligence professionals.
- Their intelligence is high on volume and low on quality or grade.

As per Richard Clarke (a top American bureaucrat in charge of American Cyber security and author of *Cyber War*), China have done all the things a nation would do if it contemplated having an offensive cyber capability and also thought that it might itself be targeted by cyber war. It has:-

- Created citizen hacker groups.

- Engaged in extensive cyber espionage.
- Taken several steps to defend its own cyberspace.
- Laced US and other countries with logic bombs.
- Established cyber war military units.

By 2003, the Chinese had announced creation of cyber warfare units housed in the Naval Base at Hainan. The techniques and weapons they developed for cyber war include:-

- Planting information mines.
- Conducting information reconnaissance
- Changing network data.
- Releasing information bombs.
- Dumping information garbage.
- Disseminating propaganda.
- Applying information deception.
- Establishing network spy stations.
- Organizing information defence.

It will be interesting to note that from 1998 to 2012 China had been precariously unstable. There have been more than 1,00,000 mass incidents per year. The coercive control of the state on the population is slipping. This resulted in an expenditure of ninety-five billion dollars on internal security for intelligence-led policing.

Chinese Operations against Terrorism

China has been facing religious terrorism by the Uyghur in the Xinjiang province (around 40% Han Chinese and 50% Uyghur population—primarily Muslims). The state commissioner for counterterrorism and security said, 'Islamist separatists pose the most prominent challenge to China's stability and security.' The Chinese Foreign Ministry emphasized its willingness to work with the international community to fight terrorism. Chinese President Xi Jinping, according to Reuters, has called for great wall of iron to safeguard Xinjiang.

The Uyghur extremism has spread to other parts of China too. In 2013 and 2014, they attacked places very close to Tiananmen Square. The Turkistan Islamic Party (TIP) supporting the Uyghur militancy wants to damage and destabilize the Chinese economy and undermine the people's confidence in the Chinese Government.

China faces a major dilemma in fighting the Islamic militancy. The militants fighting on behalf of TIP have training establishments and safe havens in Pakistan and Afghanistan. In order to eliminate the TIP influence, China needs to persuade Pakistan to neutralize the camps and support elements in her territory. Besides, China needs to join the West in fighting terrorism globally. It is here that China has been cautious. China is wary of reaction from the militant groups who would intensify attacks on Chinese establishments globally and hence weaken her economic clout.

Israel

Israel as a nation is an ancient state with around 3000 years of history. She came into existence twice during the ancient period during the Babylonian conquest followed by the Persian and the Roman rule. After the Second World War, with the decline and ultimate fall of the British Empire, Israel was carved out of Palestine based on the UN vote of partition of Palestine. During this period, Palestine itself was a British colony. Conflict with the neighbours has been a continuing part of Israel's existence post 1948. The newly born nation lost almost one percent of her population during the war in 1948. This was followed by invasion by Egypt in 1956, the Six-Day War in 1967, the Yom Kippur War of 1973, the Lebanon wars of 1982 and 2006. Israel won all these wars very convincingly.

After her formation in 1948, Israel for a brief period enjoyed Soviet patronage triggered by the Russian interest in the Middle East. This was followed by the French interest in Israel during the French struggle in Algeria. However, after the war in Algeria was over, the French lost interest in Israel around 1967. It was after the

Six-Day War in 1967 that the US came close to Israel. Since then Israel-US bond has been stable.

In all her engagements with the neighbours, Israel has had no difficulty in defeating them one-on-one as also when some of the neighbours got together to attack Israel. Historically, Israel has been unable to stand up to the threats from distant empires such as Babylon, Persia, Macedonia, Rome, Turkey, and Britain. Paradoxically, Israel—a small country—must manage external threats far outside her region. She survives so long as she manoeuvres great powers commanding enormous resources. Israel's history shows that some form of subordination is inevitable for her survival. To a very limited extent, she is subordinate to the United States now.

Israel, as a nation, is one of the most innovative, technically advanced countries in the world. In the Middle East, she is far superior to all the other nations in the region in all the competitive indices (identified by the World Economic Forum). Israel Defence Forces (IDF) have been outstanding in their performance in conventional operations in 1967 (Six-Day War), in 1973 (the Yom Kipper War) and also in 1982 across the Golan Height. But that is where the success stories (of complete victories) of Israel end. After spectacular victories in the short, swift, conventional operations of fire and manoeuvre, the prolonged engagements with the Hamas, Hezbollah bring different set of challenges in the virtual space governed by the cyber war tools and techniques. It is here that the decisive victories against the Lebanese, Gaza strip forces become illusive.

Gideon Avidor, who has been in active service in the IDF in 1967, 1973 and 1982 observes that the virtual domain of the modern conflict requires altogether different approach. First, given the proliferation of social media, the Armed Forces have to observe tremendous restraint in using its superior destructive capabilities. Second, decisive victories are now relics of the past. The forces need to brace up for a long indecisive war where the non-military participation is much more than the military participation. Lastly, the 'new end state' – the main objective as per Clausewitz cannot be defined. It is an exercise in futility as per him.

Though, the Israeli youth is very much conversant with technology and the nuances of social media, the youth on the other side in Gaza and Lebanon are equally clever in exploiting the social media and cyberspace. In their article, 'Information and Warfare: The Israeli Case', Gideon Avidor and Russel Glen observe that modern wars in the information age has three dimensions. The first is the close combat dimension characterized by fire and manoeuvre, the second is physical elements farther afield and the third is the virtual space where cyber operations are conducted. The IDF is quite capable to achieve decisive victory and control in the first dimension anywhere in the combat zone against its adversaries irrespective of their number and preparation. In the second dimension also victory can be achieved quickly and control for limited time can be exercised. It is the virtual space where victory implies controlling the behaviour and decision making of the adversary that Israeli forces find themselves in the uncertain zone.

In their operation in Southern Lebanon (2006), and Gaza (2009, 2012, 2014) the deft handling of the social media by the cyber militia of Hamas and Hezbollah convinced the international audience of their victories over the mighty Israeli forces. Use of Facebook, Twitter, Instagram in six different languages by Arab youth kept their morale high and prolonged the war. Against this backdrop, the expectations of the Israeli population placed additional pressure on the political leaders and the IDF. Though the IDF has been quite capable and quick to wrest the initiative, influence the proceeding of the short wars, gain supremacy in the combat zone; its efforts to control the behaviour and decision making of the opponents (the ultimate signs of victory) have always failed.

This is the situation for Russia in her war against Chechnya, US in Iraq and Afghanistan, India in Kashmir, China against Xinjiang, and Pakistan in Baluchistan.

Pakistan

Pakistan came into being as a Muslim-majority Islamic State, on 14 August 1947. Before this, the land mass known as Pakistan was part of India. Until 17 December 1971, Pakistan existed in two parts—the East Pakistan adjacent to the Indian state of Bengal and West Pakistan across the Redcliff line. After 17 December 1971, the East Pakistan separated from Pakistan consequent to the Indo-Pak War of 1971. Besides being an Islamic state, Pakistan does not have any independent and rational identity away from her historical past with India. Her political leaders have inadvertently defined her existence as an opposition to India. They also considered the use of Muslim proxy warriors as the legitimate tools of the state. Having lost all her wars with India since 1948 Pakistan finds the proxy war through jihadi (in the backdrop of nuclear threat) approach as the only viable option with India. This has been the biggest folly of the state. Pakistan approach to IW is in support of these clandestine non-state and deep-state actors.

Pakistan does not seem to have any elaborate doctrine or concepts on IW—as per the open source literature on the subject. Since information on the famous Inter-Services Intelligence of Pakistan is scanty, it is possible that ISI may have some methods, concepts for supporting global terrorism as also for perception management of their own population. Some of their scholars and military thinkers do mention the need for developing technologies and concepts on IW to exploit the payoffs of using IT in warfare. Specific reference in these papers is to computer network attacks and cyber security. Pakistan does have Electronic Warfare Units, good weapon locating radars of US origin, good air defence system and AWACS procured from China. The avionics in the fighter aircraft are of earlier versions of F16 and Chinese J7 fighter aircraft. The Pakistani Armed forces prefer the American weapon systems and are wary of Chinese systems due to their poor quality. As per them, the American toys are more reliable then the Chinese weapons.

Pakistani weapon systems in general are high on ordnance and low on intelligence. Strategic concepts are based on strong riposte, playing the nuclear weapon card as threat against the Indian conventional offensive. Recently the Bajwa Doctrine enunciated by the Pakistani armed forces affirms that Pakistan has done enough to fight global war on terror on behalf of US and is not going to take orders from US and the West. It is for the rest of the world to do more than what they have done for Pakistan (perhaps in supporting Pakistan in her quest for international intervention in Kashmir). As Pakistan is being jettisoned by the US, the Russians appear to be filling the vacuum to create a counter to the American influence.

Pakistan has substantial number of young people who can indulge in effective hacking of Indian websites—especially those that do not follow stringent cyber security protocols. This group, which calls itself as Pakistan Cyber Army (PCA), has in fact defaced many Indian sites including those of the Indian Government. However, Pakistan has not demonstrated advanced capability in developing and deploying advanced cyber weapons, though it may not be very difficult for them to collaborate with the Chinese to scale up cyber offensive against India.

So far, we have gone with the flow of events and the deductions that were drawn in the immediate aftermath of the Gulf War in 1991. A lot has happened since then. Hence there is a definite need to look at the events—that shaped the theories of IW—once again with a lateral view. Analysis of the epistemology will be in order.

★★★

Analysis of Epistemology

The changing global environment in the Information Age while the nature of war remains the same

The term 'Information Warfare' emanated from two sources. First, the term was defined in the US Manual 100-6. It was validated in the Iraq War of 1991. Second source is the best-selling book by Alvin Toffler, *War and Anti War*. The Iraq War of 1991 was widely publicized in the book, *The First Information War*, contributing Editor Alan D Campen. This book was sponsored by a company which was involved in manufacture and marketing of communication systems. The subject of this book caught the imagination of military thinkers and academicians involved in national security in China, Russia, India, and a host of other countries.

The theories and concepts envisaged in the book as also in the manual were accepted in all the discussions that followed the First Gulf War. The US transformed their war fighting machinery to fight this new form of war; China and Russia too added new capabilities and force structure. If we look at the sequence of these historic military events, it appears that the US theorized a new war form—Information War.

Then validated the concept by fighting one against Iraq. Rest of the world followed suite by remodelling their weapon systems and force structure on what the US had demonstrated to them. Two lesser-known American military operations before the Iraq War of 1991 are US operations in Grenada and Panama.

To summarize in brief, the theory of this new war form postulates:-

- Information in itself is a valuable resource.
- Nations wage war for dominance of this critical resource.
- Information war amounts to defending own information and stealing/disrupting that of the enemy.
- Nations with powerful and secure information systems have a shorter decision cycle as compared to their adversary. As a consequence of this competence, these nations emerge victorious in war.

The most commonly identified components of this new war form as given in various US doctrines are:-

- o Psychological Operations.
- o Electronic Warfare.
- o Military Deception.
- o Operations Security.
- o Information Assurance.
- o Computer Network Attacks.

Besides the above, the literature on the subject also includes the following as components of Information war (Martin C Libicki):-

- o Command and Control Warfare.
- o Intelligence Warfare.
- o Hacker Warfare.
- o Economic Information Warfare.
- o Cyber Warfare.

Some other authors also include physical destruction as one more component of Information Warfare.

Around the time the Vietnam War was being fought and right up to the First Iraq War, Alvin and Heidi Toffler wrote a series of best-selling books on the information age society. These are; *Future Shock* in 1970, *Third Wave* in 1980, *Power Shift* in 1990, *War and Anti War* in 1993. These books are widely referred to in military literature emanating from the American Generals (especially General Sullivan who had been the Chief in the US Army). The major issues propagated in their writings are:-

- With dramatic advances in information technologies, the global societies have moved to the third wave. This wave commenced its rise in the later half of 1960s. This also marked the end of industrial age society.
- Knowledge and information are the key resources in the third wave society.
- Nations compete and also engage in conflict for dominance of knowledge in the third wave era.
- Though Alvin Toffler did not write much about the

Information War, he did make reference to Information War while highlighting the American victory in the First Iraq War.

- Toffler also endorsed General Westmoreland's views on precision navigation and targeting in third wave wars.
- As per him, third wave wars will entail minimal collateral damage since the destruction of targets will be done by precision-guided smart weapon systems supported by sensor to shooter links.

Since the epistemology of information war is based on the above popular books and literature as also on events in history, it is that much more relevant and easy to check the fact sheet to ascertain whether the hypotheses are validated. First war in the information age—Vietnam War—was fought between the most advanced and comparatively primitive militaries. To start with, US forces lost the war in spite of all the advantages of information age. Second, the casualty to military and the civilian population was huge. In terms of sheer brutality and inhuman nature of fighting, it was perhaps worse than the two world wars. Third, the physical damage to the Vietnamese infrastructure caused by the Americans was colossal. Bulk of the physical damage was to the non-military infrastructure directly linked with the well-being of ordinary men and women. Fourth, this war was not fought for any information or knowledge dominance. The only objective of the war was to check expansion of Chinese and Russian influence in Vietnam. Ironically, six years after this meaningless destruction, China invaded Vietnam in 1979. Thus the American apprehension that if Vietnamese are left to themselves they will get into Chinese or Russian influence was misplaced.

In knowledge society the most important question, which needs to be addressed is, when should a nation go to war. Even the first and second wave theories on wars suggest that it should be waged after exhausting all the means of non-military, non-violent competition to reach a better end state. If the goal can be achieved without resorting to violence and strife to the people, and destruction of assets then war must be avoided. This appears to be the most relevant outcome of situation and goal analysis. The information sources and cognitive capabilities of the political and military leadership must answer this question correctly. There is no scope of error here especially if you are endowed with all the knowledge resources. Secondly, having started the war (based on the goal analysis and knowledge obtained from technical and cognitive resources), nations in the information age must know when to end the war so that human and material damages are minimized. Thirdly, the nation, which commences the war, must win—assuming that she has done all the calculations right based on the information and knowledge resources. Vietnam War was a huge American failure on all counts.

Let us look at the Iraq War of 1991—the First Information War. The trigger to this war was Iraqi invasion of Kuwait. This surprised the American and British political leadership! Being 'surprised' by the Iraqi move was the first failure of American establishment in terms of Information War. In 1990, both these countries had almost a century old relationship with Iraq. Right from the emergence of Iraq from Mesopotamia, the region between the two rivers – Tigris and Euphrates, the two leading nations of those times had influence in the region. The British and American efforts had propped up Iraq in the region. During the long war between Iran and Iraq, US supported Iraq by providing weapons and diplomatic support. Even when Iraq used chemical weapons against Iran for mass destruction, the Americans looked the other way.

The American oil companies were very active in Iraq (though these were later nationalized by Saddam Hussein). The CIA was extremely active in the region. And of course the knowledge era leader of the world had all the technologies at her command to monitor Iraqi moves. Hence, the failure to check Iraq in time to avoid destruction in Kuwait—especially when the US was committed by treaty to protect Kuwaiti interests—proved too expensive in terms of human lives and property. Once Iraq invaded Kuwait, the US very rightly mobilized international support and intervened at the head of coalition forces given sanction by the UN. Iraq very quickly saw reason and withdrew; accepted all the conditions set by the coalition forces. The First Iraq War of 1991 was over very quickly. We need to now look at the war from the IW perspective.

First, the entire world was against Iraq. Even her all-time friend Russia, had abandoned her. No Arab nation stood by Iraq (though Iraq had left US in favour of Arab nations during the six-days Arab Israel war). For the coalition forces Japan, Saudi Arabia, Germany, and Kuwait paid for the war efforts including wages for the troops. The combined efforts of thirty odd nations were directly pitted against Iraq. Iraq was on her own. There was no comparison between the US war-fighting technologies and that of Iraq though Iraq did have Russian and some American weapons. These were not as modern as those of the coalition forces. More importantly, the Iraqi forces were not akin to the Vietnamese or the Israeli forces. They had not taken part in any modern war except for crushing internal descent and controlling Kurdish uprising. The Iraqi people as also bulk of the Armed Forces—except for the Republican Guard—were controlled by fear and systemic indoctrination.

The Iraqi military as also the political leadership under the Ba'athist Party were acutely worried about their personal survival under a ruthless dictator known for getting his own military leaders and people killed in the most brutal manner. Hence, there was no leadership at the operational and functional levels. The strategic leadership too was totally oblivious to the ground realities.

Compare this with the US and UK soldiers with more than 500 years of experience in fighting wars under national leadership which by all standards was much more developed, egalitarian and endowed with collective wisdom inclined towards national interests as against using the soldiers for personal glory. The US forces were tested in Grenada and Panama to fight joint operations. These two operations acted as pilot projects before the major project was undertaken in Iraq. Besides professional leadership, the US and UK soldiers were well trained in joint operations and had technical orientation. Thus, the US war-fighting machine in this war was par excellence. With thirty-eight days of intense air strike undertaken by around 2000 fighter and bomber aircrafts supported by AWACs, JSTARs, and E2C Hawk Eye it was a demonstration of the most synergistic and focused attack by any air power so far. Hence, when the American combat teams moved in, the battlefield was adequately prepared for quick victory for the ground forces. It took them just four days to achieve this victory.

Though no one can deny the stunning display of American military technology and her just cause, it may not be very prudent to formulate any theory based on this war. It was a war between two unequal forces not only in terms of weapons and morale but also in terms of will to fight and the international isolation of one as compared to complete global support for the other. Hence, the coalition victory in the war was quick and complete. The tactical aspects of Information Warfare, in the short duration of forty-two days, provide a good case study to highlight the technological superiority of a modern military.

Yes, by all accounts, the Iraq war of 1991 or the First Gulf War was a great military victory by a vastly superior force over a weak and degenerated army. But, twenty-seven years after the war it becomes very evident that Alan Campen and his co-writers wrote *The First Information War* too early and read too much into the victory of US forces over the Iraqi military. Firstly, the television shows by the CNN gave a tunnelled view of the war. The real war was much less spectacular than what the Americans and the rest of the world saw from the comforts of their living rooms. Second, the Iraqi people launched the real war in Iraq after Saddam was defeated.

The war was not over after the forty-two days of blitzkrieg. It laid the foundation for another prolonged conflict for the next twelve years. To start with, the end of the First Iraq War resuscitated the almost dead Al-Qaeda in the region. As the vanquished and suffering Iraqi people saw the American troops in their country, the will to resist the American occupation created a bulge in the terrorist recruitment and their resolve to fight the Americans on ground of their own choosing. In 1993, the Al-Qaeda targeted the World Trade Center in US. This was followed by the massive terrorist attack on the World Trade Center in 2001. In 2003, the American President declared the Second Iraq War with the aim of overthrowing the Iraqi President, Saddam Hussein. Simultaneously ground operations were launched in Afghanistan.

It is interesting to note that the Second Iraq War in 2003 was not christened as the Second Information War. This time, 'two of America's most distinguished historians bring clarity and depth to the first major war of the millennium. Reaching beyond the blaring headlines, embedded videophone reports and daily Centcombriefings…,' (This is how the authors, Williamson Murray and Major General Robert H Scales Jr. of *The Iraq War: A Military History* are introduced in the book published as part of the US Armed Forces History). The authors very categorically state, 'Technology may alter how wars are fought, but it will never change the fact that wars are conducted by human beings for political ends.' Sounds somewhat similar to what Clausewitz observed two centuries ago and Sun Tzu, Kautilya postulated 2000 years ago!! The unchanging nature of war as per General Scales and Williamsons are friction, fear, emotions, and human suffering. This in fact was the case during the First Iraq War too but the euphoria about the new war form somehow suppressed this eternal fact about war, modern or otherwise. Thus, whether it is first, second or third wave war, the nature of war remains the same. Nevertheless, the political and military environments in which these wars are to be fought are very different from the earlier wars. These include:-

- Modern wars in the information age will be characterized by the interdependence of three services. Hence, the biggest challenge for the nation will be to synergize the efforts and capabilities of army, navy, and the air force. Given the strong attachments to respective turfs and generally myopic views by the field commanders, this will have to be addressed very deftly. The three services need to learn to co-opt the relevant non-military capabilities of the nation into war fighting efforts. Clausewitz did envisage this requirement when he said that, 'all the national capabilities need to be mobilized for war.' Military organizations need to learn from the corporate world where the competition has shifted to managing supply chains consisting of independent entities cooperating and collaborating together to create excellence in products and services.

- The main pillars of governance, which include central administration, political consensus, judiciary, police, research establishment, private sector, and even educational institutes, must converge to achieve the same politico-military goal. A major part of the conflict spectrum in Information War is outside the narrow domain of overt military conflict. Market domination, trade-related conflicts and open trade war (in spite of existence of WTO!), IPR infringements, cyber espionage to steal technological and military secrets, using the legal means to stall progress in the prospective enemy country, subverting the loyalty of citizens of the target country (through netwar) etc. are all means to achieve military and political goals without fighting. Hence, all the citizens in the nation including the critical institutions listed above must understand their respective roles in national security. Their efforts must converge to make the nation strong and secure. The governments need to invoke the spirit of supply chain management—'independent entities cooperating and collaborating to achieve common goals'.
- Modern military conflicts (as also modern business) do not

need large monolithic outfits with long, rigid hierarchies and strict rules. The combat as also conflict environments change very rapidly. The leaders need to be more concerned in creating the right capabilities at the right time and place rather than sticking to the same capability irrespective of the threat and the conflict environment. This will entail creating a culture of tri-service jointmanship at the strategic level and combined services and combined team functional environment at the forward edge of the combat zone. The strong affiliation to respective units and commands must give way to identification with the common vision and goals. Organizations will be ad hoc for a limited period of time in consonance with the task at hand.

- Speed of operation will create friction for the enemy and facilitate own operations. Thus, velocity of operations should replace 'mass'. Fast, well-equipped troops, quick to acclimatize and operate with efficiency will outclass slow-moving massed troops, high on quantity, and low on adaptability, mental mobility and flexibility. There will be a need to prepare the rear area troops to engage in active fighting to defend themselves.
- The information systems on the modern battlefield should be used in conjunction with physical contact with the adversary to convert information into tacit knowledge. In a large number of cases, the US troops in contact battles knew much more about the adversary than all those personnel at the strategic top who had access to modern technological means.
- Precision in IW has two facets. First, during the conventional operations where the precision is biased towards target acquisition and neutralization without collateral damage. Second level of precision—which is more difficult to achieve—is during the post hostilities operations against the terrorists or hostile resistance in the captured territory. This would involve

locating the real terrorists and identifying their state of morale and future planning. This capability of precision in identifying and targeting needs to be acquired by the infantry and the police. To achieve this, the troops, need to be equipped with cognitive ability as also with technical means. To assimilate and apply this capability the troops need to be trained at different levels of skills, aptitude, and intellectual maturity.

- Information operations pay rich dividends when launched simultaneously across various domains. This involves launching precision destruction of target in physical (kinetic) military operations, psychological operations, administrative and political support at the desired levels coupled with operations directed at providing healing touch to the population suffering from the ravages of war in their homeland. There need to be proper plans to integrate the population of the target country with the mainstream socio-political activities. The American forces (by their own admission) failed to envisage this last phase of operation in Iraq as also in Afghanistan. On the contrary, creation of Bangladesh by the Indian forces in 1971 has been a sterling example of this integration of conventional military operations with the humane approach to provide healing touch and stabilize the new nation as a democracy.
- The extended ranges of the information systems along with the need to safeguard the troops from highly lethal, non-nuclear weapons of mass destruction entails that the troops need to be widely dispersed. Also smaller mass must be given greater capabilities. This dispersion of small teams both in time and space equipped with greater ranges to 'see', 'understand' and influence will help generate greater combat power if the principles of network-centric war are adapted.
- War is not a continuous process. There are uneasy lulls in between for troops, which are widely dispersed. Such

empty battlefields, with long periods of inaction under fear of death and destruction, at times creates conditions where troops are overwhelmed by fear and fatigue. Adequate psychological preparation needs to be done to protect the soldiers from these adverse psychological effects. It may be of interest to note that the number of American troops who suffered from the psychological ill effects of Iraq wars was much higher than those killed and wounded. Against about 4000 troops killed in action from 2003 to 2011 more than tens of thousands of troops were made ineffective due to psychological impact. Thus while planning psychological warfare against the enemy it may be worthwhile to prepare own troops also to sustain the psychological impact of modern war.

- Notwithstanding the massive amount of information available to technologically advanced Armed Forces, the conditions on ground will invariably be different from those given in the plans. The real enemy and his moves will be different from what has been envisaged before joining battle. Hence there is need to inculcate the capability to fight the 'real enemy' and not the plan.
- We have seen earlier that starting ratios do not decide the outcome of battle. The Israelis were always less in number, both in terms of troops and weapons. Also, the Israeli weapons were not vastly different from those of their adversaries. Same has been the case in India–Pakistan conflicts. But the outcomes of conflicts have always been in favour of Israel and India. Thus, in modern wars (even in the earlier wars!), quality scores over quantity. Who decides quality? In the business world, it is the customer. In war, the outcome of the war in terms of longevity of sustained peace decides the quality of politico-military engagements.
- General Scales and Williamson underline the role of

training, leadership, and education of Armed Forces to fight and win the information age wars. Iraq did have sophisticated weapons; they did not know how to use those weapons. This was because of technical ignorance as also cultural deficiencies. As an example, the Iraqi troops had radio sets from a multitude of countries (Russia, US, France, Germany, UK). Many of these radio sets did not interoperate. At times when the radio sets could interoperate, the Iraqis kept the frequencies of communications in the same unit different from one component to another. Thus, when one of the battalions was overrun the brigade commander did not come to know. This was done intentionally to keep Iraqi troops from fleeing in the face of the enemy. Such a culture will definitely ensure defeat.

- After the intense phase of operations was over in Iraq, the American ground troops did not know how to handle the civilian population. The Americans also failed to bring normalcy to civil administration. This highlights the importance of education of junior officers and troops to deal with the civil administrations of different cultural hues and belief system.

Besides the military environment, the global political environment too has changed since 1991. The US made a very clear attempt to prove to the world at large that she has the capacity and the will to defeat a rogue state and confront those who threaten the vital interests of the US. But, where the Americans failed—both in Iraq and Afghanistan—is how should the military act after quick decisive victory. It was very easy to overthrow and even hang Saddam Hussein. The difficult part has been fighting the prolonged war since 2003. Even before the Bush administration launched the Second Iraq War, Senator Robert Byrd had outlined the strategic failure of American intervention in the Gulf. As per him, 'Americans are being seen with distrust in the entire region since the American administration and military demand obedience rather than seeking cooperation.' He also maintained that there was no conclusive proof linking 9/11 with Iraq. The American intervention in Iraq has made Saddam Hussein a hero instead of a demon. The US is seen as imposing Western values on the Arab culture. The turmoil in the region and the world cries for diplomacy not for war. In his opinion, the bombings by the Western forces in Bosnia, Somalia, Kosovo, Sudan, Afghanistan, Pakistan, Syria, and Iraq resulted in large-scale killing of Muslims. This has boosted fundamentalism. Well, all these may not be true; but this certainly provides an important and unbiased alternative course.

This brings us to very important questions pertaining to warfare, which need to be answered with better clarity and accuracy in the information age by the knowledge societies of the third wave:-

- Since wars have seldom benefitted the citizens of the victors and the victim, the first question should be on avoiding war. Thus, 'how should nations exist in peace and harmony so that full benefit of the information technology can be enjoyed by humanity in general,' should be the primary concern.
- The second aspect must address the means of creating wealth and evolving market conditions to ensure efficient supply chains to reduce inequalities and causes of conflict.
- Nations need to evolve a very high threshold for allowing competition to move to the region of conflict.
- Based on the experience from the bitter war against the terrorist organizations springing out of the two Iraq wars, the US Department of Defence laid more emphasis on cultural, ethnic, linguistic, religious, and regional aspects of prolonged war in regions with complex balance of power amongst various tribes, religious affiliations, and regional imbalances. Cognitive capabilities became more important than technological supremacy. Inspirational and transformational leadership, morale, appropriate behaviour of ground soldiers

with people in the region of conflict became more important. The role of special-forces changed from deep strike for destruction of select targets to deep and prolonged insertion for the purpose of indoctrination, training, crucial human intelligence. It emerged that there is need to coordinate air operations in conjunction with Special Forces.

- As the sample size increased in 'time' and 'data units', a new realization emerged. February 1991 and March 2003 do not mark the culmination of Iraq Wars I and II respectively. These dates mark two events as part of a bigger continuum reflecting the start of a prolonged conflict in a much wider region.
- The era of short, swift wars between militaries of nations resulting in decisive victories is over. It is almost impossible to predict decisive victory no matter how powerful a nation is in terms of weapons, economy, and even technology.
- In spite of overwhelming technology and information dominance—fear, emotions, leadership, physical violence, psychological damage to own and enemy forces, loss of human lives, elements of chance, and friction etc. which constitute the essential nature of war remain the same in the information age. However, the nature of global political environment as also military environment has changed.
- It is almost impossible to bring in political, cultural, societal changes in any region of the world by using military power howsoever superior in technology and operational capability. In such cases, swift victories during the conventional engagements follows prolonged involvement of invading troops in counter-terrorist and counter-resistance operations where the casualties to invading troops are much higher than that suffered during the initial engagement.
- The predominant role of media in the First and Second Gulf Wars appeared to be hyped. Within a couple of years of the First Gulf War, the other side of the popular stories came up

in the public domain. These were found to be true and more authentic. The credibility of the mainstream US and even global media took a massive hit. The tunnelled view provided by the mainstream media and the spin doctoring by the 'experts' was countered. This is the time the social media came into its own and occupied the space ceded by the mainstream media.

- By 2016, the Russians could exploit the social media to influence the presidential election in the US. Similarly, the militant groups ranged against the mighty Israeli Defence Forces could claim credibility against the most potent military in the region. In Afghanistan, the militant organizations countered the 'tech savvy' global media and the information systems of the superpower using primitive means of sharing information using local dialects and sentiments.
- The roaring success of Western Air Power in 1991 came a cropper in Kosovo. The NATO forces had estimated five to six days of air strike to subdue Milosevic. It took eighty-eight days of air operations resulting in huge adverse effects and loss of credibility. Milosevic backed out only when threatened with ground operations by NATO.
- Another factor, which emerged in the 1999 NATO operations in Kosovo, was the importance of reading the situation before the conflict. The ethnic strife was brewing up in Kosovo right from 1990. Deft handling of the situation when the Albanian Serbs and Muslim communities in Kosovo were at their initial stages of ethnic strife could have averted use of so much violence. Milosevic could not have exploited the turbulence to his advantage.
- The launch of American and British troops in Second Gulf War of 2003 became a case of blatant dictatorship in the most powerful democracy of the World. Inputs from all intelligence agencies negated the primary cause of the War—possession of weapon of mass destruction by Iraq. The NATO allies—

except for UK—refused to be on board. The UN did not approve military intervention. More than 73 percent of the Americans opposed the military intervention. In spite of all these hard facts and information, the American President launched US troops into another war in Iraq in 2003.

- In spite of all the physical destruction, loss of lives and the extravaganza of two Gulf Wars, none of the political as also military objectives were achieved. But at the global level, the Second Iraq War brought in the fearful misuse of information, irrelevance of UN as an organization in preventing a superpower to act in such a brazen manner against all democratic and political norms. It is also a warning to emerging and third world countries that it is very important to adopt rational geopolitical posture and maintain internal harmony in their respective countries. Continued internecine violence, insurgency, suppression of select groups, economic deprivation, use of military in subjugating internal dissent, and proxy war are always dangerous and invite external intervention.

In essence, nations must build up war avoiding capabilities. These capabilities should be in military as also non-military domains. Ideally dual use capabilities that can be used for generating wealth/ sustaining peace as also for winning wars will be most relevant.

Between 1991 and 2005, it appears that the events and deductions completed full circle and came back to the point where we were few centuries back. Apparently, the theories of first and second wave wars are no different than the most modern and widely talked about IW, sans the technology part. Nevertheless, a closer look at the old theories and the way these evolved will be in order.

★★★

Comparison with 1st and 2nd Wave Wars

It took four to five decades studying the first wave wars fought over almost a century to formulate the theories of war in 300 BC. Bulk of these theories are relevant even today

All these developments that 'heralded the advent of IW' took just over two decades from 1991 to 2012. In contrast, the theories of first and second wave wars took centuries to develop and were based on tens and hundreds of wars, conflicts spread over many countries and continents. There are two specific periods in history when these theories were developed. The first period being from 454 BC to 300 BC and little beyond when Sun Tzu and Kautilya developed the first known theories of war in the most developed civilizations of the world (in the East) at that time. The second period belongs to Clausewitz and Liddell Hart in the middle of the nineteenth century and the beginning of the twentieth century in the post-industrial revolution in the West. It may be interesting to scan these theories to identify as to what exactly is so 'new' about modern wars.

Kautilya's Arthashastra

The Arthashastra written by Kautilya was almost lost to the modern historians till Professor RP Kangle discovered the original writings in the prevalent language during the Maurya Empire. He was the first to translate the treatise followed by Dr R Shamasastry. Dr LN Rangarajan further edited and rearranged the work to make it easier for laypersons to understand the relevance of the work in modern societies. The timing of creation of this work by Kautilya is 300 BC as per most of the Indian historians and 150 AD by some Western historians (Trautman). However, there is unanimity among all historians that Chandragupta Maurya was enthroned in 320 BC. Also it is a generally accepted fact that Chandragupta Maurya was Kautilya's disciple. For purpose of our study, Kautilya's period definitely belonged to the first wave agrarian societies.

Arthashastra written by Kautilya is about an ideal state. This type of state may not exist in reality. However, in case there is an ideal state then it should be what Arthashastra describes. Second, the work is in the form of instructions. The nation states and societies that existed in 300 BC or 150 AD were vastly different from those existing today. Arthashastra contains a chapter on prostitution, which appeared to be a legitimate and legal activity. He explains the rights a citizen or a king has on prostitutes. Also he justifies assassination of kings, treachery in certain cases and expansion of own empire.

Kings ruled societies during that period. Dynasty was important. All these are not accepted in modern societies though these are practiced covertly by many nations. The Chinese concept of unrestricted war includes many of these techniques, which as per the Chinese are quite acceptable in war. Nevertheless, all the teachings or instructions of Kautilya's work may not be relevant today. At the same time, many of his teachings about statecraft and war are very relevant even today. For our purpose his teachings on leadership (king), defence, and war are relevant.

The King

'The king and his rule encapsulate all the constituents of the state.' We may substitute the king by the apex leadership in a country. 'A king must give up lust, anger, greed, conceit, arrogance, and foolhardiness to attain self-control.' As per him, sole aim of all branches of knowledge is restraint over the senses. A wise king:-

- 'Must keep his eyes open through spies.' This is where information, intelligence, knowledge, and wisdom figure in.
- 'Be ever active in promoting the security and welfare of his people.' Thus the ancient monarchy was also expected to be 'for the people' or the citizen was at the centre of all activities of the state.
- 'Should improve his own learning in all disciplines of knowledge.'

- 'Should endear himself to his people by enriching them and doing good to them.'

As per Kautilya, 'only a just king commands the loyalty of his people. The subject of a just king, attacked by another, will follow him until death even if he is weak. On the other hand, when a strong but unjust king is attacked, his people will either topple him or go over to the enemy.' Kautilya's instructions to the king on economics are, 'King shall be ever active in management of economy. The root of wealth is economic activity and lack of it brings material distress. In the absence of fruitful economic activity, both current prosperity and future growth will be destroyed. A king can achieve the desired objectives and abundance of riches by undertaking productive economic activity.'

Kautilya enunciates three important approaches to security of the state. These include power, enthusiasm, and intrigue where power is depicted by military power in terms of number, weapons, training etc. Military leadership, and morale of the soldiers, would depict enthusiasm. Intrigue involves diplomacy, the essence of foreign policy. Intrigue is given highest priority in securing the state followed by enthusiasm. The last in priority is military power. This is what General Starry of American Army meant when he said, 'starting ratios do not decide the outcome of battle.' Israel, Vietnam, Germany, Japan and a host of other nations have proved this point time and again in many battles and wars. Coming back to intrigue ie. foreign policy Kautilya makes very important observations which are relevant even today:-

- A prudent course will always be adopted.
- Peace is to be preferred to war.
- A king's behaviour in victory and in defeat must be just.

It will be relevant to recount the six methods of foreign policy enunciated by Kautilya. These include:-

- Making peace.

- Hostilities, which are of three kinds.
    - Open War.
    - Secret war.
    - Undeclared war.
- Staying quiet.
- Preparing for war.
- Seeking protection.
- Making peace with a neighbouring king so that another king can be attacked with his help.

While writing about use of violence in warfare of any kind—overt or covert—Kautilya advocated that minimum casualty needs to be suffered and inflicted to own as well as enemy soldiers respectively. Does it sound like 'precision in application of force to minimize collateral damage?'

Sun Tzu 'Art of War'

The great Chinese General philosopher Sun Tzu's is believed to have written, *Art of War* sometimes around 450 or 354 BC. He was born into an aristocratic military family. As a young man he became an adviser to the warlord of the state of Wu and helped him defeat his more powerful rivals from the state of Chu. Though Sun Tzu's work precedes that of Kautilya's, the socio-political situations in India during Kautilya's time and in China during Sun Tzu's time appear to be similar. In India, Kautilya witnessed the decline of Nanda dynasty and continuous fighting by Chandragupta Maurya and other kings to establish their empire for the next few centuries. In China, Sun Tzu's work finds mention during the period of warring states (476-221 BCE). Establishment of Quin followed by Han and Chu dynasties in China were based on adherence to the teachings of, *Art of War*. It is also believed that Chairman Mao Zedong was an ardent follower of Sun Tzu during his struggle against the Kuomintang forces of Chiang Kai-Shek.

Like Kautilya, Sun Tzu also believed that warfare is a serious business of the state and hence must be studied by all. The cost of war as per him is very high and hence it needs to be avoided by achieving the state objectives by other means. Sun Tzu advocated swift victories by manoeuvre and avoiding long wars, seizes. For effective manoeuvre he emphasized blending and harmonizing all elements of the army. This in today's parlance may indicate joint operations, collaboration, and inter-operability. Long wars in his opinion will always bring misery to the people and the soldiers. Here again the concern for the ordinary citizens. Another similarity between Chanakya and Sun Tzu is the use of spies. Sun Tzu has categorized five types of spies, local, inward, converted, doomed, and surviving. Thus the importance of information and what you do with it.

Sun Tzu also advocated least casualties even to the enemy. He advocated, 'Take enemy country as a whole and intact. To shatter and destroy it is no good. Capture an army intact than to destroy it.' A similarity to abhorrence to excessive destruction.

While comparing the forces, Sun Tzu identified seven critical components, which decide victory in battle; moral law, generalship, weather and terrain, discipline, strength, training, constancy in reward and punishment. Thus leadership was important then as it is now.

Clausewitz 'On War'

While Kautilya in Arthashastra and Sun Tzu in Art of War have covered the subjects in the form of instructions and at times philosophies, Clausewitz has written *On War* spread over two decades in the form of essays, which were later compiled. His widow published the book, On War one year after his death. Clausewitz—son of a Prussian Lieutenant in internal service—encountered war in 1793 as a twelve-year-old Lance Corporal. The years of war that Clausewitz saw during the period 1806 to 1826 were in the backdrop of French revolution, Napoleon's rise, long wars between France and Prussia. The French Army also captured Clausewitz during their war against Prussia.

It was his pure genius that he saw war as interplay of means and purpose. His observations on linking political goals and war, friction in war, mix of timeless elements and temporary features of warfare, psychological aspects, emotions, and feelings in war are very much relevant even today. The Americans (as per their own admission) appear to have re-learnt it post 2003. Being close to the modern times in relative terms, it is easier to relate his concepts and theories on war to the present day wars amongst nations.

In the context of current theories on IW, some of his observations are very profound and caution us against drawing hasty conclusions. He said, 'The variety and constant changes in war could never be fully caught by a system. Any dogmatic simplification that victory depends on control of key points, for instance or on the disruption of opponent's lines of communications only falsified reality.' This needs to be noted by those who suggest various templates or causal theories for certain victory in war. Fog of war is a law.

Clausewitz also limits the importance of theories and concepts and observes that talent and experience are the two more critical aspects that make a theory actually work in war. He laid great importance on the psychological aspects, emotions, and feelings of own forces in war. As per him managing psychology and emotions of own forces is more important than trying to impact the psychology of enemy troops. He urges military leaders and soldiers to achieve intellectual mastery over the complex areas of human activity. At the same time, he observed 'most men are neither capable nor interested in this pursuit.' Hence, knowledge was the key element of warfare even in early nineteenth century. And how do you manage psychology and emotions of own forces? Leadership appears to be the most effective means.

Clausewitz brought about the concept of 'friction' in war in a very lucid manner. He said, 'to conduct war resembles working of an intricate machine with tremendous friction so that combinations that are easily planned on paper can be executed only with great effort. Consequently, the commander's free will and intelligence find itself hampered at every turn and remarkable strength and intelligence are needed to overcome this resistance. Even then many good ideas are destroyed by friction, and we must carry out more simply and modestly what in more complicated form would have given greater results...'

'Friction' in fact is a commonly used term in classical physics in Newton's theory of motion. 'A body in motion continues to move at the same velocity on a frictionless surface unless an external force is applied to accelerate or retard the motion.' There is no frictionless surface in nature. Hence, the friction between the body and the surface on which it is moving de-accelerates the body and if external force is not applied the body comes to rest.

In the context of war, the command and control network or channels from the commander to the troops under command carries the accelerating force. Clausewitz talked of negative and positive friction. While effect of weather, low morale, deficiencies in training amongst own troops and so on are causes of negative friction or de-acceleration; confusion amongst the enemy ranks, their lack of leadership, poor equipment, and lack of enthusiasm amongst their rank and file act as accelerating forces for own troops.

To overcome friction, Clausewitz recommended genius in leadership. His concept of genius was, 'the harmonious combination of exceptional gifts and by extension intellectual and emotional qualities in general.' Clausewitz himself was a reformist; hence, he never found favour with the monarchy and people in position of authority. He was posted to a relatively less important position where he got ample time to write and reflect.

Clausewitz emphasized the use of violence in war. In the absence of violence in a conflict, it (the conflict) cannot be considered as an act of war. As per him, 'violence is the essence of war.' Also, 'ideally war must be waged with extreme violence.' While teaching the Prussian prince he observed, 'If war was an act of force…no logical or internal self-imposed limits can be on the use of force. War always demanded fullest mobilization of resources and their most energetic exploitation.' This observation by him must be based on his experiences in the long wars with very high loss of human lives. Surprisingly, the earlier philosophers and military writers on war did not preach extreme violence. Kautilya, as well as Sun Tzu, spoke of winning without fighting. Kautilya went to the extent that human casualties to own as well as enemy's forces must be minimized by skilful use of diplomacy, intrigue, and movements. Sun Tzu had similar views for the conduct of overt warfare. Societies in the East, ie. India and China appear to be much saner, almost 1800 years before Clausewitz wrote On War. Even Liddell Hart during the later years at the start of the twentieth century did not profess extreme violence. However, notwithstanding Clausewitz's approach of maximum force, in practice limited force was used during that period customized to the situation.

Liddell Hart

Liddell Hart—the famous British military historian—is famous for his work on mechanized warfare. He and JFC Fuller were the pioneers in developing the strategy and operational art of employing armour along with air power and anti-air weapon systems for creating shock through surprise and speed. His theories were vehemently resisted by his own countrymen but were widely appreciated by the Germans and the French military thinkers. The Germans employed his armour warfare strategy during the Second World War. The German blitzkrieg is derived from theories formulated by Hart and Fuller.

Like the British, the Indian Army too has ignored Liddell Hart and Fuller's theories and have followed the British approach of using armour—more as an antitank weapon and less as a decisive force used boldly, achieving surprise through speed and application in an area where it is least expected by the enemy.

In the context of war in general, Liddell Hart's book, *Thoughts on War* written in 1943 is very relevant. His ideas and arguments are very similar to what has been said by Kautilya and Sun Tzu.

In a very reflective way, he talks of the physical and spiritual world. In the physical world, everything is temporary. The destruction of physical world leads to the spiritual world. Then he makes a very profound and realistic statement. 'Any reasonable man must hope that war has no future. But experience does not lend encouragement to hope.' Hence avoiding war as far as possible is a wise choice. But avoiding it at any cost is not realistic and such a nation that shirks war at the cost of national honour will have to pay a heavier price. He further says, 'If you wish for peace, understand war.'

Thus, Liddell Hart someway defines the pre-conflict part of the spectrum indirectly. We need to so prepare ourselves that as a nation we are free to live our lives and conduct business without any external or internal hindrance through violent means. But, if war is the only option then it must be fought in a manner that we achieve quick and decisive victory. Liddell Hart was against wars that inflict unnecessarily heavy casualties to humans, and that destroy disproportionately large chunk of civilian infrastructure. Again, there are similarities between him and the Indian, Chinese thinkers.

On the question of idealistic peace-loving individual he says, 'I share the idealistic repugnance to war, but I have also repugnance to their all too frequent disregard to reality.' It may be interesting to mention his view on democracy—perhaps drawn from his British experience. He says, 'Democracy has commonly put a premium on conventionality. By nature, it prefers those who keep step with the slowest march of thought and frowns on those who may disturb the conspiracy of mutual inefficiency.' This is an important observation in our context. Indian democracy has borrowed heavily from the British. While the British may have reinvented themselves after the Second World War and have moved on we have been slow. Culturally our democracy has imbibed all the qualities of inertia and inefficiency that Liddell Hart observed in Britain of 1943.

Liddell Hart expanded Clausewitz's definition of strategy, 'art of employment of battles as a means of gaining objectives of war' to 'art of distributing and applying military means to fulfil the ends of policy.' In the IW context, we need to go beyond the military means and perhaps beyond policies to national power and core values.

Lessons from First and Second Wave Wars

The theories on the first and second wave wars took almost a century each in developing and maturing to a level where these became relevant and enduring. The essence of these theories is:-

- War is an affair of the state. It needs to be studied and understood by all citizens.
- It is the nation that goes to war not only the military. Hence, the entire resources of the state must be available as per the requirement.
- Keeping in mind the violence and consequent loss of lives and properties, wars must be avoided as far as possible but not by sacrificing national values, pride, and interests. Timidity at national level inflicts greater loss of lives and prestige.
- Economy plays a major part in national security.
- It is the economic and creative productivity of people that makes the nation strong.
- The involvement of military in war when it becomes imminent should be for short duration but with maximum intensity so a position of advantage is achieved.
- The nation must adopt means other than war to ensure peace at acceptable terms.
- Political leadership plays extremely important role:-
    - In winning without fighting.
    - Launching the military in a manner that is conducive to quick decisive victory.
    - Terminating the war on terms that ensure prolonged peace for the nation.
- The military leadership is critical in winning the war in a

comprehensive manner as per the political directions and objectives.

- The political and military leadership must act in complete harmony.

The above discussion brings out very clearly that war is an affair of the state. Also the entire national power must come into play before, during, and after the war. The first priority must be to achieve the stated goals without having to engage in violent war. It is only when the other measures fail that war becomes a necessity. In this context it is important to analyse what constitutes this 'national power'. We will address the aspects of Comprehensive National Power (CNP) in the next section.

★★★

Comparison with the Theories of Comprehensive National Power (CNP)

China formulated the concept of CNP: It hinges on the power to coerce. For a totalitarian state it works since there are no rules of engagement for China for dealing with their own population or other nations

When we bring in the discussion on CNP in this study, are we digressing from the main theme—'India's strategies for IW'? Yes, in case you still look at IW as an exclusive premise of the Armed Forces. No, if you (by now) realize that IW involves the entire resources and the might of the nation. The preceding discussion should have cleared the air on this issue. IW or warfare in general is an affair of the nation and every citizen is on board. Second, and more important aspect is that avoiding war is extremely important as long as a nation can achieve her political ambitions through means other than war. Scholars have identified a number of means in this part of the spectrum centuries ago. Kautilya propagated diplomacy, intrigue, and statecraft to achieve the desired end state without fighting war. Sun Tzu implied the same when he said winning a war without fighting depicts the highest level of leadership.

In the information age, a state has a number of other instruments where it can dominate internationally. The World Economic Forum (WEF) identified the pillars of competency. However, WEF for obvious reasons does not talk about coercion. A Chinese scholar formulated the concept of CNP—which in essence suggests that the capability of a nation to 'coerce' another nation (there needs to be a Chinese touch in the author's writings!!) without having to commence a violent and destructive war lies in number of factors inherent in her resources which in turn can be quantified. Hence, CNP may help us explore that part of the IW spectrum, which precedes violence.

The CNP Concept

There are numerous modes of dealing with the environmental factor in the context of a nation. CNP index defined in the Chinese military writing is one of these. Wu Chunqin, at the Academy of Sciences, Beijing, writes, 'The discussion of warfare in Chinese ancient literature embodies national power thinking...China's wise ancient strategists never advocated only relying on military power related to war in order to get an upper-hand.' According to Wu Chunqin, calculating CNP can aid a nation not just for war but also to 'coordinate a political and diplomatic offensive, to psychologically disintegrate the enemy forces and subdue them.' CNP has a wider coverage, stressing comprehensiveness in all aspects, apparently including material strength, ideational ethos, and international influence. While CNP stresses material strength or command power, it does not ignore completely the importance of ideational ethos. Ashley J Tellis is the senior fellow at the Carnegie Endowment for

International Peace specializing in international security, defence, and Asian strategic issues. He defines national power as a product of the interaction of two components, that is, the capability of a country to command its economic innovation cycle at a given time, and use such command power to form effective military capabilities and, in turn, to create a stable political environment, intensify the existing economic advantages, and provide basic conditions for maintaining its strategic advantages and seek gains in the international system. He identifies political realism, national performance, and military capability as the major components of national power. In his opinion, performance is the key to deriving national power and performance depends at the state-society relations and capacity of rationality in national action. As regards military capability, Ashley is of the view that even if military capability is not an effective predictor of regional outcomes it does matter. National power is material in nature and hence is necessary but not sufficient condition to achieve desired national objectives.

CNP, as per the Chinese concept, may be simply defined as the comprehensive capabilities of a country to pursue its strategic objectives by taking actions internationally. The core factors to the concept are strategic resources, strategic capabilities, and strategic outcomes, with the strategic resources as the material base.

CNP is based on economic resources, human capital, natural resources, capital resources, knowledge and technology resources, military resources, and international resources. Each of these major factors would have sub factors adding up to a total of twenty-three indices. The calculation of indices is done as percentage of global resources in each index. The sum total gives a figure that denotes the overall CNP. The US has been at the top of the ladder since 1990. China has been closing the gap with respect to US and now has one third of US power. India comes at third place. Russia is way behind China. Israel does not exist among the first ten! Nations at the higher rung of CNP are expected to be more secure and insulated from global turmoil.

However, the theories of CNP ignore some other factors:-

- The entire process is based on numbers. Numbers do not tell the whole story. The US outranked Vietnam in all indices in numbers from 1965 to 1975. It could not influence Vietnam in spite of direct and most violent involvement.
- China in 1979 outranked Vietnam. She could not force Vietnam to pull her forces from Cambodia in spite of direct military action.
- The combined CNP of Arab nations outranked Israel in 1967. They suffered the most humiliating defeat against Israel.

There is another ranking done in Business Insider, which ranks countries as per alliances, influences, and leadership. This again places the US at the top. In this ranking India ranks fifth and Pakistan twenty-second, China is third. Surprisingly, Singapore is twenty-fourth, Sweden is eighteenth!! One of the major anomalies, which appears in all these ranking processes, is the obsession about influence or coercion. Let us look at some data to highlight this anomaly:-

- Nations collaborating with each other in win-win spirit create synergies, which ensure sustained development and indirect benevolent influence over each other. ASEAN, NAFTA (before the Trump administration disturbed the balance), European Union (minus Greece and UK), create a more sustained coexistence of nations in the current networked global communities than those where stronger nations use their CNPs to influence/coerce other nations (US Vs Iraq, Syria, Saudi Arabia, Afghanistan as also Chinese forays in Pakistan, Sri Lanka, Mongolia, Tibet; Russians trying to coerce Chechnya, Estonia, Georgia).
- The concept of CNP does not appear to be in synch with the UN Charter and vision where all nations are sought to be helped in a manner that none of these lose their individual

culture and sovereignty to govern themselves.

- There is enough scope for nations to compete within rather than getting into race with others. It is no case for India to mimic China ship vs ship, tank vs tank, guns vs guns. So long as India can insulate herself from external influence to ensure that she follows the core ideology and vision set by her people for the well-being of her people, it does not matter whether she is equal, more, or less in the number game.
- There are enough examples of David vs Goliath where numerically superior nations in all indices have lost to those who do not have number on their side. Blind pursuit of numbers is one of the paths, which can lead to disaster. This would be causing self-destruction. Pakistan, Iraq to some extent, erstwhile USSR and Libya are some examples. In case China continues to compete by her approach of unrestricted warfare (using drugs, cyber theft, misinformation campaign, Intellectual Property Right infringements, coercing Western MNCs, legal misadventure by creating meaningless legal battles in free democracies where the state does not have coercive power like China), it may be quite possible that China gets isolated and blocked from access to technology and more importantly foreign markets. The US has not gained from this CNP concept and China may follow suite.

Going back to Ashley Tellis's remark that 'material aspects of national power though necessary are not sufficient to achieve strategic objectives,' there appears to be some more abstract and intangible components that add on to the material components (of national powers) to make the sum total of power to achieve strategic goals. These aspects may include the way societies in a nation are integrated, their sense of self-esteem, pride in belonging to the nation, self-appraisal in relation to other countries in the world, inherent sense of national securities[1], political leadership, societal and national resilience to adapt to changes and so on.

A detailed discussion on the comprehensive national power to include the tangible and intangible components is not within the scope of this study. However, we may list out some important events/achievements and failures of select nations and then look for behavioural trends that indirectly explain the national power fault lines of the concerned nations. For obvious reasons the discussion given below will highlight some of the issues and detailed study on these lines can be taken up separately. For this study, we will take US, China, and Pakistan as sample units.

US

In March 1984, during my Defence Services Staff Course at Wellington (Tamil Nadu-India) we had an American officer on the course. We used to get along well. During one of our casual conversations I asked him, 'Why did the US nuke Japan when they had almost surrendered?' 'We wanted to punish them,' he said with sudden change in his facial expression, with grim face and clenched teeth. 'They attacked us at Pearl Harbor,' he said, 'without any provocation; no one dare do that to America.' I was shocked. What a magnitude of punishment!

But when you reflect on the American history, that response to Japanese unprovoked attack on Pearl Harbor falls in place. In 1861, one of the greatest American Presidents of all times made the famous statement, 'A nation cannot survive half free and half slave.' Americans fought a bitter civil war for four years (1861-65). 6,20,000 to 7,50,000 men died in that war. A total of 2.4 million people were killed. 10 percent of northern population (men aged twenty to forty-five) and 30 percent of southern population (men aged eighteen to forty) died.

1 (https://www.nbr. org/wp-content/uploads/pdfs/publications/sa15_overview_telllis.pdf). Accessed 4 March 2019.

In Korea, the US intervened militarily to check North Korean offensive (which was supported by communist Russia and communist China) against South Korea. The bitter war from 1951 to 1954 resulted in killing 37,000 and wounding 92,000 US troops. At the same time the Allied troops inflicted massive casualties on the Chinese and North Korean militaries (1,10, 000 Chinese were killed and 3,80,000 were wounded; 5,00,000 North Koreans were killed. More than 20,00,000 Korean civilians died in this war).

When the US felt that the spread of communism and Russian and Chinese influence in Vietnam was dangerous to their security, they fought a ten-year long war in the region. They lost the war. Sacrificed more than 58,220 soldiers. The entire region including neighbouring Cambodia was devastated. This happened to be the darkest period of American military history. In terms of ideology, what we need to note is that the effort went on for ten years. Three American presidents were part of this effort!

In 1991, the US intervened in Iraq—the much-publicized First Information War. This was to evict Iraq from Kuwait. This war was followed by the 2003 offensive in Iraq to get Saddam Hussein alive or dead. Consequent to the political imbalance created in the region, the US has suffered huge casualties in the region (Syria:59, Afghanistan: 127, Iraq: 4541). Though as per Wikipedia, the American military casualties in Afghanistan are much higher at 2732. Another painful fact is that after the swift victory over Iraq in 2003 where the casualties suffered by the US was around 140, the subsequent yearly casualty figures have been in the range of 800 plus per year. This casualty rate was sustained from 2006 to 2009. Thus every year the US military was losing a battalion plus size force in Iraq!!

The above data on American casualties is not to judge military efficiency or effectiveness of any country. It is just to assess the risk appetite of countries in pursuing their perceived national security goals. The goals may be right or wrong for rest of the world but for the nation, it reflects their belief system.

We may look at other relevant parameters pertaining to the US:-

- The US has three times the GDP of the next ranking country (China). The US has had the highest GDP in the world for many decades.
- They are the biggest exporter of arms and ammunition in the world.
- Their defence expenditure is more than the next ten countries put together. This trend also has been for many decades.
- Their per capita income at $58000 is eight times that of India and more than three times than that of China.
- More than 60 percent of the top 500 MNCs are based in the USA.
- The US dollar is the most traded currency in the world. In spite of float system of currency exchange rates, dollars remain the most influential currency. Decisions taken by the Federal Bank in the US impact global economies within minutes.
- The US has the strongest hold over almost all the UN organizations.
- As per the World Economic Forum, the US has been among the top five countries in the world since the time WEF commenced the global survey in 1994. It has always been an innovation and research driven nation—the highest level of developmental ladder.

So what do we conclude? Did the US rely on CNP to get to their national goals without violence? In a number of cases, the US could have done just that. But, it did not happen. Primarily the cumulative or collective leadership of the nation is conditioned in a certain way, which does not prompt them to use the CNP in a more civilized way. This is where Ashley Tellis' comment becomes relevant. How you exploit your resources is more important.

China

The journey to formation of People's Republic of China on 1 October 1949 has been through thirty years of guerrilla warfare led by Mao Zedong. Mao had followed the famous Chinese general and military strategist Sun Tzu for the conduct of war against the Chiang Kai-Shek forces. Let us look at the activities and macro level thought process of the Chinese government as they came to power:-

- One of the first announcements Mao made on 1 October 1949 was to make Tibet as part of China. Thus, China made expansionist intentions very clear. They also expressed in a very unambiguous manner the way China under Chairman Mao wished to secure her national security interests.
- Within one year of formation of this new nation, the Chinese leadership faced the biggest challenge. General McArthur's forces crossed the Yalu River during their war with the Democratic Republic of Korea. This was too close to the Chinese borders. China warned the American President (Truman) that if the US forces do not stop the advance, the Chinese would enter the war against them. President Truman (under McArthur's advice) did not believe in the threat. The US wanted to call the bluff. On 25-26 November 1950, the Chinese Army entered the Korean War. China suffered heavy losses. 1,10,000 soldiers were killed and 3,82,000 soldiers were wounded in the war. But they made it clear to the world that no one should take the Chinese threat lightly.
- Fresh from the moral victory in 1953 from the Korean War, Chinese troops invaded Tibet in 1954. China lost 2000 soldiers. Around 87,000 Tibetans soldiers were killed. Once again, the Chinese reiterated their intent.
- In 1962, war with India was preceded by a series of aggressive but smaller moves by the Chinese. First, they built the road in Aksai Chin joining Tibet with Pakistan Occupied Kashmir.

Then there were border skirmishes with the Indian patrols in Barahoti and other regions across the McMahon line. India adopted forward posture by deploying small bodies of troops (of the size of platoons—thirty to thirty-seven troops) along the inaccessible heights (without adequate logistic support). The then Indian Prime Minister made a statement in the Indian Parliament, 'I have asked the Indian Army to throw the Chinese out.' China launched massive offensive. They inflicted humiliating defeat on the Indian Army and reached the foothills. China lost 700 soldiers and 1300 were wounded. As against 1300 Indian soldiers killed and around 1000 wounded. In the bargain, China attained an unassailable position against India. Till now everything was going in China's favour at least militarily.

- During the Indo-Pak War of 1965, China started pressuring India to vacate her forward posts at Nathu La and Jelep La in East Sikkim. During the war, India did not accede to their demands (Late Shri Lal Bahadur Shastri was the then Prime Minister of India). In 1967, the Chinese again started bullying India to withdraw. This time the Indian Government buckled under Chinese pressure. Hence, the Corps Commander of Indian 33 Corps gave orders to his divisional commanders to withdraw from the posts at Nathu La and Jelep La. The divisional commander at Jelep La—commanding 27 Mountain Brigade—withdrew promptly. The Chinese occupied Jelep La. But, General Sagat Singh, the divisional commander 17 Mountain Brigade, responsible for Nathu La refused to withdraw affirming that the McMahon Line, which runs along the watershed depicts Nathu La on the Indian side. Besides, withdrawing from Nathu La would compromise Indian positions to the West of the border. During the tussle, the Indian and the Chinese troops fought across the Nathu La. The Chinese lost 300 to

400 soldiers while India lost 80 soldiers. After this battle, the Chinese withdrew from Jelep La also. It was the last time the Chinese and the Indian troops fought anywhere along the Sino-Indian border.

- Due to presence of ethnic Chinese community in Cambodia and their relations with Prince Norodom Sihanouk as also with Khmer Rouge, the Chinese did not like Vietnamese invasion of Cambodia, which overthrew Khmer Rouge regime. Thus, China attacked Vietnam to teach them a lesson! However, the Chinese could not achieve any of their war aims. Vietnam did not pull out their forces from Cambodia. They also did not oblige the Chinese by engaging in conventional war. Instead, the Vietnamese forces resorted to guerrilla war. Between 7000 and 50,000 Chinese were killed in this war.
- China has border disputes with almost all her neighbours and that includes North Korea and Pakistan as well—countries that are considered her all-weather friends. The countries with which China has border disputes include North Korea, Russia, Mongolia, Kazakhstan, Kyrgyzstan, Tajikistan, Afghanistan, Pakistan, Nepal, Bhutan, Myanmar, India, Laos, and Vietnam. This gives us a feel of the Chinese perception of their territorial extent and the strategic need to keep the disputes alive.
- Besides, China is in active confrontation with the US as also some of the Western countries, in the South China Sea. Though, the US and some of the British naval vessels did ignore Chinese claim and hence the situation remains volatile. With the advent of Trump Administration, the US approach has been more explicit and aggressive. The US President did approve the two-nation theory for China in respect of Taiwan and also spoke to the Taiwanese President on phone—a departure from the accepted norms.

Nonetheless, the Chinese leadership has not shown any signs of buckling down though they have also not done anything, which could aggravate the situation.

- China has been busy establishing naval bases in Indian Ocean to encircle India. She has also sent her warships close to the Andaman Islands in the Bay of Bengal.

The other non-military parameters pertaining to China, which give us a glimpse of her leadership decision-making style and hence the core of their strategic intent are as under:-

- The first two decades following the founding of the People's Republic of China in 1949 were marked by periods of substantial growth in per capita GDP growth, the growth of output per person, followed by sharp reversals. Soviet advisers helped establish and operate the 156 large-scale capital-intensive Soviet-assisted projects, significantly increasing the pace and quality (productivity) of industrialization in the country. However, it was followed by the Great Leap Forward (1958-1962), which undid many of the gains through worsening of incentives by banning material incentives and restricting markets. These reforms were then unwound between 1962 and 1966, leading to another period of productivity and per capita GDP growth, before the events of the Cultural Revolution (where strikers clashed with the authorities) set the economy back once again.
- The GDP growth rate increased from 6 percent between 1953-1978 to 9.4 percent between 1978-2012 but also increased the pace of urbanization as workers were drawn from the countryside into higher-paying jobs in cities. This process of market liberalization led to the establishment of China as a major global exporter. It eventually allowed for the reopening of the Shanghai stock exchange in December 1990 for the first time in over forty years and, ultimately, to

China's accession to the World Trade Organization

- China today has per capita income of around $16000 per annum, the Gini coefficient for in-equality is 477 (average value 2007-2017), which is higher than that of India. In WEF ranking (WEF 2017-18) China ranks at 28 while India is at 39. Thus, though China is at higher level in competitiveness she has a more un-equal society. China today is an efficiency-driven economy.

Again, in the context of CNP, the Chinese propensity in precipitating the disputes into armed conflicts at least from 1949 to 1979 does not support their own philosophy of winning a war without fighting. Except for the Korean war in 1951, all other goals could have been achieved without violence. In 1962, the Indian leadership was very considerate and many times submissive to Chinese geopolitical ambitions. Not much happened from the Indian side when China annexed Aksai Chin. The then Indian Prime Minister did not even inform the Indian parliament immediately. He made a statement that not even a blade of grass grows in the area (implying why bother for its loss). Hence, the 1962 war with India was unnecessary. In 1967, the Chinese got Jelep La without fighting. This should have been enough to buttress their ego. Provoking someone like Sagat Singh and then getting a bloody nose was not warranted. In 1979 when China wanted to teach Vietnam a lesson, they learnt a bitter lesson instead.

Hence, how CNP is applied is a function of what type of leadership you have, and what your assessment of the adversary is. Numbers do not count.

Pakistan

Partition of India—based on the two-nation theory (Hindus and Muslims in erstwhile integrated India)—resulted in the birth of Pakistan on 14 August 1947 as an Islamic nation. The state of

Jammu and Kashmir in the north initially opted to be independent of Pakistan as well as India. Pakistan was ill disposed to the fact that a Muslim majority geographically contiguous region was not part of Pakistan. They sent tribal raiders to annex the state for Pakistan. This forced the Hindu King of the state to accede to India that paved the way for the Indian Armed Forces to commence military action to secure the new state of Jammu and Kashmir. First Indo-Pak war followed:-

- **First Indo-Pak War 1948:** The war resulted in defeat of Pakistani desire to add Jammu and Kashmir to her territory. It is estimated that she lost 1500 men and bulk of territory, which the raiders had captured. As per Peter Almos Kiss's paper, by the end of 1948, the Pakistani Army was in full retreat and Indian Army was poised to crush the remnant of Pakistani forces in Kashmir. At this juncture, Nehru, the then Prime Minister approached the UN for ceasefire. The dispute continues till date with huge casualty of people and loss of public property on both sides.
- **Operation Gibraltar by Pakistan 1965:** On the heels of the humiliating defeat of Indian Army at the hands of Chinese Army in 1962, Pakistan launched operation Gibraltar. Pakistan lost 450 tanks (many of these famed American Patton tanks were captured in serviceable conditions), 5800 men, and 1920 square kilometre of territory. This was the last time Pakistan attempted conventional overt operations against India.
- **Liberation of East Pakistan 1971:** Despite claiming to be the Islamic state–champion of the religion, the internal fault lines in Pakistan emanating from ethnic, regional, tribal, linguistic differences and animosity dominate their political affairs and rivalry. During the 1970 elections, it was Sheikh Mujib who had won. Bhutto—the Prime Ministerial aspirant, refused to respect the mandate. The Pakistani Army supported Bhutto

being a West Pakistan leader. Thus started the mindless and cruel killing of Bengali Muslims in East Pakistan. The 1971 war was initiated by India to get the refugees from erstwhile East Pakistan back to their country of origin. The short, swift war defeated the Pakistani Army and created a new nation—Bangladesh. The biggest Pakistani loss in this war was their military reputation for their home audience. In all other wars, though Pakistan lost they managed to convince their citizens that their brave army had actually won! Pakistan lost 8000 soldiers and 25,000 were wounded besides 93,000 Pakistani soldiers were taken as prisoners of war.

- **Events leading to Kargil 1999:** Pakistan displayed her treacherous cunning in launching the Kargil operations. 'Even as India was being feted with an olive branch and promise of a negotiated peace that climaxed in February '99 bus ride by the Indian Prime Minister Late Shri Atal Bihari Vajpayee to Lahore, the deception continued through March when the two foreign ministers further cemented what was thought to be the beginning of a new relation at the margins of SAARC meeting at Colombo.' (From Surprise to Reckoning: The Kargil Review Committee Report). However, after the initial surprise sprung by Pakistan on India it was India's turn to surprise Pakistan with the quantum and intensity of response by the Indian government in evicting the Pakistanis from those impossible heights and getting the entire international opinion on India's side. Besides, the winters subsided earlier. The intervention by the Indian Air Force was unnerving. Pakistan Army listed 453 soldiers killed in Kargil war thus admitting that it was the regular Pakistani Army soldiers (Northern Light Infantry) who took part in the operations and not the Mujahideen. The political parties in Pakistan declared more than 3000 casualties with 200 Pakistani soldiers buried on the Indian side. Kargil was a massive failure of Pakistan as a nation especially since within two years of Kargil 9/11 happened and the entire international ecosystem pertaining to Pakistani misadventure changed overnight. Nevertheless, the Kargil operations by Pakistan fall into the same trend and habit displayed by the Pakistanis in 1947 within days of her emergence as a new Islamic nation!

The other non-military parameters depicting the economic growth and well-being of the citizens, which depict the decision-making trends and culture of Pakistani leadership are as under:-

- In 1947, Pakistan started as an agrarian economy, with literacy rate of about 10 percent. The emphasis was on protecting own economy against foreign competition and helping the farmers.
- In 1950, Pakistan joined the group of most rapidly growing economy. She was a major beneficiary of the Korean War from 1950 to 1953. Besides, Pakistan got lavish aid from the US ($500 million from 1955 to 1959).
- Between 1960 and 1970 Pakistan maintained good GDP growth at 6.7 percent though the 1965 war with India did cause a temporary set-back to the economy.
- During the decade of 1970s Pakistan did try her hands at socialism and hence the economy suffered through the decade. However, they quickly revived the economy from 1980 to 1990 reducing the poverty to 29 percent and unemployment to 3.7 percent.
- It was in 1990s that the Pakistani economy started floundering due to debt crisis and when they entered 2000, their economy was in serious crisis.
- As per 2018 World Economic Forum Report, Pakistan ranks at 107, four ranks below Bangladesh at 103 while India has climbed to fifty-eighth rank. While India is improving her ranking (went up five places) Pakistan has been steadily going down economically. It may be noted that Pakistani

proxy war in Kashmir received renewed impetus after 1991. That also is the timeline when Pakistan started their downward movement in economic growth.

- Pakistan has been a favoured nation by the US from 1947 to as late as 2001. There has been large-scale economic and military aid flowing from the US to Pakistan. This peaked up in 1979 in the wake of Russian intervention in Afghanistan and US resistance through Pakistan. Also, China has been using Pakistan as a proxy against India. As the foreign inflows in the form of aid were choked post 9/11, the Pakistani economy too slowed down. It is surprising that the Pakistani Army has a strong stranglehold on their economy. The Army controls most of the lucrative enterprises. This makes their enterprises inefficient.
- This is what the Pakistani newspaper *Dawn* says about the WEF Report of 2018, 'With an overall ranking of 107 out of 140 countries, Pakistan was at 109 for institutions; 93 for infrastructure; 127 for ICT adoption; 103 for macroeconomic stability; 109 for health; 125 for skills; 122 for product market; 121 for labour market; 89 for financial system; 31 for market size; 56 for business dynamism; and 75 for innovation capacity. In 2017, Pakistan ranked 106 out of 135 countries. GDP per capita stands at $1,541.1; 10-year average annual GDP growth at 3.6 per cent; five-year average FDI inward flow as percentage of GDP at 0.7 per cent. In the area of the freedom of press, the country's score was worst with ranking of 112. In judicial independence, where 1–7 is considered as the best, Pakistan ranked 70, while in budget transparency the score was 77. In respect of terrorism incidence, Pakistan was further close towards the bottom.

How do we view Pakistani behaviour in the context of CNP? For a very long time everything appeared to be favouring Pakistan—

economy, international support, geography, strategic importance in terms of superpower rivalry. India—her perceived arch enemy—on the other hand had most of the CNP numbers going against her. Poor economy, increasing rate of extreme poverty from 1947 to as late as 1974, not so supportive international support from the quarters where it mattered most, military humiliation in 1962, weak governance and so on. What did Pakistan achieve with her higher or even comparable CNP?

In case of Pakistan, the military adventurism has destroyed the national power to leverage in the international arena. She has also suffered high casualty coupled with great strategic losses. There are many takeaways in case of Pakistan in the context of our study:-

- Does the two-nation theory hold? If Pakistan by her own admission declares that she has suffered more deaths due to Islamic terrorism—Muslim against Muslim—then where is the justification for creating a nation based on religion.
- Have the Pakistani people and their leadership identified correct value system? Hate India is not a value system. Solidarity with the Kashmiri Muslim community does not gel when Muslims on their western borders are being killed by their army. Partition of Pakistan into two was a direct result of their internecine conflict between Punjabi and Bengali Muslims.
- In spite of being a leading economy for well over three decades after they came into being (and hence enjoying better CNP numbers), the advantage was frittered away. Today they are at the rock bottom as per the WEF report.

The problems of CNP concept

What we can conclude from the above discussion on CNP and other methods of ranking is that all these relative positions are based on past data and tangible factors. These reflect the trend of the past which may not dictate the future since the state of relevant environments for the nations may change where past trends become meaningless. In other words, the past sales or profit figures do not necessarily forecast the future sales or profits because the customer taste or the market conditions may change. The real competitive edge depends on seeing the future first and adapting to it in time. This aspect is the domain of human capital and leadership. This also helps us in identifying the most important pillar of our strategy—the people and the leadership.

So far, we have been scanning the external environment in 'non technology' realm. Nevertheless, knowledge and technology play very significant role in IW. There is no dispute on this issue. All the nations, leading the IW movement accept this fact and are actively strengthening their knowledge and technology capabilities. Hence, it will be prudent to scan this aspect in some detail.

★★★

Technology Base Knowledge and IW

Technologies and Knowledge for Information War

The cognitive capabilities of a nation as a whole is critical in winning modern wars and sustaining peace

Convergence of AI, Communication and Big Data

AS PER THE popular discourse on the subject, the heading should have been technologies for information war. But understanding and conducting the affairs of war needs more than technology; it needs constantly increasing and at times changing knowledge. Understanding war involves prevention, conduct, and termination of war. Traditionally, technology is defined as use of scientific knowledge for specific purpose. Generally, we use the principles and concepts of basic science to develop machines, tools or systems to achieve the desired goals in a more efficient and effective manner. In academic circles, engineering and applied science disciplines are expected to meet the above requirements. For Information War, we need to focus on knowledge as also technologies. This approach would give us more variety and comprehensive capability to achieve the purpose of IW.

Our next question is what is the specific or range of purposes for IW? Once we are clear about the purpose, we will be able to develop suitable knowledge for achieving the same. There can be another approach. We look around for or develop technologies and knowledge for wealth generation and then adapt these for IW. The latter approach would give us the flexibility of dual or multiple use technologies. In the information age society, the second approach is more suitable. As Alvin Toffler said in *War and Anti War,* 'The means of generating wealth and fighting war converge in the third wave knowledge era.' The network-centric approach was first adopted by business enterprises to scale up market reach, product excellence, competitive edge, growing customer satisfaction and linking together business entities across the globe. The network-centric war followed.

Coming back to our earlier question? The purpose of IW is to so prepare the nation that war is prevented. In case war becomes imminent then develop military capabilities to achieve reasonable dominance over the adversary so that we can dictate the desired new end state. Finally use the military dominance, international clout, and psychological advantage to terminate the conflict in such a manner that for the next few decades the nation does not have to get involved in a violent conflict with the same or other adversaries.

The first stage of IW is to win the war without recourse to violence. Maybe some sort of CNP without the coercion part. In other words, get the state of peace most suitable for the nation to pursue her growth trajectory as envisioned by the people. This would involve:-

- Optimization of human capital:-
    - Identify and proliferate shared values, which are not only accepted but also cherished by the widest cross section of people.
    - Enable the people to be innovative, creative, productive, collaborative, resilient, and agile.
    - Create healthy, happy, and enlightened societies. Harmonize ethnic, religious, and regional differences by creating oneness among the people of the country.
    - Create conditions for productive, internationally competitive economic activities in harmony with ecology.

- Identify internal and external threat vectors and develop means for eliminating the threat in a proactive manner to minimize the cost of such intervention.
- Establish and nurture international relations through trade, culture, and security alliances to enhance the level of deterrence.

The second stage as envisaged above involves conduct of war through violent means. In the information age with networked global societies:-

- Violent wars must be short and swift.
- Collateral damage to the people and civil infrastructure (own or that of the adversary) must be minimal.
- The war fighting capabilities of the adversary must be crippled both in material and in psychological dimensions.
- All the above objectives would be achieved by following the concepts of network-centric war.

The third stage would be conflict termination on terms that gives us better end state than the one at the commencement of the war. The capabilities required for this phase are:-

- The war objectives or goals must be clearly defined and understood by all concerned including the citizens of the nation right in the beginning.
- Entire capabilities and resources of the nation must be available for war. This would include science, technologies, laboratories and expertise, psychological preparation through media and social network, dual use systems such as satellites, logistics, supply chains, communication systems, hospitals, cyber security and cyber offensive capabilities, and so on.
- Cognitive capability of the political leadership and netwar for perception management of the adversary and

international community.

- Cyber intelligence and espionage capability to keep the adversary under constant threat till such time the negotiations are over and sufficient confidence is built for sustaining the new end state.
- Enhanced intelligence and surveillance capabilities to monitor the state of peace after conflict termination.

Sustaining the Existing State of 'Comparative Peace'

Given the state of turbulence India has been in for the past seven decades, state of complete peace at the moment appears unreal. Hence the use of the term 'comparative peace'. By this, we would imply that the cost of crime, homicide, and terrorism to economic activities in the country is about one quarter of what we are incurring now. Thus in 2018, as per the WEF, we were ranked at a lowly 137 in incidents of terrorism slightly better than Pakistan at 140. We should aim at climbing to first thirty in the next five years. This would be very ambitious considering that even the US is at 128th position and China is at 111th rank. But we can take inspiration from Israel at twenty-sixth position in incidence of terrorism. Also the US suffers because of her global presence and active involvement. China suffers due to totalitarian regime.

On the parameter of faith in police, we fare better than China (at sixty-fifth place). However, it will be worthwhile to aim at rising to twentieth position emulating US who are eighteenth rank. In impact of homicide on economy, we are at seventy-fifth position, lower than China. We should aspire for being among the top twenty.

What is the knowledge base and technologies required for achieving these?

- Reducing the incidence of terrorism:
    - o Digitization of social interaction, policing, border management, much more effective and efficient administration and judicial processes so that social

capital in the region is appropriately nurtured and external involvement is minimized. Social interaction can be very effectively done through organized and social media, select groups trained in psychological and perception management. Police must be trained in adaption of ICT for crime prevention, detection, and for preparing the case in swift culmination of judicial processes. Border management forces must adapt to use of sensors, exploit data integration and data fusion technologies. Security forces for combating terrorism should be enabled with cyber intelligence gathering capabilities, precision targeting, lean logistics, Non-Lethal (NL), Less-Lethal (LL) weapons, highly manoeuvrable long range precision small arms as also effective weapons for close combat engagements, drones for surveillance and so on.

- Improving the faith in police: This would need improving the cognitive ability of the police force, eliminating political interference in policing and introducing a mechanism for swift redressal of grievances among the people. There is a need to generate consensus on long-pending police reforms and implement the same to resolve the ugly spat within the government (state versus the centre). There is a need to engage the village/panchayat/mohalla level organizations in ICT adaption for education, training, grievance redressals, and extension of online social welfare schemes to the citizens. Huge amount of pilferage has already been checked by invoking the Direct Benefit Transfer (DBT). There is a need to introduce human intervention at appropriate levels to ensure that other issues related to skills development, crime prevention, law enforcement, etc. are also addressed through fixed lined or mobile networks.
- By making the police efficient in use of ICT and educating

them in better communication skills, human psychology, forensic science, etc. the impact of organized crime and homicide on economy will be minimized. This will make the human capital more creative, innovative, agile, and collaborative.

- Productivity, creativity, innovativeness, agility, and collaborative culture among the human capital are critical aspects to generate national wealth and provide resilience to the nation against external aggression and internal turmoil. It is here that we need knowledge and technologies for preventing diseases, means and technologies for treating diseases at affordable cost, creating and sustaining a culture of healthy life style, efficient manufacturing technologies and management systems and creating a harmonized society to encourage collaboration and cooperation.

Conduct of IW

War has always been a very expensive and violent business. In many cases, human suffering and economic cost of war are much higher today than what they were during the period of the two world wars. Hence, before a nation enters this part of the conflict where disruption is overtaken by destruction a few tenets become important:-

- Wars in the information age are seldom declared. In case of India, we have been at war for a long time. It is only the intensity of violence, which rises and falls.
- Advance means of generating wealth and those for waging war converge in the case of developed nations. Thus sensors, communications systems and networks, logistics systems, materials, supply chain management efficiencies, innovative and creative culture, collaborating nature, understanding the core values and sticking to these no matter what the price to be paid is, and so on are some of the parameters required for creating a prosperous and happy nation as also

for supporting Armed Forces.

- It is very critical to be very clear about the goals for the unavoidable war. The new end state must be visible to the largest cross section. There must be absolute clarity and willingness to pay the price for reaching the new end state and sustain the national pride. The nation needs to be psychologically as also economically prepared for this shared understanding.
- It must also be understood that no matter what means of intelligence, surveillance, and reconnaissance we have there will always be large segments of uncertainty where the decision makers' personality and belief systems will prevail. Hence the need for sterling qualities of character and leadership at the highest political and military levels.
- The international opinion at the commencement of the war must be on our side. Even the superpowers seek international support for this purpose. Nevertheless, economically superior and militarily strong nations wield greater leverage. In case of India, our ancient historical ties, inclusive culture, highly visible diaspora in the developed nations can create the desired leverage.

As regards knowledge and technologies during war, the focus must be on the following:-

- Intelligence, Surveillance and Reconnaissance (ISR).
- Communication.
- Precision guidance munitions.
- Remote sensing and communication by satellite based systems.
- Underwater sensing and communication as also guidance systems.
- Signal processing, data integration, data fusion.
- Robotic, material science, nanotechnologies and particle physics.
- ICT enabled supply chain management and logistics

technologies.

- Clear understanding of modern organizational dynamics, human psychology, and leadership.
- International relations, macro and political economy.
- Relevant aspects of legal framework both at the national and global levels.
- Military affairs of major and relevant Armed Forces in the world.

Conflict Termination

This is an important and often neglected part of the conflict spectrum.

Though, it is not technology intensive, for many reasons it contributes much more than actual victory in war. It is here that the negotiation skills, the wisdom of creating a win-win situation even for the vanquished, sagacity to see the distant future more clearly, and an understanding of war as well as peace become the principle ingredients for the political and higher military leadership.

Synergizing Knowledge and Technologies of the Three Stages

Even a brief enumeration of actual technologies and knowledge base required in the three stages will be very lengthy and beyond the scope of this study. Besides these are subjects with well-defined knowledge bases and theories which the readers can access. Hence, we will make an effort to synergize the efforts in terms of technologies, knowledge, and wisdom applicable to the three stages. This synergy is inherent in the use of artificial Intelligence (AI), communication (as applicable in the AI environment) and big data (in the context of exceptionally large amount of data being created by social media, internet of things, and all other sources in an unstructured mode at an extremely fast pace). Thus, a very brief discussion on these three niche areas is in order.

AI

The human mind takes inputs from all sources (sensors) which it is trained to receive. An alert and trained mind is also capable to rationalize, learn, and if required act on the data. In a very large number of cases, the human mind prefers to collaborate and cooperate to make sense from the stimuli and for taking decisions. With every iteration in the given domain of knowledge, the mind keeps on adding tacit knowledge and hence becomes more effective with more use. This is what AI systems are expected to do.

But there are limitations. The human mind is an exceptionally powerful and complex tool. Also it is not designed by humans. Since the time humans emerged as a civilized society, there has been intense research on understanding the mechanics and power of the human mind. In case of AI, the systems are designed by the humans as per their understanding of how the mind functions. The complexities of AI are well understood (by some hard work and average intelligence!) whereas understanding complexities of human minds is still 'work in progress'. However, the use of AI in its present state of evolution is restricted by the ingenuity, imagination, and skills of people who design the system.

In essence, AI systems are computer models or programs that are written in such a way that with every use the program learns on its own to perform better and faster in the next iteration. It works on specified problems under well-defined constraints or ecosystem. It is the job of the programmer to define the goals or objectives. Also the human masters define the ecosystem that the AI program will encounter. An AI system designed for the ISR ecosystem will learn the mechanics of data collection, collation, integration, diffusion, and transformation for intelligence pertaining to military decisions. However, this system will not be capable to learn beyond the ISR ecosystems designed for its use.

Thus, AI is an interdisciplinary field of cognitive science that brings together computer models and experimental techniques from psychology to try to construct precise and testable theories of working of the human mind. The foundation of AI is based on a variety of knowledge domains. These include:-

- Philosophy: The subject deals with wisdom (literal meaning of philosophy is love of wisdom). Understanding self and nature around us through logic and observation is part of philosophy. AI systems can be designed around this field.
- Mathematics: Is an exact science. It has many techniques and tools at getting to quantitative understanding of different phenomena. It includes:-
    - o Algorithm: Dealing with the techniques of solving a problem. Techniques, which can be repeated by different persons without affecting the solution.
    - o Probability and decision theory: Decision theory can be applied to three different situations. One, when the payoffs and penalties in future state of nature exist without ambiguity. Two, when the probability of future state of nature is known. These probabilities can be calculated from past occurrences. Three, when there is complete uncertainty about future state of nature.
- Game Theory: When two or more players (competitors) with mutually competing interests engage in decision making, the outcomes of these decisions result in payoffs and penalties for players in this game. Game theory is systematic study of projecting the payoffs and penalties of respective competitors during the competition. This sounds very close to the military conflicts involving two competitors.
- Operation Research (OR): The origin of operation research dates back to the beginning of the Second World War. This body of knowledge was created to find out optimal deployment of radars and submarines. OR involves optimization based on objective functions in given set of constraints. In case of more than one objective function, the OR techniques use goal programming using prioritization

of different goals. Solution of OR problem so formulated will give out the resource allocation for the optimal solution. Other techniques used in OR are transportation models, replacement solutions, and so on. All these techniques can be used through appropriate software.

- Neuro Science: Deals with the way human brain functions. As per the latest theories on the subject, the brain is considered to be the seat of consciousness. This knowledge existed with the Indian philosophers since ancient time.
- Psychology: This field of knowledge deals with the human behaviour and response mechanism. In the context of IW, study of human psychology is critical for insulating own troops against the psychological operations of the adversary as also facilitating own psychological operations.
- Cybernetics: Involves the study of computer modelling.

Concept of an Agent in AI

An agent is a computer system that is situated in some environment and that is capable of autonomous action in this environment in order to meet its delegated objective (Wooldridge). An agent takes sensory input from the environment and produces as output actions that affect it. The interaction is usually an on-going, non-terminating one. Thus, the system consists of perception, decision, and action.

There are intelligent, collaborating, and cooperating agents, which have different characteristics. A combination of three types makes smart agents that continuously learn from the environment in each of their transaction. Learning agents allow themselves to operate in the unknown environment and then become more competent as they learn from the environment in each transaction. Agents also have different levels of autonomy. No agent has complete autonomy since this type of autonomy can only be available with the humans. Good AI systems have adjustable autonomy where the control of decision-making is transferred from the agent to the person whenever certain conditions are met.

How will 'agent' help in IW environment? The simple answer is, in many ways. Intelligent agents can be used for decision support and for transactional activities that involves bulk of the junior and mid-level staff work. It will involve routine logistics, transportation, and resource allocation work of simple nature. Collaborating and cooperating agents will come handy for inter-organization synergy. The smart agents will help the higher-level command and decision support functions. The added advantages of using these agents will be better training of staff, more efficiency of agents with each use, and speed of operations. Besides there can be major reduction in the size of headquarters. More personnel will be available for actual functional and operational roles.

Concept and Types of Environment

The environment for an agent is in terms of tasks specified for which the agent has to find a solution. The environment can be any of the following:-

- Fully observable and partially observable: Let us assume that the agent is interacting with an environment created by integrated sensors in a well-defined tactical area. The entire area is fully covered by various types of ground-based, airborne, and space-based sensors. The agent interacts with each piece of data made available by the sensor-networked environment. This case will be somewhat close to fully observable environment. In case any gaps are left the case will be for partially observable environment.
- Deterministic versus stochastic: If the next state of the environment is completely determined by the current state, then the environment is deterministic. If the environment is partially observable, then the environment is stochastic. If we are observing through the social media, then through partial observations probabilistic results can be drawn.
- Episodic versus sequential: In episodic environment the

agent's experience is divided into atomic episodes. Each episode consists of agent perceiving and then performing the task. The next episode does not depend on the task performed in the earlier episode. In sequential environment, current action may affect all other tasks in the sequence.

- Static versus dynamic: If the environment can change while the agent is deliberating, then we say that the environment is dynamic. Fluid combat situation such as air-to-air combat or fast-paced armoured battles come in this category. Bulk of the forward zone battles are going to be dynamic. Besides, anti-terror Special Forces operations by conventional or Special Forces will also be dynamic in nature.
- Discrete versus continuous: It deals with the state of environment the way time is handled and to the precepts and actions of the agent (taxi driving). Discrete environment has finite number of actions with respect to time (game of chess).

Communication in AI

In AI environment communication has a very different meaning. It depicts an 'agent's' request for action or taking over some function. This is also called speech act theory or communicative act theory, since it has little specific connection with spoken communication. The main insight behind communicative act theory is that communication is a form of action. Specifically, we can think of communicative acts as those where 'saying makes it so.' For example, when a military task is handed over to a unit or person it is implicit that the task has been accepted. When the gun position officer speaks the word 'fire' it is understood that the gun crew will take all the actions of loading, aligning, pulling the lever/trigger and ask the observation officer for effect. Speech in these cases are taken as actions. It emphasizes that although what is being communicated may or may not be within the control of the communicator, the fact that the agent chooses to inform, request, or promise another agent is entirely within its control.

In AI, communication is an action. An agent can undertake emailing, skywriting, and using sign language by any means so that working in a multi-agent environment, two or more agents cooperate and coordinate to help arrive at a joint plan. The communication can be any one or more of the following:-

- Query: Asking about particular nature of the environment.
- Inform: Informing each other about the world.
- Request: Ask other agents to perform the task.
- Acknowledge: Send back OK once the agent has been requested.
- Promise: Commit to the plan.

The agent environment interactions as also communications among the agents can be used to address simple problems as also complex problems. Accordingly, the agents are configured. Thus following types of agents are programmed:-

- Simple Reflex Agent.
- Model-Based Agents.
- Goal-Based Agents.
- Utility-Based Agents.

A very basic description of the last two types of agents will be helpful in understanding the general mechanics, strengths, and weaknesses of the system. A utility-based agent looks for the best utility (happiness) in performing the function expected from the program. In other words, it homes on to doing an action in better ways. In case there are multiple goals the utility function describes the trade-off. In case there are several goals but none of these goals can be achieved with certainty then the system defines the likelihood or probability of achieving a given goal.

Besides the above mentioned agents, there are learning agents that work in an unknown environment and then become more competent than what its initial knowledge would have allowed. A learning agent has four conceptual components:-

- Learning element designed for ensuring improvements.
- Performance element programmed for selecting external actions.
- Critic element for auditing the efficiency of performance.
- Problem generator that will lead new and informative execution.

Big Data

Traditional method of analytical processes involved identifying the 'question' or the 'research problem' and deciding the type of information required to answer the question or solve the research problem. The information gathering process consisted of the value chain activities of identifying the source of data keeping in mind the relevance, accuracy, and randomness in case of very large population. The data was then arranged in some convenient order or in some appropriate form. The next step involved forming a sample from the data so collected and applying appropriate statistical technique to analyse the sample data in a manner that the results so obtained apply to the population from where the sample data was gleaned.

To start with, the entire process was manual. Great results were achieved during this period since the people involved were very few, highly dedicated, and honest to their professions—the earliest statisticians. Then came the software for analysis—Statistical Package for Social Science (SPSS) and R (Linux based open source free software developed by Robert Gentleman and Ross Ihaka) for statistical analysis, graphic representation and reporting.

Big data buzz started in 2002. It does almost the same in a very different manner, at a much larger scale and at exceptionally fast pace. Here are the major differences:-

- The data here is infinitely large compared to what was handled manually or even through SPSS or R.

- Most importantly the data is un-related, unstructured, continuous and hence very complex.
- Generally used to identify trends, market state. However, the only limitation to its use is the imagination and ingenuity of the users.

Characteristics of Nature

Big data has four dimensions in terms of its characteristic nature. First the volume of data is so large that no conventional or even the SPSS, R types of software can handle this volume. Imagine data pouring in voice calls emanating from billion odd people in a geographical area or the data coming from all types of ground, surface, and space-based sensors coming to a single receptor round the clock.

The second characteristic is velocity. The data streams in at the speed of light. Millions of bits per second from one source. Since the sources of data in big data architecture range from pictures to terrain maps, tweets, voice calls, e-mails, weather update and so on, the velocity gets multiplied many times. Secondly, it is concurrent with the process of analysis. There is no discernible time gap between the arrival of data and its analysis.

Thirdly, the data comes in variety in terms of sources and also form. It consists of voice, pictures, maps, mails, audio thermal impression, RADAR signatures and so on. The earlier systems generally handled one type of data at a time. The variety of data adds on to the system complexity.

Lastly, the veracity of data. This aspect is extremely important in the context of IW. The data that is being analysed by big data tools may be fed to us intentionally by the adversary. If this aspect is not known, then the analysis can be very easily hijacked to mislead the receiver into taking wrong decisions. Thus checking for veracity of the data becomes very important. In the earlier system, veracity and relevance were the first two attributes of data that were checked before commencing with analysis.

Dimensions of Use

Like the characteristics of nature, big data has four characteristics of use. First, the characteristics of totality. Unlike in the earlier usage, the user does not depend on samples of data. The urge is always to use the entire range of data in all the formats. The user does not want to miss out anything from the population.

The second dimension of use is the exploratory nature of research. The user first develops the query and then puts big data techniques to use. This is somewhat similar to what the traditional methods used to be.

The third characteristics of use is frequency. In the quest for real time intelligence or not to miss out on any vital piece of information the frequency of analysis in big data is much higher compared to all earlier means of analysis.

Lastly, as in the case of traditional means, the cost factor is equally important in the big data mode. The user will only invest in the big data infrastructure if the analysis is dependable.

How can Big Data be used in IW?

The US Argus ground surveillance system collects more than 40 GB of information per second. It is an Autonomous Real-Time Ground Ubiquitous Surveillance Imaging System and has 1.8 gigapixel video camera with 12 frames per second (fps) and 368 sensors. Collects 6000 terabytes of data/imagery per day and feeds it to Homeland Security. Post 9/11, this has served as a big deterrent.

Memex developed by DARPA, which stands for combination of 'memory' and 'index' is a high-tech Internet tool for internet crawling, internet searching, data aggregation, data analysis, data visualization, data extraction, and image analysis. Data flowing in the networks of USA is analysed on a real time basis for proactive actions.

The Green Line Vessel Selection System (VSS) helps analysts and decision-makers identify targets of interest and make interdiction decisions. Complementing existing Command and Control Systems

(C2) with operational analysis, VSS develops a holistic maritime picture by integrating data from multiple sources, such as terrestrial and satellite based ship position/AIS data; vessel and company characteristics data; entity or vessel watch lists; and agency databases containing details on vessels cargo and crew. This data is analysed and presented in a user-friendly interface which supports a collaborative work environment.

Can big data be used in the Indian context too? Yes, it can be used. It will be of much more immediate and long-term value. If appropriate queries can be formulated (the way traditional intelligence problems and source tasking are done) and right network environment (social media and Internet) can be hooked on to big data analytic tools, the security forces will get real time intelligence round the clock. The option of storing or acting on the information will be with the concerned agencies at different levels.

What the US is doing with the sensor networks can be adapted to Indian conditions as part of border management very easily. We can hook the systems to the police, military, or other intelligence agencies' networks.

The most fertile domain for all this is cyberspace—a domain, which can create colossal wealth and also become fertile space for all treacheries.

★★★

ICT Adaption: Peace and War in Cyberspace

A phenomenal engine of growth and quagmire of dirty wars

Given the title of this study 'cyber war' would have been more appropriate heading for this section. There are a few reasons to name the section as above. First, cyberspace has emerged as an immensely effective catalyst for creating and distributing wealth. Second, cyberspace connects continents, countries, societies and people without discrimination or any prejudice. To that extent, it can be the most effective guarantor of world peace. Third, the global supply chains of giant multinational companies (MNCs) with assets generally greater than many of the underdeveloped and some of the developing countries depend on cyberspace. Hence, most MNCs would welcome peace. At the same time, the inherent human failings of greed, hatred, violence, and perversion in general make cyberspace a fertile arena for crime and conflicts. Thus in the order of occurrence, first peace and then war—as has been the case with many other inventions and discoveries.

The basic facility that cyberspace provides is a network. As we expand spatially, network of networks helps in creating cyberspace. While network is a physical entity 'networking' becomes an essential culture for exploiting the networks. Important aspect here (both in peace and war) about networking is that it is an essential attitude for inter-operability, synergy, collaboration, and cooperation. It is the non-military equivalent of combined arms and combined services teams and cooperation. Businesses have already become network centric. The military has no choice but to adopt network-centricapproach for harnessing the power of cyberspace.

Network-centric Business

We may address two disparate questions germane to the study. What are the common factors in the business dynamics of Zara, Dell Computers, and Li & Fung? Second, how are these business dynamics relevant to us? The answer to the first question is that all the MNCs mentioned above exploit cyberspace to derive their respective core competence and hence business strength. These are not the only MNCs that do so. All business firms that matter—MNC or not—use cyberspace to compete. Those who know how to use cyberspace better than others win the race. Second, if we wish to use cyberspace for military purpose (in network centric war) then we cannot ignore to look at the way these MNCs started harnessing the net for generating business power. Let us look at Zara, Dell, and Li & Fung very briefly.

Zara, a Spanish firm established on 24 May 1974 at A Coruna, Spain, produces apparels for kids and young people. Though, with the inclusion of 'Massimo Dutti', they now have a range of products for men and women up to forty years of age. The target segment is highly fashion loving with very fast rate of change in customer taste. Bulk of the production facilities for Zara are in Western Europe. Hence, though the cost of production is very high, the productivity as also quality compensates the high human resource cost. There are four sets of people that work for Zara. The tech-savvy youngsters, who go to fashion shows, nightclubs and such places where they can pick up new trends in apparels. These scouts capture those designs in photographs and use technology to create variations. Link this with information gathering. This input is then given to the design people who have higher expertise to fuse the input into something more attractive. Conversion of information into intelligence comes in here. This is then given to the decision makers to activate the production system. In terms of IW, it is selection of a course of action. The decision makers go into the cost benefit analysis and give executive orders to the fourth team involved with manufacturing. The manufacturing department has highly flexible manufacturing equipment in terms of design and quantity. While manufacturing process is on, the environment is highly controlled to ensure output as per plan. This is akin to command and control. With this model,

Zara takes just two hours to convert the basic input into working design for manufacturing. Its lead time to the market is twelve weeks. Call it decision cycle loop. It hardly sells its produce at discount. Its stuff goes straight to the retail outlets. It has been among the market leaders in such a volatile, competitive market. Its annual sales are in the range of twenty-one billion euros (2015); the sales are spread over five continents and ninety-three markets. This confirms that for remaining competitive in the market (war) you need to be within the decision cycle loop of the adversary.

Dell is an American multinational company (MNC) established by a college student (Michael Dell) in 1984. Its strength is to provide highly customized computers and related products direct to the customer. Hence the name Dell Direct. Dell production facilities are spread over thirty-four countries and it sells its products to people across the globe. Its annual turnover between 1994 and 1999 increased 30,000 percent. It relies on IT. However, as per Dell's founder, Michael Dell, the real power of Internet is its ability to transform relationship within the traditional suppliers, vendors, and customers chain. For Dell, Internet is not just an add-on. It is part of their strategy. What he has not said explicitly is that the supply chain partners (in thousands spread across many continents) are bound together by commitment to a common goal and not through tight control. There is no hierarchy of Annual Confidential Report channels. Achieving synergy of efforts is the hallmark of network-centric operations.

Li & Fung of China was established in 1906. It works with its customers to design, develop, source, and distribute products sold over forty markets worldwide. Though it was established much before the Internet came into being, today it exploits cyberspace to generate a turnover of 20.7 billion dollars (2014 figures). The company does not own any means of production. Some of Li & Fung's notable clients include Walmart, Sears, Target, Juicy Couture, Lucky Brand Jeans, Quiksilver, Calvin Klein, Coach, Hudson's Bay, Tommy

Hilfiger, DKNY Jeans, Kate Spade, American Eagle, Aéropostale, and Sean John. Li & Fung maintains access to a network of over 15,000 suppliers from which it sources products for its customers. From this snippet on Li & Fung, it is very evident that:-

- To exploit cyberspace or to become network centric the organization must possess the capability to embrace change at a rapid pace with the changing operational environment. The military cannot be an exception.
- The emphasis shifts from 'command and control' to collaboration, cooperation, and synergy. Individual people or entities do not win or lose. The entire supply chain does.
- The core philosophy or the vision of principle supply chain owner is non-negotiable; rest everything is up for change.
- Geography is not very important; the network and networking culture are.
- Physical movements are minimal. Movement of processes in the network are maximum. Hence the speed of operations.
- Operations and customers may be local but the approach and strategy are global.

Why did we choose these three MNCs?

- First, their locations—three different continents.
- Second, their journey through time—from pre Internet era to the information age heralded by the expansion of Internet.
- Third, their unmistakable dependence on managing supply chains through collaboration, cooperation, commitment, and synergy as against through controls and transactional approach.
- Fourthly, all these MNCs stuck to their core values while everything around and within changed.
- Fifthly, all these grew consistently and at times dramatically (Dell Direct registering 30,000 percent growth!) without suffering any major setbacks.
- Lastly, they used the network as part of their strategies. The

network decided their organization structure and culture, relationship, mode of logistics and operations and so on.

What are the unique features of these MNCs despite their disparate product lines and business models?

There are four areas where these MNCs—located in different continents, serving different customers and comprising of very different types of people—are strikingly similar. These include their strategic approach, organizational culture, and process dynamics:-

- **Strategic Approach:** The core values or the vision of these MNCs did not change while the external environment specific to their business changed resulting in changes in their internal environment. They survived on four pillars. First, the 'sensors' who sensed the customers, market environment, and created a mosaic from the information so acquired. Second, the component that synthesized the mosaic with the core values, mission, goals, and objectives. Third, those who evaluated options and selected an option for execution. Fourthly, those who executed that option by flexible, efficient, and effective process. Once the option was executed, back to the sensors. The supply chain entities establish partnership in information transformation; use Internet as part of strategy and not an add-on. The supply chain entities strive for synergy though interoperability, commonality of core ideology, and commitment to excellence in managing the supply chain.
- **Organizational Culture:** Despite being spread over several continents and in the absence of direct control and most often without direct interaction, the organizational culture across the supply chain is based on shared vision and commitment. The structure has minimal hierarchies and is characterized by speed and objectivity in decision making. Besides, the decision-making is distributed and participative in nature.

- **Process Dynamics:** Different pillars from which the MNCs derive their stability and competitive edge are decoupled and work in autonomous mode. Their contribution or the use is not sequential in the process. Simultaneity of functions by the sensors, evaluators, decision makers, and executors in the market place makes the process fast and comprehensive. Waste, in terms of time and resources, is minimized, and conversion processes are flexible within the limits of vision and goals. Finally, the processes ensure concentration of efforts rather than concentrating resources.

Network-Centric War

In the backdrop of very simplified and brief picture of network-centric business the pertinent question would be, how does it affect war? Since war is a very different type of activity, there is a need to first identify the major differences before any attempt to conceptualize network-centric war.

War, to start with, is characterized by violence—at times extreme violence and destruction. Second, since it does not generate wealth and well-being for the people, it needs to be avoided as far as possible. Should it become inevitable in the light of national values and ambitions, the duration of wars and hostilities needs to be as short as possible. The environment after the war and resultant negotiations must be conducive to prolonged peace in the region or at least between the nations that participated in the activity.

The components of network-centric war comprise of the sensors, command and control nodes, weapon platforms/shooters (troops in contact), and most importantly the network plus the networking culture. Thus to define network-centric war we can visualize generating combat power by interlinking war-fighting enterprise. It provides the capability to synergize geographically dispersed forces or war-fighting entities to obtain shared battlespace awareness and ability to concentrate their efforts with minimal or no physical movement.

Network-centric war is about humans and organizational behaviour based on collaboration, cooperation, commitment without control, and total synergy in efforts. The universal environment for network-centric war is information infrastructure.

The information infrastructure for network-centric war comprises of sensors, networked together decoupled from the other components. These sensors include space-based, airborne, ground-based sensors with ranges from thousands of kilometres to say few hundred meters. Based on their range and combat requirements, the sensors are networked into smaller networks, which in turn get connected to the data fusion and data integration centres for creating relevant situational awareness. This enhanced situational awareness with increased resolution is fed to the command and control component on a continuous basis.

At command and control nodes, the battlespace awareness is situational awareness in terms of terrain, logistics, and own and enemy entities. The decision-support systems in the nodes help to generate ranked order options for execution along with likely payoffs and penalties for selecting each option. This can be done through expert-based systems, artificial intelligence systems, and neural networks. The decision makers select options and issue executive orders to the components responsible for execution.

The actors in the network-centric operation are the weapon platforms, forces, or functional troops in contact (guns, aircraft, ships, companies, combat teams and so on). Once the actors receive the execution orders, they are also privy to the battlespace awareness relevant to them for execution of the task and also the relevant part of the decision support systems for the tasks. Thus, the weapon platforms or the shooters get far superior sensor feed than what would normally be available to them through their own sensors or decision support systems. The characteristic capability of the fighter aircraft in its head-up display (available to the pilot) is limited in scope due to obvious reasons of range, resolution, space constraint, etc.

However, the same picture provided to the pilot on her/his weapon release display board through the integrated sensor network using data links, will be far more superior and of very high resolution. This enhanced situational awareness also helps in reducing the probability of blue over blue fire where the pilot may fire at friendly forces due to inability to identify friend from foe.

Hence, the power of information infrastructure provides the forces the capability of netting the sensors by fusing and integrating data and information management techniques. This will vastly enhance the battlespace awareness. As the entities in the battlespace get the same awareness, the scope for collaboration and self-synchronization increases manifold. Considering the ranges of the sensors and weapon platforms, precision-targeting capability and vastly improved logistics, the tempo and effectiveness of operation is enhanced exponentially. The commanders get the capability to simultaneously engage targets/forces at tactical, operational, and strategic levels. This gives a different level of combat effectiveness.

The simultaneity of operations at all the levels effectively cuts down the overall time for completing the operation as also bringing the war to an early end. However, once the conventional state versus state war or conflict is over and the vanquished adversary chooses to continue the fight in small teams widely distributed across own or even other countries, the environment changes drastically. That is what happened in Iraq, Lebanon, Kashmir, Somalia, and a number of other places, where nation states are fighting against forces in a situation of asymmetry or a situation of proxy/hybrid war. Once this happens, the network-centric approach needs to evolve different components and vastly different approach.

Metcalfe's Law and Network-Centric War

Metcalfe's law highlights the importance of number of nodes in a network. The power of the network rises exponentially in relation to the number of nodes that are added to the network. Thus, if the number of nodes in the network rise from five to six, the power of the network rises to exponential value of square of six.

However, the catch here is that simply increasing the number of entities or nodes will not automatically increase the power of the network. A network can only be exploited by corresponding transformation in the organizational behaviour, synergy, and formulation of appropriate doctrine. Without matching organization and doctrine, the network itself will be of little use. It is quite likely that archaic organization and poor doctrine can cause more harm in network-centric environment. Thus to derive maximum benefit from the network-centric approach, the basic tenets to be remembered are:-

- Focus on goal; change the rules as per the battlespace environment.
- Reduce hierarchies to the minimum.
- Think out of the box.
- Increase speed of decision making.
- Decouple shooters/weapon platforms/actors from the sensors and information infrastructure.
- Keep the platform light and supporting systems heavy—follow thin client approach.
- Constantly monitor the environment and adopt operations to changing environment.

Cyber War and Network-Centric War

Cyber War is an ongoing conflict in cyberspace. It need not be accompanied by violence. It is seldom declared. Attribution is a major problem. A large number of criminal and harmful activities in cyberspace may be initiated without any complicity of the state. Even if the state approves such activities, the approval may be covert. However, both cyber warfare and network-centric war use the network or cyberspace. That appears to be the only similarity between the two.

Cyber War and Information War

In a very large number of military and academic writings, cyber war and information war are considered to be synonyms. This is a major error. Cyber War is a component of information war. But, it does not substitute information war. For the purpose of this study, it is essential to bring out major differences between, information war as a universal set and cyber war as its sub set:-

- Primitive information systems did exist much before the advent of modern ICTs. These information systems based on drums, messengers, pigeons, light signals, smoke signals, and so on were used in the ancient time during war and peace. Thus, information war (making sense of data, converting it to information and intelligence for the purpose of taking operational and strategic decisions in war and learning from the feedback) did exist earlier also. Post 1985, the means have become much faster and potent. The advent of cyber war dates back to proliferation of Internet, as we know it today. Information war can be fought without the use of modern means of information systems. The same is not true with cyber war.
- The means and techniques of information war are embedded in all forms of wars. Thus physical destruction, operational security, military deception, economic war, netwar all encompass the concepts of IW. In case of cyber war, physical destruction of infrastructure can only be done through cyberspace if the relevant part of the infrastructure or weapon platform is connected to the network components. Infrastructure, weapon systems not connected to Internet are immune to cyber weapons. Thus, while spoofing, misleading and denial of information can be done within the realm of cyber war, use of destructive force to physically destroy say power systems, nuclear installations, surveillance

systems by triggering explosive devices or missiles through cyber network will not be strictly under the domain of cyber war unless these targets are connected to the Internet in some way.

- Much higher level of cognitive abilities is required to wage successful information operations since such operations have well-defined, long-term goals. Cyber war on the other hand is an ongoing process primarily aimed at securing own network and monitoring that of the competitors to be in perpetual state of advantage.

Hence, it will be prudent to discuss cyber war in some detail here. The terms, cyber, cyberspace, cyber war and cyber warfare mean different things to different groups of people. To start with, the word 'cyber' was coined in a fictional work in the 1980s. William Gibson first used this word in his short story, *Burning Chrome* and then in his novel, *Neurometer*. The author defines cyberspace as, 'A consensual hallucination experienced daily by billions of legitimate operators, in every nation, by children being taught mathematical concepts...' Before this, cyber was used as a prefix in 'cybernetics'. This usage was much before the advent of Internet.

As regards cyberspace, there are a number of definitions or explanations of the word. 'Cyberspace is all of the computer networks in the world and everything they connect and control. It includes Internet and other networks that are not connected to the Internet. It also includes transactional networks which facilitate flow of money as also networks that form part of control systems that allow machines to speak to each other and with human interface like pumps, elevators, generators, automated home appliances (Internet of things), and so on.' (*Cyber War* by Richard Clarke). Cyberspace, meant to evoke a digital virtual world of computer networks that users will be able to jack into through consoles...is an effective buzzword...evocative and essentially meaningless. This is what

Thomas Rid extracted from William Gibson's writings. (*Cyber War Will Not Take Place* by Thomas Rid). As per IDSA, 'Cyberspace though technically restricted to Internet is now increasingly linked by convergence to every communication device. With greater connectivity…every citizen or aspect of life is vulnerable. (IDSA Task Force Report 2012).

Richard A Clarke has delved into the subject very comprehensively in the American context in his book, *Cyber War: The Next Threat to National Security and What to Do About it*. Since Clarke served in the White House for four presidents (Ronald Reagan George HW Bush, George W Bush and Bill Clinton appointed him as the National Coordinator for Security and Infrastructure Protection), his account of the general ecosystem and future road map for US for addressing cyber war issues are very authentic. How far his observations are relevant to India is another matter.

As per him, the US Air Force (USAF) in their doctrine first incorporated the word. They looked at cyberspace as an additional domain besides 'air-space'. As per the USAF concepts, cyberspace is in the domain of air force!! It took some time for the US Department of Defence to convince the USAF that the job of controlling or operating in the cyber domain is not the exclusive right of the USAF since it is a much bigger pie for which USAF neither has the capability nor the mandate to control! Meanwhile the US Navy had developed techniques and doctrines to operate in cyberspace without claiming any bragging rights and without even announcing it. The US Army as per Richard Clarke was oblivious to all this. The US Army was to be coaxed to take note of the threat emanating from cyberspace.

In the Indian context the Indian Navy, Indian Air Force and the Tri-service doctrines do talk of military cyberspace. Though in the context of national and global cyberspace it may be very unrealistic to look at military cyberspace as a different entity, for the sake of some delineation of responsibilities we may define military cyberspace. As per the tri-service doctrine, 'military cyberspace is to include all networks, communications, and data centres specifically used by the military.' This cyberspace is in isolation from the non-military users. It should also include weapon platforms (aircraft, tanks, missiles, logistics elements in installation and on the move, networked soldiers in combat). Besides the social media network in the area of interest and influence, the digitized national media reporting on the military activities must form part of the military cyberspace.

Coming back to Richard Clarke, he makes very important observations for preparing the nation (The United States in his case) for cyber war. His six broad observations are as under:-

- **Bring the subject in the education system by initiating broad public dialogue about cyber war:** In the US, there are major security policy schools such as Harvard's Kennedy School, Princeton's Woodrow Wilson School or Texas's Lyndon Johnson School. As per Clarke, cyber war was not being taught at any of these schools. In case of India, we do not have any institute in the public domain where national security issues are taught in some reasonable detail and focus. There are training institutes of the three services where the officers of the respective services or all the services (in case of tri-service institute) are trained. Since bulk of the conflict spectrum in the information age wars will be in the non-military domain, it is time that the youth in the country is taught the nuances of national security especially in the non-lethal or less-lethal part of the conflict. In the West, a number of academicians have written good books on IW and cyber war. The subject has not caught the imagination of the Indian academicians. The Indian academicians still nurture some very unrealistic and naïve ideas of national security.
- **Establish a defensive triad by securing the Internet backbone of the country, harden the control systems of services connected to the Internet, and increase the security of the defence network:** In our case, work is in

progress for the last part. The Indian Navy and the Indian Air Force have done substantial work in this domain; the Indian Army is catching up fast. However, the backbones and the services driven by the Internet are not secure. This can be easily verified by the quantum of low-grade cyber-attacks on the Indian banking, railways, CBI, commercial entities etc. A number of cyber-attacks on the Indian civilian systems are not being reported in order to save reputation or customer confidence.

- **Reduce Cyber Crime:** Cyber-crime has been proliferating as a very low-risk and high-gain activity of the sophisticated criminals. Firstly, hacking tools are easily available on the Internet at a very low cost. Besides, given the inherent security lapses in the software (especially Microsoft software), the cyber criminals write their own codes to hack the systems. Since the police and other law enforcing agencies are still coping with the proliferation and sophistication of this crime, the common citizens as also the state are at the receiving end. A concerted drive needs to be launched to plug the loopholes in the legal system and train adequate number of young people in cyber forensics, cyber security, and ethical hacking to check the menace.
- **International Cooperation:** There has been a gradual awareness among the nations—including China—that it is in the interest of every nation to cooperate to check cross-border cyber-attacks. Also given the difficulty in attribution in case of cyber-attack, the countries are now more willing to check any non-state actor indulging in their respective countries to conduct cyber-attack on another country. There is a pact between China and Russia to prevent any cyber-attack from their cyberspace to the partner country. Efforts are being made by US and China to sign such a treaty between them. The UN is working towards an international

legal framework where member nations will be expected to ensure that their cyberspace is not used to launch cyber-attack on other nations.

- **Modernize Internet to make it safer against cyber-attack and crime:** The TCP/IP protocol was developed as an Open Source Interface with packet switching communication system. Authentication and prioritization of packets are not included in the protocol. If the TCP/IP protocols were modified to include authentication and prioritization, it would be easier to check cyber-crimes since attribution would become very easy. Also, if software companies are forced to write error-free software so that the hackers are not able to breach these then the situation will further improve.
- **It is the national responsibility:** Cyber war, cyber security, and cyber power are all national responsibilities. These cannot be left to the defence ministry or any service or even to tri-service headquarters as insulating the country from this new threat would involve checking the cyber-crime, safeguarding the net-connected services, preventing losses to the business entities, and most importantly protecting the common citizen from harm due to fraud, violence, indoctrination, ethical animosity, and so on. The government must declare very stern measures against any state indulging in cyber-attacks on India. At the same time, there should be prohibitive penalties and punishments against individuals who indulge in cyber-crimes for fun or profit.

Military Cyberspace Vis-à-Vis Civilian Cyberspace: The military cyberspace generally is not connected to civilian cyberspace—Internet or even to the strictly Indian cyberspace, which includes NIC (set up in 1975), INDONET, NICNET and VSAT Network set up between 1986 to 1988. However, such a separation may not stand a deliberate state-sponsored cyber-attack. Attack on the Iranian nuclear plant

(Stuxnet) and even on the Syrian nuclear installation by penetrating the Syrian Air Defence (Kill Switch) are cases in point. With proliferation of 4G mobile network and growing number of Internet users, which includes military personnel, the prospective adversaries can very easily launch targeted cyber-attack or wage cyber war using the civilian network as a stepping-stone for penetrating the military cyberspace. Hence, there is need for very strong, structured collaboration between the civilian agencies responsible for securing the civilian cyberspace and the organization for military cyberspace.

The IDSA task force report 2012 contains a detailed 'proposed coordination structure for the purpose.' (IDSA Task Force Report 2012). At the apex level, NSA and National Information Board can provide overall guidance. The National Security Coordination Secretariat receives and coordinates inputs from MHA (related to cyber-crime and cyber terrorism), MEA (for international cooperation when required), NTRO (for critical infra protection), DRDO (for R&D), and DIT (for interface with the private sector). This will form the policy layer.

Relevance of Social Media for Cyber Warfare at Cognitive Level

Cyberspace essentially has three distinct dimensions—physical, software or logical, and cognitive. It is the cognitive dimension that is most suitable for the social media due to three very obvious and distinct factors.

First, as we move to the higher generation bandwidth (from 3G, 4G and finally 5G) there will be no difference between mobile network and Internet. Each mobile handset is an Internet device.

Second, with the growing efficiency of artificial intelligence and big data, the task of perception management, subversion, degrading trust factor in the government by DDoS attacks, lowering the morale of troops/population and degrading the. Leadership capability will become easy for a reasonable timeframe.

Third, social media will become a lucrative and open source for gathering vital intelligence using the same tools. Exploiting the opportunities provided by social media will need multi-disciplinary, highly-trained, and experienced cyber warriors in the leadership role. This task will have to be undertaken by a team of trained and experienced personnel from the cyber operation organization.

Preparing for Cyber War

Internet and the cyber technologies are comparatively new technologies and knowledge domains. These are extensively used for creation of wealth as also for intra and inter-societal communications/ transactions. At the same time, adequate knowledge about their operations, possibilities, and security threats is available to a very small group of professionals.

Generally, people and many a time nations remain oblivious to the grave threats to their economic well-being and societal harmony emanating from cyberspace. Thus, nations and individuals need to arm themselves with relevant and adequate knowledge as per the specific requirements. The sequence of action should be, first identifying the knowledge domain followed by focus areas for knowledge management and finally vulnerabilities and types of skills and knowledge required at different levels.

Framework for the Knowledge Domain

The framework for the knowledge domain must be based on the functions to be performed at various levels for the relevant cyberspace security and deterrent. The American National Institute of Standards and Technology (NIST) devised a Framework for Improving Critical Infrastructure Cybersecurity investing both in the traditional preparation and protection phases as well as in the detection, containment, and recovery from cyber-attacks. Within this framework the organization is defended from attack, while its capabilities to detect a successful attack, contain it, and recover with minimum impact are augmented.

Focus Area

The focus of knowledge management would be on identifying and protecting vulnerabilities in cyberspace, creating escalating levels of expertise for cyber security, high level of multidisciplinary expertise for deterrent capability and developing advance knowledge for the future.

Vulnerable segments of cyberspace include:-

- **Traditional computer networks:** Cyber security is the primary responsibility of organizations that use a workstation, Local Area or Wide Area Networks, or the Internet. Though it is rare that an organization in the military environment will be using a standalone workstation, it is important to note that even standalone workstations can lead to major security breaches if proper security precautions are not used.
- **Weapon platforms and things connected to the network:** Besides personnel using an IT enabled weapon platforms, networked logistics appliances or military power supply systems, standalone generators with networked control systems, sensors or GPS enabled racks, trucks, robots, and so on are also responsible for the cyber security of the systems that they are using. Modern fighter aircrafts, gun control systems, surveillance systems etc. have large number of platforms connected to the military cyber network. These platforms are vital targets for cyber-attacks. These can be spoofed, slowed down by infecting these platforms with malicious malware or even botnets can be injected for activation later. There can be trapdoors in these platforms; the software can contain codes, which could be activated later. In view of all these threats, thorough checks on these platforms (at the time of induction) from cyber security aspects and periodic checks while in service must be instituted.
- **Mobile phone users:** With the exponential increase in the use of mobile phones by military and non-military users, the Internet extends to the skin ware in uniform. Thus, what the

potential adversary cannot get from the insulated military networks can be gleaned from the vast amount of data being generated in the mobile network. Since the fourth and fifth generation mobile networks are already connected to the Internet and follow Code Division Multiple Access (CDMA) protocol, this cellular network provides a lucrative target for espionage, psychological war, and analytics. Mobile network in conjunction with artificial intelligence and big data can be very effective tool for intelligence gathering and waging various components of cyber war and even information war.

There is a need to establish some organization at the national level to streamline and synergize various activities for preparing the nation for cyber war and in case the need arises, wage a pre-emptive cyber strike. The US was the first country to set up cyber command along with strategic command and revise its military doctrine. The US has declared cyberspace the fifth dimension of warfare. Any attack on the US cyberspace will be considered as attack on US Forces and US reserves the right to retaliate in any manner including a 'military strike'. Such a doctrine makes global security a very complex issue since cyberspace cannot be attributed to an identified person or state. However not many countries have established cyber command on the lines similar to those of US.

UK established Joint Forces Cyber Group and Joint Cyber Reserves Force to provide support to two cyber units. The Ministry of Defence Global Operations and Security Control Centre (GOSCC) has taken the lead in coordinating network defences which in fact is traditional IT security role (James A Green *Cyber Warfare: A Multidisciplinary Analysis*). The Defence Cyber Operations Group (DCOG) is under United Kingdom Joint Forces Command and will most likely focus on cyber war fighting (Green).

The Dutch Ministry of Defence has established a cyber command with offensive and defensive capabilities. The Germans had been conducting covert Computer Network Operations (CNO) by a group of sixty personnel, since 2006. They acknowledged the existence of this group in 2012 (Green). Estonia—after suffering the cyber-attack by the Russians in 2007—have taken Home Guard approach to cyber warfare. Cyber security experts from the industry have been working together for sustainable cyber resilience.

Israel has Unit 8200 responsible for cyber-attack and cyber defence. This is the unit, which took part in Operation Olympic Games (Cyber-attack in 2010 on Iranian nuclear reactor in conjunction with the US).

In China, Unit 61398 has been identified for carrying most extensive cyber-attacks across the globe. China has been carrying extensive cyber-attacks (stealing sensitive data on weapon system like F35 fighter aircraft) as reported by the US cyber experts. Around 35 percent of cyber-attacks on Indian websites in 2017 were rom China[2]

In the case of Pakistan there is no specific mention of any cyber warfare units even in their modernization plans[3] Another book by Ayesha Siddiqa where she analyses Pakistan Armed Forces[4] does not bring out any formal organization in Pakistan, which is responsible for cyber warfare. However, there is mention of Pakistan Cyber Army (PCA, an amateur and perhaps rogue group who indulge in hacking many Indian sites including those of ONGC and CBI). PCA also boasts of hacking the Chinese and Bangladeshi sites. An Indian group 'Indian Cyber Army' has been hacking the PCA sites and has identified the PCA members. However, this information is not properly analysed and documented. Bulk of the cyber warfare related

2 (Indian Express, 23 August 2018 quoting National Security Secretariat Report http://indianexpress.com).

3 (Pakistan Army: Modernization Arms Procurement and Capability Building by Dr Shah Alam,Vij Book India Pvt Ltd 2012).

4 (Military Inc: Inside Pakistan's Military Economy Pluto Press 2007).

activities in India and Pakistan are conducted in this grey field. In many cases, even the state agencies crowdsource cyber offensive activities to these unknown amateur but very efficient hacker groups. The Russians in Georgia did this during the 2009 cyber-attacks.

India's vulnerability to cyber warfare—as per Internal Security Threat report—is ranked third in the world. The most vulnerable being US, followed by China. In response to this vulnerability, the US has established a Cyber Command as stated earlier. China has a dedicated organization for information assurance and information security. She also has a unit for conducting cyber-attacks on other nations. In fact, China ranks among the top aggressor in cyber warfare on US as well as in Indian cyberspace. In case of India, home secretary Rajiv Gupta while speaking at FICCI on 'Smart Policing Partnership with Corporate and Academia', is on record stating that though India is vulnerable she is not capable of fighting cyber-attacks.[5] The major aggressors on Indian cyberspace are China: 35 percent, US: 17 percent, Russia: 15 percent, Pakistan: 9 percent, Germany: 5 percent. There are also attacks from some other countries possibly carried out by Pakistani or Chinese hackers.[6] Bulk of the attacks are on ONGC, IRCTC, NIC, Center for Railway Information System (CRIS), Punjab National Bank, Oriental Bank, State Bank of India. The geographical locations of these attacks are in Maharashtra, Madhya Pradesh and Karnataka. Bulk of the attack weapons is spam, bots, ransomware and coinmining. Other means include malware, phishing, network attacks, web attacks and cryptominers.

It may be prudent to understand the difficulty in identifying the location from where the cyber-attack originates and the type of cyber weapons. Cyber-attacks traverse several computer systems located in multiple countries. As per Russian author, SP Rastorguev, an

5 www.indiatoday.in 31 May 18.

6 http://indianexpress.com 23 August 18.

information weapon is, 'A means directed at activating (or blocking) information system processes in which the subject using the weapons has an interest. An information weapon can be any technical, biological, or social means or system that is used for the purposeful production, processing, transmitting, presenting, or blocking of data and or processes that work with the data.' An information weapon must be used on an objective with maximum speed as compared to another type of weapon; cause the necessary damage to the objective within the allotted time period; be sufficiently cheap and simple to produce, as compared to another type of weapon of the same action class; and be capable of mass production. They offer a great increase in the effectiveness of the impact of information. The latter is due to the emergence of sophisticated theories in the areas of programming for computers and neuro-linguistic programming for social systems, to include many methods and means for exerting an information-psychological effect.

What needs to be done for establishing credible Cyber Deterrence?

On 12 April 2019, the VIF Task Force headed by Lt General Davinder Singh presented a report on 'Credible Cyber Deterrence in Armed Forces of India' to the then Raksha Mantri, Ms Nirmala Sitharaman. The report was appreciated and the Indian Defence Minister promised to address the issue very soon after the Indian elections for the Parliament. The report is available on the VIF site. It suggests development of cyber power for India based on seven pillars comprising of policy and strategy, doctrine, organization, human resource, technology, integration, and international engagement.

Use of Cyberspace: Fear against Confidence

As per Richard Clarke and World Economic Forum Report, the US is most wired nation in the world. Her ICT adaption is amongst the best. The US is also the most attacked and most vulnerable country against cyber-attacks and cyber weapons. The safest country against any kind of cyber-attack is Afghanistan. She is the least wired nation—a tag Afghanistan may not be happy with. Afghanistan would like to be more wired even if this makes her more vulnerable to cyber threat.

On 12 April 2019, India's then Defence Minister addressed two task forces at Vivekananda International Foundation. Her vision and optimism on 'Make in India' approach in the defence sector were encouraging and revealing. She said that the government has analysed the inherent capabilities of some of the private sector entities based on a number of factors and performances in select pilot projects. Based on these indicators, the government is keen to allot them prestigious defence projects. She was willing to bet on the supply chain efficiencies of these entities without bothering too much on the security 'suspicions' against the private sector so conspicuous during the last several decades. We need to note that supply chains are operated and monitored by extensive use of ICT enabled Internet.

On the same day, the chairman of a task force on 'Make in India'[7] study spoke on the possibilities and approach to enhance the 'Make in India' profile. Talking about incorporating eProcurement processes for defence procurements he observed that 'these (eProcurement processes) cannot be used for defence procurement since our orders can be easily monitored by our adversaries and we will lose out on security.' We need to remember that eProcurement has the potential to cut down time overrun and cost to almost one tenth of the cost and time overrun suffered in the current sequential approach. Given our procurement budget, using eProcurement platforms (these can be secured), India can very easily save billions of dollars per year even after catering for the additional cost of cyber security for these networks.

7 https://www.vifindia.org/sites/default/files/vif-task-force-report-make-in-india_0.pdf accessed 12 May 2019.

Our approach to formulate India-centric strategy in the context of 'cyberspace' needs to cater for the aspects of wealth generation and cyber deterrent that threatens our endeavours to prosper as a nation. The broad aspects of 'developing credible cyber deterrence in Armed Forces of India,' are covered adequately in the VIF Task Force Report referred above. However, we will discuss some additional aspects that were not within the scope of the above mentioned report in the final section of this study under the IW pillar of 'cyberspace'. These issues relate to the following:-

- The concept of deterrence in general with its inherent complexities
- Cyber deterrence in the Indian context
- Options for escalating the levels of deterring punishment: gradual or massive
- Deterrent and alliances

One of the elements of deterrence is denial through prophylactic measures. This brings us to cyber security. An extension of cyber security in the domain of IW defence is information security. If the adversary knows that penetrating Indian system is very difficult, involves prohibitive cost, and attracts automated or certain debilitating response, the attacker will be deterred. Hence, the first step towards acquiring cyber deterrent is to address cyber security as a subset of IW defence.

★★★

Information War (Defence) Information and Operations Security

In addition to technologies, organizational culture and discipline help securing information

Robust and offensive defence is considered as the first level of deterrence to any prospective aggressor. In the context of cyber threat or offensive IW, we need to develop IW defence with an offensive mindset at all levels. Information security and cyber security are important components of IW defence.

Definitions and Concepts of Information Security

In its simplest form, information security implies that unauthorized people cannot read or worse yet, modify messages intended for other recipients. Another way of looking at information security is to think of security as a problem of managing risks. 'There are three reasons for this approach. First, security needed is a function of what is being protected. Second, additional security always comes with additional cost, inconvenience, or delay. Thirdly, a chain is as secure as the weakest link in the chain. Hence, there is no point making one part of the system very secure and neglecting the other part.'

Another aspect of information security arises from the question—Is information security all 'technical'? The answer—as most of us would realize—is 'No'. A more comprehensive definition especially from the military perspective is that information security encompasses the full range of disciplines to provide security, protection, and survivability of information systems from attack.

These are measures and controls that protect the information infrastructure against denial of service and unauthorized (accidental or intentional) disclosure, modification or destruction of information infrastructure components including data. Information security includes consideration of all hardware and software functions, characteristics and features, operational procedures, accountability procedures and access control at central computer facility, remote control, and terminal facilities, management constraints, physical structure, devices, personnel and communication control needed to provide an acceptable protection level for an infrastructure and for data handled by an infrastructure for a given period of time. At the same time, we need to remember that nothing can be secured permanently.

It will be prudent to derive the sense of information security from the functional compulsions. In the context of countering the adversary's attempt to gain information as part of their Observe, Orient, Decide, Act (OODA) activities, information security would entail hiding all that contextual and critical information required by the adversary to reach the action stage in the time frame which is critical to us. With this approach, the concept of information security goes beyond the scope discussed above. It is not limited to information infrastructure or information systems. There is a much wider field from where the adversary can gain the desired information.

To start with, open source inputs or information available in the public domain do give away a lot to an intelligent and observant adversary. How to deal with this? Plenty of sensitive information will be available with people who had been part of such critical organizations that handled operational information. The media would try their best to procure such information on the sly for enhancing their TRP! Media in a democracy is independent and hence cannot be part of government's information system. Similarly, the ever-increasing social media would be a trove house of information of all types and by employing the converged systems of artificial intelligence (AI) and big data, the adversary can prepare a fairly accurate picture.

The situation given above leads us to a number of measures to be taken to ensure denying the relevant information to the adversary necessary to plan and conduct operations within their desired OODA cycle. These would include:-

- Counterintelligence operations.

- Counter-espionage.
- Flooding the open source public domain with vast amount of contradicting and confusing information (Russians practice this).
- Sensitizing own personnel and citizens.
- Deception measures to mislead interpretation of information.
- Operational security measures.
- Technical measures to mislead the adversary's sensors and surveillance networks.

Develop a capability that cannot be copied

Learning Curve Based Security

While we are taking all these measures to deny information we must realize that no matter what we do no information can be hidden from a determined adversary. Information security has time limit. But there are ways of making own organizations and even nations immune from the loss of information. Some real life examples will elucidate this:-

- Toyota Production System is easily accessible on the public domain. It has been there for a very long time. How many car makers have been able to challenge Toyota by learning from the unique and globally acclaimed lean manufacturing practiced by Toyota? None. The reason lies in the organizational culture and learning curve of Toyota.
- The quality gurus—Juran, Crosby, and Deming postulated the theories of Total Quality Management in the US. However, the Japanese were the first to use these theories and beat the American car makers in their (US) markets. The Americans have not yet been able to match the Japanese when it comes to quality at minimum cost.
- Liddell Hart and Fuller were British citizens who formulated the mechanized war theories just after the First World War.

The British never used these theories in the Second World War. The Germans mastered the art of using armour based on the theories formulated by these British citizens and beat the British and French Armies in most of the encounters they had.

- AWACS were first made by the Americans in the seventies. No nation so far has been able to match the capabilities and sophistication of AWACS till date inspite of massive theft of information by the Chinese and perhaps the Russians.
- We have been buying a number of weapon systems from Russia for the last several decades. None of our defence production units have been able to manufacture even spares for these systems.

Another way to beat the fear of information loss is to develop the knack of overwhelming speed of operations and decision making so that even if the adversary comes to know there is precious little they can do.

There are certain other abstract factors critical to winning battles and wars such as leadership, proactive culture, tech-savvy troops, innovative and creative culture, sound intellect that are immune to loss of information. Once these capabilities and cultures are developed in the nation then there is less to fear from information security related issues. Proven capabilities in these intangible domains act as a deterrent. Think of Israel from Arab perspective. Think of China from Indian perspective till 1967.

In comparison to the stand-alone sensors or/and open source information, cyberspace provides the most lucrative source of sensitive information to the prospective adversary because various sub-systems of information infrastructure operate in cyberspace. It may be relevant to look at the threats emanating in cyberspace.

Vulnerabilities in Cyberspace

Cyberspace vulnerabilities include people doing it for fun as also people indulging in cyber-crime for illegitimate gains. States also crowdsource from within or outside their countries to launch cyber-attacks on the target countries or societies. In terms of inherent vulnerabilities of cyberspace emanating the way Internet came to the present shape, following aspects are noteworthy to plan comprehensive measures to fix the threats:-

- **Evolution and structure of Internet:** When Internet opened up from defence and academic use to society at large, accessibility and interoperability became the key requirements. Hence, the entire architecture was hinged on easiest access, lack of identification, authentication, repudiation, and ethics. Since the defence personnel were using the Defence Advanced Research Projects Agency (DARPA) net in coordination with the academicians and students in select premier institutes, no one imagined that as the net opened up to general use criminals, anti-social elements, terrorists, and pornography enthusiasts would outnumber those who use Internet for gaining knowledge or for business purpose. As the net grew with astonishing speed after it was commercialized, regulating it was not planned right from the beginning. Though countries like China have tried to regulate the net to a very large extent, it has not reduced her vulnerabilities. China is the second most vulnerable country after the US!
- **Proliferation of mobile network:** As the mobile spectrum moved from 3G to 4G and is now galloping towards 5G, the distinction between mobile and fixed line internet disappeared. Add to this the exponential growth of the social media, which is least regulated and which also hates regulation of any kind; the vulnerability of cyberspace multiplied manifold. The type of people who use smart phones are not keen or capable of understanding the security issues.

- **Internet of things:** With growing clamour for online operations, control, and repairs, the Internet extended to every single appliance, platform, system that could be handled through the software. This included almost everything that we use in our daily life or for war-fighting. By automating the Supervisory Control and Data Acquisition (SCADA), the threat spectrum moved from disruptive to destructive zone.
- **Emergence of supply chain management (SCM) concepts in manufacturing of hardware:** In order to enhance the potency and capability of the systems, computer hardware as also all other products and services are being provided through managing supply chains involving a very large number of independent enterprises spread over many countries in several continents. These enterprises are bound together by financial and inter-SCM competitions. The competition today is not inter-enterprise but it is inter-SCM. Thus during military conflicts the national loyalties overtake business ethics. The manufacturers may leave trapdoors in the hardware to be used later. Alternatively, they can share the hardware vulnerability with unauthorized agencies or persons.
- **Software design:** The Internet as also the mobile network is packet switched network. The packets are made up of bits, which are logic zeros and ones. The software too is written in similar logics of zeros and ones. As the Internet traffic (messages and software) moves through the network as packets along various routes, gaps or discrepancies in the software is exploited by cyber weapons or codes to harm the network or the attached systems. These discrepancies occur unintentionally as well as are introduced by the software designer to be used later when required.
- **Open source and closed source systems:** An open-source

software such as Linux discloses the source code and hence makes it easier to check for vulnerabilities and fix these. A closed-source software such as Microsoft does not give source code hence the vulnerabilities are difficult to find and fix. Richard A Clarke in his book *Cyber War* brings out the clout Microsoft wields over the American Congress due to the funding the politicians receive from it that any type of regulation on Microsoft is impossible. Microsoft has been forced by China to reveal more than what the corporation has revealed to the US authorities.

- **Internet service providers:** Generally, there are three levels of switching or service providers at the national level starting from the backbone service providers to the local ISP. Besides, the Wi-Fi routers in the houses provide another level. At all these levels, there are inherent security concerns as also opportunities to plug the loopholes.

Threats to Network

Since Internet is a network of networks, it may be prudent to look at the threats to network security also. These threats can be divided into four intertwined areas. These are secrecy, authentication, non-repudiation, and integrity control. Secrecy involves keeping the information from falling in unauthorized hands. Authentication entails determining the identity of the person to whom information is to be revealed. Non-repudiation deals with digital signatures and is more applicable to e-commerce. However, it can as well be applicable for military purpose in terms of operational orders and instructions conveyed on the net. Integrity control deals with the accuracy of the message. For military purposes integrity as also availability of information of the message are extremely important. Availability is in fact information assurance on a time slot basis to meet mission requirements. Threat to the network can be posed by people, physical effects and vulnerabilities of the individual, PC operator error, software or programming error, unauthorized disclosure, unauthorized use, fraud or embezzlement, modification of data, alteration of software, theft of assets, and induction of viruses. Physical threat includes electrical power failures or disturbances, hardware failure. Stand-alone PCs are vulnerable to theft of data through USBs, hard disks and during repairs.

Cyber Weapon

Thomas Rid, in his book *Cyber War Will Not Take Place* has defined a cyber weapon as a 'computer code that is used or designed to be used with the aim of threatening or causing physical, functional, or mental harm to structures, systems, or living things.' When we link this with cyber war then the element of instrumentality must be factored in. As per Rid, most of the cyber weapons as defined above lack the instrumentality aspect.

How are Cyber Weapons Developed?

Developing a cyber weapon can be extremely easy and exceptionally difficult. It depends on the type of use and the target. A cyber weapon like the Stuxnet used by the Israeli and American cyber experts took many years to develop by the best brains in Unit 8200 of Israel and the US cyber team. Malware developed by the Russians or the Chinese in the Distributed Denial of Services (DDOS) in Estonia, Georgia, Chechnya (by the Russians) and against the NATO forces as retaliation against bombing of Chinese embassy (by mistake) by the NATO air forces in Kosovo operations were relatively very simple and could have been designed by an average cyber hack.

The basics of cyber weapon development are derived from the vulnerabilities in the Internet software, hardware, and most importantly the ignorance/carelessness of the average users of the net.

The software, which runs the Internet, applications, internet devices, runs into millions of lines of codes. These codes are written by a very large number of IT employees, working across the globe.

The codes do contain unintentional errors, which do not affect the functioning of the software as such but provide an opportunity to the cyber criminals as also hackers to insert small programs for doing things for which the software is not written. Say for example these programs inserted by the unauthorized person are such that will follow instructions by the hacker or the criminal. These codes can send requests for information from someone who is not a genuine user. These can change the address codes in the Domain Name Server (DNS) to misdirect the request for a given website to a fake website. These simple weapons are malware. These include viruses, worms, bacteria, Trojan horse, logic bomb, unintended bots, and trapdoors.

Besides the above weapons which are internal to the network, there are external weapons too which consist of microbes, nano-machines, non-nuclear electromagnetic pulse (NNEMP), high energy radio frequency (HERF), high energy laser (HEL) weapons, high energy particle weapons, passive conducive device, and passive conducive measures. A brief description of all the above cyber weapons is given in the glossary.

What Can Cyber Weapons Do?

This depends on who has developed the weapon, for what purpose, and level of risk the user is willing to take. In the most fundamental and easy use of cyber weapon DDoS, stealing information from insecure systems or from ignorant/careless users can be done by an average hacker. This will impede the information infrastructure and inflict financial loss. This will also impact the target psychologically. However, the target will revive from such easy, generic, and basic attacks by elementary cyber weapons.

In case the cyber weapon is designed for a very specific high-value and well-protected information infrastructure, the design will be highly complex and will require considerable time and funds. Such weapons will not inflict collateral damage and are mission specific. 'Stuxnet' used against the Iranian centrifuges and 'kill switch' used against the

Syrian air defence systems (in conjunction with the Israeli air force) are such highly targeted weapons. Nevertheless, Stuxnet did corrupt large number of other networks for which it was not intended!

In case of destructive cyber weapons, there are important pre conditions. First, the target should have some systems wired to the Internet for functioning, control, and maintenance. These can be electricity generation systems, pumps for the gas or oil pipelines, weapon platforms, hydroelectricity systems and so on. Once these pre conditions are satisfied the attacker must find out the SCADA systems of the infrastructure to be destroyed. Once this is done, various techniques can be used or vulnerabilities exploited for destroying the infrastructure.

How to Secure Information and Infrastructure from Cyber Weapons?

There is enough historical data to suggest that no secure system has actually been fully secure all the time. Hence, it is always prudent to assume that whatever security systems we adopt especially in cyberspace, it is not going to be 100 percent safe all the time. At some point of time, someone is going to compromise the security. Hence, keep updating and changing as also plan for contingencies. It should also be clear that vulnerability can even be in terms of people who can get compromised.

Hence, the first principle is 'keep monitoring and changing/ upgrading.' At the same time if someone attacks our vulnerabilities we must build up credible deterrent. This deterrent can be in terms of our capabilities to find the attacker and punish the organization, individual, or even the country that sponsored the attack. This deterrent need not be limited to counter cyber-attack. The deterrent policy should be well publicized and there should be no hesitation in executing the threat when the need arises. Remember China and even lesser known North Korea have retaliated against the might of the US.

We need to build capability to isolate critical networks as and when the need arises. Placing far too many systems on automation has its own risk. Hence, operational alternatives must be built in. We can also plan to feed information to the prospective adversary if the intention of the enemy is to gain information only. Seemingly relevant information can be made available.

For extremely sensitive information infrastructure, physical security measures against non-nuclear EMP, Van Eck Radiations, high energy radio frequency (HERF) and high energy lasers (HEL) weapons must be built-in. At the same time, we need to have credible international alliance to identify cyber-attacks or protect against cyber-attacks. Even with the prospective adversary, it will be much safer to enter into mutually beneficial treaty to desist cyber-attacks from their respective territories. Such confidence building measures will help all under the umbrella of international efforts to safeguard the global cyberspace for obvious reasons.

Cryptologic Attack Techniques

In its simplest form encryption deals with three elements. First, the original message known as the plain text. Second, the function or code used to transform the message known as the key. Third, the transformed message known as the ciphertext. The art of devising cipher is cryptography. The process of breaking the cipher is cryptanalysis. Both these activities combined together are known as cryptology. The efficiency of the key and the method or cryptography lie in the fact that if an intruder picks up the ciphertext he or she is not able to transform it back to the plain text—within a stipulated time and cost. The two factors, which lie between the plain text and the cipher text, are the key and the method (or algorithm). Of these, the algorithm is of more permanent nature. Many a time the algorithm is made available commercially at a cost. The key to change the plain text to ciphertext (using the algorithm) is of temporary nature. Firstly, this is kept secret and secondly it is periodically changed (since nothing can be kept secret indefinitely).

During the time when cryptologic methods were applied manually, the sheer accuracy and alertness of mind required in the process entailed employment of specialists. The number of such specially trained people always remained limited especially in a military environment. With the introduction of computers, the algorithm can be now fed in the hard disc or given on any external device.

The key like a password is available to the user. Invoking algorithm and super-imposing the key to encrypt the message does not need any high level of cryptologic skills. Any average literate person can be trained on it. If the algorithm is strong (a number of them are available commercially), and key length is long then the transaction in the net is fairly safe. A key length of about 256 bits is considered adequate.

However, there are two anomalies in this arrangement. First, a commercially available algorithm for military purposes is not completely safe though the companies selling such algorithms promise its security. Secondly, as the number of persons holding the key increases, the security of the system as a whole especially in a government organization decreases. This problem has been partially obviated by introducing the public and private key system. In this, a strong algorithm is chosen. The key to encrypt a message is made public. Everyone in the concern uses the public key. However, decoding the message is done by the private key, which is available only with the concerned person.

Again, the strength of the algorithm and length of the key enhances the secrecy of the transaction. In most of the literature on the subject, it is claimed that such a system is totally secure. However, a close look at the arrangement would reveal that if adequate effort is made (which is quite possible for a hostile state), the arrangement can be cracked. The commercially available algorithm will definitely carry some trapdoors. Thus, penetration into the algorithm can be made through a program known only to the vendor. Secondly, with the help of parallel processing techniques and employing very fast processors even the private key can be cracked. However, this cannot be done by an amateur. A large number of systems, which have long been compromised, are still being used in banking and other organizations. A military grade system needs something more than the key systems described above. Nevertheless, for lower grades of secrecy the system works. In fact, the RSA algorithm used with 128 or 256-bit key is extremely safe. The probability of its compromise is very less. Needless to say, we need to develop our own algorithm for military use.

General Precautions and Politics Information Security

When Microsoft entered the software market, their intention was not to power high-security military or the government systems with their software. Microsoft was for low-security commercial use. This approach gave Microsoft cost advantage (since expensive security standards and checks were not required), market share, and huge profits and hence tremendous clout. As the American military became cost conscious (or were 'talked-in' by the Microsoft marketing team), the military systems too started using the Microsoft software. Countries like India with L1 mindset (lowest cost tender) and pliable political leadership did not require much of lobbying. This resulted in huge savings in terms of cost. So what is wrong? There is a flip side to the story.

Microsoft operating systems have low-grade coding with plenty of opportunities for miscreants in cyberspace. Also, Windows are known to crash more often. Secondly, Microsoft does not give source code of their software to the buyer even if they promise. China being an exception since the Chinese threatened them that they would switch over to Linux platform for all their software needs. Bill Gates knew that the Chinese could do it. Hence, he could be coerced by the Chinese. Also, the Chinese know how to deal with the lobbyists or anyone whom they perceive to be not toeing their line. The Americans never succeeded though Bill Gates is an American citizen. More importantly, he funds both Republicans and the Democrats. In the absence of source-code, it is almost impossible to secure the system on your own. So what is the way out?

It is right there in our grasp. Linux is an open-source system. It is available for free. Obviously there are no well-dressed marketing teams to market it. Linux platform can be used to design operating software. Apple does it for their systems. Where do we stand?

Human Resources for Creating Cyber Power Capability in the Armed Forces

While building up appropriate infrastructure and culture for information security at the national level, we also need to consider creating defensive and offensive capabilities in the cyber war domain for the Armed Forces. The VIF Task Force Report on Credible Cyber Deterrence referred above gives out detailed modalities for the purpose. Specific aspects related to identifying skill sets and career progression of personnel in this organization are given below:-

- **Cyber literate:** Basic aspects of cyber security to be practiced by all those who use a device or system (Operators' skills). Entry level: Ten plus two with IT literacy: Concerned unit in the respective services using centrally prepared online modules explained by trainers selected by formation commanders/Cos.
- **Cyber operator:** Cleaning of devices, systems and networks of malware, virus. Inserting security patches, social media monitoring, website security and unit level cyber security audit. Nodal military institutions like MCTE, Army War College, CEME under Army Cyber Group.
- **Cyber warrior:** Maintain cyberspace information of select adversaries/targets, prepare operating systems on open source languages such as Linux, identify resources for crowdsourcing of cyber operation if required etc. IITs, Forensic Science University Gujarat, JNU (for psychology and behavioural economy).
- **Cyber leader:** Army-level cyber expert on big data, machine learning, AI, psychology, psychology forensic. These leaders

need to be trained by premier academic institutes with active involvement of concerned government organizations tasked for the role.

- **Coordinators in National Cyber Security Board (to coordinate with the civilian cyberspace):** Some of the select think-tank organizations need to be dedicated for this purpose.

Till as late as 2014, we were seen as a soft state with very moralistic or unrealistic view on national security. That ecosystem has changed. Many encouraging signals emanated from the new model of governance. But, a lot needs to be done. India needs very massive investment in terms of leadership time and people involvement in enhancing our knowledge and technology base. We also need to work on establishing credible deterrence in cyberspace.

(Updated from the articles published on, 'Information Security' in the USI Journal 2002 by the Author)

***

Cyber Deterrence

The word deterrent is derived from 'deter', which means discourage (from some specific activity). Thus, deterrent for a criminal activity would mean clear knowledge of unacceptable degree of punishment once the crime is committed (and detected, attributed). In this context, effectiveness of deterrent depends on rational thinking of the prospective criminal, degree of certainty of detection, attribution and probability of being punished for the crime within relevant time frame.

Thus for someone thinking of committing massive financial fraud or such crime where sizable fortune is made through embezzlement (cyber criminals as also nations are capable of doing this), deterrence will have three preconditions. First, prospective criminal needs to be rational. This would mean that she/he understands and is afraid of the cause and effect relationship of the crime. Second, the criminal believes that the crime will be detected within a short time frame. Third, the agencies involved will quickly resolve attribution accurately and quickly. Finally, the perpetrator of the crime knows punishment will be severe, certain, and administered quickly.

Complexities of Cyber Crime in the Context of Cyber Deterrence

The above discussion addresses the complexities of deterrence in a very simple case of ordinary crime and punishment. Cyber-crime or cyber-attack by no means is so simple. In the earlier sections, we have seen that our cyberspace is exposed to very complex and wide spectrum of threats. Peculiarities of cyber threats in the context of deterrence are as under:-

- The perpetrators of cyber-crime in most cases are not rational. Thus, a terrorist, 'cyber-crime-for-fun' amateur, or a rogue nation state is not rational. Terrorists whom we face have suicidal tendencies and nothing much to lose, the amateurs do not realize that they are committing any crime and rogue nations generally do not have any concern for their citizens and are ready to suffer huge costs for minor gains.
- Detection of many types of cyber-crimes is extremely difficult if not totally impossible. Thus if a Trojan is inserted but not activated, it will be extremely difficult to detect till it is activated. Once the Trojan is activated, detection will be a case of 'too late and too little' effect. Similarly, large number of cyber weapons can be inserted in the target network with a view to activate these later. Detection of these weapons will involve sustained and disciplined effort.
- Attribution of cyber-crime is extremely difficult. A number of countries should be genuinely willing to cooperate in order to help attribution. In the absence of attribution, it will be risky to counter attack.

- Almost entire range of cyber offensive action or cyber espionage come under the envelop of covert operations. Since deterrent by definition must be explicit, it becomes difficult to respond to cover operations in an overt manner. If we make the deterrent policy explicit, its implementation will be very complex and it will be tedious to maintain credibility of explicit deterrent.

Difficulty in Formulating Cyber Deterrence as a Strategic Option

Going by the definition of deterrent it is extremely difficult to formulate a workable and credible policy for cyber deterrence. No country has credible deterrent against cyber or any other attack including the US, Russia, China and even Israel. If they had credible deterrence, they would not have suffered so many cyber-attacks from countries much weaker than them militarily. The US has been subjected to cyber-attack by North Korea and China several times. China ranks among the top five nations in terms of magnitude of cyber-attacks. The difficulty lies in the nature of 'not-so-desirable' activities in cyberspace as also the types and number of people, organizations, and states involved. Unlike in the case of nuclear or even conventional conflicts, cyber confrontations are too amorphous and ambiguous.

In a nuclear attack there is not even an iota of doubt about the magnitude of damage that will be caused by the least potent kiloton device. It does not make any sense to take the risk of retaliation. Nevertheless, it must be accepted here that countries have worked around the nuclear deterrent also. China was the first to call the bluff in Korean war. Vietnam took on nuclear US from 1967 to 1973 and fought nuclear China in 1979. There is a justifiable repudiation of the concept of nuclear deterrent.

Similarly, it is quite evident what a million infantry soldiers, few thousands of tanks, supported by hundred guns and combat aircraft can do to a country. The rebels in Kosovo knew this, so did Saddam Hussein. Since all wars do have certain degree of asymmetry, the less endowed nation does not take the risk. Hence, even conventional deterrent works though with lesser certainty than the nuclear deterrent. Again as in the case of nuclear deterrence, the conventional deterrence has its limitations (amply proved in various wars).

Cyber deterrence is the most uncertain leverage. If India decides to create a capability for cyber deterrence, then following questions become very important:-

- **Strategic policy-related issues**
  - o What are the red lines after which the retaliation should be executed?
  - o Should the capability be made explicit or be kept implicit?
  - o If cyber-attacks are carried out by a non-state third party with reasonable support from the state where these actors are harboured, should the retaliation be carried out against the state also?
  - o What should be the magnitude of retaliation—massive to start with or graduated response as per the attack by the target source?
  - o Should it be immediate or after careful analysis?
- **Issues during the execution:** If decision is taken to retaliate to create deterrent effect some questions become important:-
  - o Why did the cyber-attack happen on us? Was it due to blatant laxity at own end, by accident, or by concerted high-level planning by the adversary to achieve defined objectives?
  - o What was the impact? How much damage was caused?
  - o Who did it? Are we certain?
  - o Should we destroy the source of attack or just neutralize the cyber-attack capability or retaliate in kind but inflicting higher level of damage?

  - o If the situation escalates to higher levels of cyber engagement or even into conventional war domain, are we prepared?
- **Post-execution issues**
  - o What damage has been caused to the target during the retaliation?
  - o Has the retaliation been severe enough to deter future attack of this kind?
  - o Should we be prepared to repeat the retaliation with more severe intensity or maybe launch another cyber-attack, combined with conventional forces?

Planning for cyber deterrence in the context of threat spectrum faced by India

We listed general issues pertaining to the complexities of cyber deterrence very briefly. To be more specific in the Indian context we need to look at the following:-

- What are the threats we face and from whom?
- What do our prospective cyber offenders think of us?
- What perception we wish to create among those who interfere with our cyberspace?
- Investment-benefit analysis of investments in cyber security and cyber deterrent.

Threats India Faces in Cyberspace

Any deterrence is a function of what threats the deterring nation wishes to deter. In other words, whom do we want to dissuade from harming us. Consider this. The US demonstrated her nuclear capability in August 1945. First nation to go nuclear militarily. Communist Russia was the next nation to develop military nuclear capability. Obviously, Russia considered the capitalist US a major threat that needed to be deterred. Russia—as also most of the pro nuclear deterrent think tanks—assume that the Russian nuclear deterrent worked. Though, this belief is not universal!

In the context of cyber deterrence specific to the Indian situation, the response may not be that simple and linear. Let us look at the trends in the Indian cyberspace and threats. Dr VK Saraswat of NITI Aayog while briefing at the 'Cyber Security Conclave' in Vigyan Bhawan[8] on 29 October 2018, made some very pertinent observations pertaining to the complexion and spread of Internet in India and the pattern of threats.

Indian Cyberspace 2020

Dr Saraswat observed that there has been six-fold growth in the number of Internet users from 2012 to 2017. This establishes a compounded growth of 44 percent during this period. Of the 730 million Internet users in 2018, three-fourth new users were from rural India. Of these new users, 75 percent used vernacular languages. The online shoppers in 2018 were 175 million. The e-commerce transactions via mobile were around 70 percent of all commercial transactions. Almost 50 percent of travel-related transactions were online. In terms of technology, the speed of chips (microprocessors) doubled every twelve to eighteen months. The storage (memory) and bandwidth (capability to carry content) doubled every year. At the same time, the price for higher levels of technologies fell thus making it affordable as also pervasive.

What do these numbers mean? First, with the affordability of smart phones, and extension of 3G to 4G cellular systems in India at a vigorous pace; more and more average Indian citizens will belong to a networked society. This will have positive impact as well as raise issues pertaining to perception management and

8 (https://niti.gov.in/writereaddata/files/document_publication/CyberSecurityConclaveAtVigyanBhavanDelhi_1.pdf) Cyber Security Innovations and Challenges 29 October 2018. Accessed 03 April 2019

spread of fundamentalist terrorism. Second, as people interact peer to peer as also with the banking/other financial entities for monetary transactions online, 'stealing money' through cyberspace frauds will become lucrative and will grow exponentially. Third, the extensive use of vernacular languages in cyberspace will warrant a different class of experts to make sense of what actually is going on. The elitist English-educated experts may not be proficient in understanding the social engineering efforts being made by various groups through cyberspace. Israel learnt it the hard way when the less-educated Arab youth proved to be more than a match to the Israeli cyber warriors in perception management through social media (using a multitude of Arabic languages and dialects). With the advent of 5G (though Dr Saraswat did not mention this in his presentation), the Internet of things (IoT) will become ubiquitous. It will make life easy at the cost of adding disruptive capability to cyberspace. The cyber criminals or the hostile groups/nations will be able to use cyberspace to blow up power stations, ignite PNG (Piped Natural Gas) pipelines, damage refrigerators and airconditioners, misguide cars and trucks on the road, and so on.

Trends in Growth of Cyber Threat to India

At the outset, we need to resist looking at cyber threats from purely military perspective. As a rule, military cyberspace in any nation would be comparatively more secure. Also, breaches in the military cyberspace would be riskier and relatively easy to trace. Hence, though military cyberspace remains a very lucrative target, it is the national cyberspace in general where most of the threats continue to proliferate.

During his presentation at Vigyan Bhawan on 29 October 2018, Dr Saraswat traced the growth of cyber threats in terms of number and types. There has been a sudden exponential growth in cyber threats since 2005. This was not only in terms of number of attacks but the likely damage these attacks would cause. Thus, insertion of Trojan Horses and worms (which could be activated later) started and increased very rapidly since 2008. Saraswat also informed that from 2012 onwards phishing and identity threats increased. Cyber espionage and cyber war related attacks (computer network exploitation) increased since 2010. The attacks pertaining to Denial of Service (DoS) and Distributed Denial of Service (DDoS) increased since 2016. The advanced cyber weapons' threats increased post 2017.

He also elaborated on the relative numbers of these threats. As per him phishing, spear phishing are most common types of threats. Whereas DoS, malware and ransomware are not very common. However, numbers as usual do not tell the whole story. Since the fact that phishing and spear phishing are most prevalent can lead us to believe that most cyber criminals are interested in unauthorized access to personal and private data to commit financial frauds or corporate espionage as part of competition. Well both these threats can also be more ominous than this. These can lead to perception management, psychological indoctrination, or stealing sensitive information for future use. Similarly, malware may be considered a small percentage but it is almost impossible to ascertain the exact quantum of malware inserted in our network. Since we do not know what has been inserted in the system we do not know what harm the malware (Trojans and all) will cause when these are activated. Iranians did not know the presence of Stuxnet when it was inserted. The Syrians did not know that their RADARs have been programmed to go blind for the specific duration when the Israeli F16 would be flying over their watch on that fateful night! Also, the fact that more advanced cyber weapons are being used is alarming.

Another panoramic view of threats through the social media has been depicted in an IDSA Monograph Series No. 55 of November 2016, *The Social Media Challenge to National Security: Impact and Opportunity: A Conceptual Overview* by Shruti Pandalai.[9] The

9 https://idsa.in/monograph/social-media-challenge-to-national-security (Accessed 10 April 2019).

monograph brings out extensive use of social media by the ISIS to recruit, train, and brainwash people through this media. The target audience is not the poor, illiterate rural population but comprise of upper middle class elites, fairly educated. This section does not look like the traditional would-be terrorists and this adds to the threat. The problem may look very familiar and simple but the solution is much more complex than what it appears at the surface. In the context of deterrence how do we prevent this phenomenon to start with in the first place? Once it starts, how to neutralize it from the roots. Catching a few or very many 'converts' to ISIS may not help in the long run. It is here that we need deep thinking, heavy investment, sustained commitment, synergistic action plan across many departments including the security forces and leaning heavily on indirect approach. However, so far nothing much has happened in terms of scale—at least for the past five years.

We may feel very safe and smug that nothing is happening to national security. Suddenly, one ominous day our systems start failing, people start getting subverted, weapon platforms start malfunctioning, space-based sensors give wrong data and so on. Cumulative effect of all these will be catastrophic. Nevertheless, the reality is that this type of catastrophic failure and utter disaster has not happened to anyone so far. One of the reasons for this fact can be that nations under threats have some sort of preparation and the prospective adversaries know it. Also all major military powers have shown enough indication that they have the will and capability (in that order) to retaliate with more than equal measure.

Strategic Approach to Cyber-deterrence

In view of the threat that we face and the complexities of cyber deterrence our strategic approach must be based on the following:-

- Deny, detect, analyse, attribute, retaliate.
- Everyone involved in denial, dedicated force for detection, analysis, attribution, and retaliation.

- Continuous training and upgradation of skills in view of the fast-changing threats capabilities.
- Top priority to creating indigenous knowledge base, technologies, and processes.
- Reduce 'idea to application' time cycle.

Denial: This part deals with information security in general and cyber security in particular as discussed in earlier sections. The first two levels of skill sets discussed earlier will be adequate to perform this function across all organizations. The characteristic features here are scale, commitment, strict discipline, and propensity to report once security is breached. However, with the rapid growth of social media, the challenges of denial have increased and become more complex. The adversary will use the social media for indoctrination, recruitment of terrorists, training, propaganda, perception management, and so on. They will also use language skills not available in general with the retaliatory force. The Israel-Lebanon social media confrontation is a case in point. Hence dedicated teams of personnel, who know the language and culture, and are aware of the security concern and profile of the terrorist organizations, trained psychologists and market research experts, IT experts etc. will have to be formed. They will constantly watch the social media environment in conjunction with the agencies that host these uploads, run pilot tests, identify targets, plan neutralization using appropriate means or just keep the database for subsequent use. Some new subjects like social engineering, modes of indoctrination, and their appropriate counters will have to be studied. This conflict in the social media will also require a different type of forensic. Cyber warriors and cyber leaders discussed earlier will have to take on this task.

Detect, analyse, attribute, retaliate: This sequence requires high degree of expertise, multidisciplinary teams, automated tools like machine learning, AI, big data to go through the chain of activities. There may be cases where conventional force (generally known as kinetic measures these days) will have to be used if the attribution is very clear and the attacker does not learn from non-violent retributions.

In order to make this part of the deterrent credible, prior cyber-preparation will have to be done in cyberspace of the target organization/country. This will involve infesting their networks with Trojans, bots, worms, other malware, trapdoors in the hardware during no-conflict period so that once the deterrence is to be activated these dormant weapons can be fired. It needs to be remembered that once we use a particular cyber weapon, it loses its effectiveness if used again. Hence, the range of actions undertaken during each retaliation will have to be different.

Continuous training and upgradation of skills in view of the fast changing threat capabilities: The type, range, and lethality of cyber weapons is increasing every ten to twelve months. Thus, the people involved in countering cyber threat through retaliation (as also by denial) will have to be in continuous learning mode. Thus, things like learnability, innovative approach, creativity, and disruptive thinking will constitute some important traits among the people tasked for this role.

Top priority to creating indigenous knowledge base, technologies and processes: This is where our institutions of higher education, government policies and investments in these institutes, R&D, skill councils and general culture towards 'learning to excel in action' as against 'learning to get a degree or certificate' will come in. At present, we are far behind. Our universities and research centres do not prepare for this talent. Most of our academic institutions do not spend enough time and energy on issues related to national security.

Reduce 'idea to application' time cycle: We as a nation suffer from exceptionally high degree of procrastination. While countries like the US, China, Israel, and Russia take few months to a year for operationalizing ideas we take decades. This tendency will not work in cyberspace conflict. It will not work anywhere in the knowledge society. We need to get our act together to evolve processes to convert ideas into pilot projects and pilot projects (if successful) to new operational systems.

When we think of deterrent, the scope of activities goes much beyond using existing capabilities. It includes being competitive in creating new capabilities and becoming an important upstream participant in global supply chain of niche technologies and knowledge especially in the ICT domain. Emergence of 5G wireless provides one such case.

★★★

Fifth Generation Wireless Technology (5G) and its Impact on IW

Rolling out of 5G infrastructure by China, the US and some other select countries provides us an ideal case for this study. The phenomenon showcases almost the entire range of activities involved in preparation and conduct of IW. It highlights the importance of—national vision/ ideology, political will (of the top leadership), centrality of political economy, international relations, wonders of dual use technologies, cyber war and network-centric war using high speed digital synergies—in the realm of IW. However this is not the first case, which highlights the full IW spectrum. Before the First Iraq War all factors did come into play but it somehow remained obscured from the public gaze thanks to the tunnelled view provided by CNN.

Let us look at a brief explanation of the above statement. China has a vision of dominating global affairs—military as also non-military. Irrespective of what vision they had, the execution never lacked political will—be it the infamous great leap forward or the much-praised economic as also military transformation. As China moved up the ladder militarily, the economy did not lag behind. They rose to be the second highest economic power from being an underdog till as late as 1980-85. As regards international relations, some of the Western European countries—NATO allies of the US—are leaning towards China ignoring the US advice to the contrary. The 5G technologies are considered to be the most potent enablers for massive boost to economies in terms of productivity, jobs, penetration into almost all the domains of economic activities of people from farming to robotics. It also opens the floodgates of cyber war through intentional or 'inadvertent' trapdoors or software patches. It also provides new dimensions to battlefield surveillance, decision-making prowess, and situational awareness so critical during the conduct of network-centric war.

What is 5G? Technology and Economics

Different generations of mobile communications are based on the frequency bands that are used as carrier frequencies in wireless communication. Frequency in wireless communications impacts a very large number of factors. On the positive side, frequency improves data speed, content, miniaturization, functions, applications, relative immunity to jamming and so on. It also makes the propagation more difficult (higher attenuation), infrastructure becomes more complex and difficult to design and produce, more number of pieces of infrastructure (base stations, towers etc.) are required as we go to higher frequencies.

The fifth generation wireless communication will give data transfer rates of 3 to 10 gigabits per second (giga is 10 raised to power 9). When we compare the data transfer rates of 4G (300 Mbps) then 5G will give us a twenty times increase in the rate of data transfer. These speeds of gbps ensure real time transfer of data of any type, from images to high-resolution pictures and imageries without any latency (LTE) factor. Latency is delay in arrival of the data at the point of interest. Remote instruction given on a data link to a robot, surgical instrument, or a shooter will take some time before these are executed. In 5G, this delay will become insignificant for these highly real time operations. Such a rate of data transfer opens up the era of massive machine-to-machine communications for industrial Internet of things boosting up efficiencies and productivity at very high quality by many orders.

Other data-intensive applications such as operations in smart cities, advanced medical imagery, virtual reality for training and gaming, water and soil conservation in farming, will become possible under 5G infrastructure. All these will enhance the overall economy by a factor of three to five. As per the European estimates, 3.3 percent of their economy is supported by ICT enablers. In case of India, higher ICT adaption in our economic activities can introduce a multiplication factor close to 10 since our current ICT adaption is way behind the international standards.

Defence Application of 5G

High speed data in defence application will entail very high degree of resolutions (sensor networks, terrain maps, weather imagery), connect regional networks to theatre or national defence network (better situational awareness, help in decision support systems, enabling the sensor to shooters capability, improve precision guidance during the trajectory and at the target end), and automate logistics and support functions (provide massive speed of work across disciplines, improve logistics). Besides the capability of virtual reality can help in 'near realistic' training thus cutting down on cost. Virtual realities also help in simulated war games that help in decision making or organizing various contingencies in rank order.

The evolutionary stages and interplay of national vision, political leadership, economics and international relations

During the first three generations of wireless communication, the US was the undisputed leader. They invented it, operationalized the technologies, and marketed it to the rest of the world. In the bargain, the US private sector made huge profits from 1980 to as late as 2010. The first mover advantage was definitely with the US. The only competitors were the European companies who wanted GSM to prevail as against the CDMA technique being used by the US. However, by the time 3G matured, GSM standards were almost out and we now have CDMA for all subsequent infra.

In 2015 China decided to change all this. They envisioned self-sufficiency in semiconductor production by 2025. The 'Made in China' thrust started in 2015. Since then China has outspent the US by $24 billion. In their National Integrated Circuit Investment Fund, they already spent $31.5 billion. Besides, in their five-year plan they have pledged $400 billion in their 5G related investment. Meanwhile Huawei their biggest company in 5G—and under the eye of the storm—enhanced its profits from $28 billion in 2009 to $107 billion in 2018. In 2009, all the top ten Internet companies were American. In 2019, four of these companies are Chinese. So much for having a national vision and displaying the political resoluteness, and leadership to realize the lofty vision. Now the security concerns and international relations.

US realizes the cyber war threats but fails to convince her allies to boycott China

In case of all wireless communications up to 4G and even 4G LTE, the US was the market and technology leader. This changed in 5G. The five companies that lead the 5G rollout are Huawei and ZTE of China. Ericsson of Sweden, Nokia of Finland, and Samsung of South Korea. Of these, the Chinese companies offer great cost advantage in all the spheres—technology, devices, service and software. Besides these companies operate in the 3 to 6 GHz band which is being used by the US Department of Defence. The Americans felt that fielding Chinese infra and software for 5G rollout will compromise their cyber security at all the levels starting from the hardware (trapdoors) to software. They do not trust the Chinese assurances to the contrary for very valid reasons. This is what the Americans used to do to the CISCO components when CISCO had market monopoly in network devices and related software! Nokia did the same to the Chinese. If China does this to the US now through 5G, they would be just returning the favour.

However, Germany and UK do not seem to agree with the idea of banning Chinese 5G companies. Considering the huge cost advantage, they feel that the security concerns can be managed. Italy too are hesitant in imposing complete ban on Chinese 5G companies. India has declared her own ambition to compete in the 5G rollout. It is here that the Chinese appear to have made inroads in Western Europe and parts of Asia. Also, the non-military usage of 5G is so big that the Department of Defence in US does not have the buyer's advantage. Even if the US decides to block 5G rollout by Huawei in the US, the Chinese have big enough market to recover the cost and make huge profit. The US government is unable to stop their own private sector from dealing with the Chinese 5G companies. The presidential order to US companies, to not deal with ZTE, was revoked within five days since China blocked 200 US companies in retaliation.

The impact of Chinese dominated 5G is much bigger than the dreaded cyber war. With growing ICT adaption for rapid economic growth, the Chinese will control global economy through their 5G rollout. This is something US had been doing for a long time. Also, the bulk of high value-added supply chain in the ICT sector will be controlled by companies of other nations and by the US companies. The supply chain risks of 5G will include the radio frequency (RF) components, integrated chip sets, devices as also the services. All these will be included in the Chinese supply chain. In order to exploit cost advantage, the US DoD will have to use commercial off-the-shelf (COTS) equipment with all the attendant risks. Even if the US avoids this route, the NATO allies (except Australia, New Zealand, and Japan) will not ban 5G from China.

Ironically, the Chinese could develop all this through very generous US help. The Americans established research labs in China as also hired Chinese talents for research in related technologies (of course cost and market expansion were the two main driving factors). As of now, one of the options for US is to explore the millimetre wave part of 5G ie in the range of 24 to 100 GHz. This will have challenges of very expensive equipment at a very large scale. Also mm waves have propagation challenges. The second option would be to realign the 3 to 6 GHz 5G supply chain in favour of US interests. Once the US commences with her action to reverse the control of 5G supply chain, there will be new tensions as also emergence of new nations in the supply chain who can be trusted alliance partners of US. Can India figure out in this changing equation?

Options and Impact on Indian IW Preparation

In terms of presence on the spectrum of 5G supply chain at the global level, India does not figure at any recognizable level in terms of owning sizable part of the supply chain or market share. But, we have made some path-breaking progress in chip development. Signal chip of Bengaluru launched the first semi-conductor chips for 4G/LTE, 5G New Radio (5GNR) modem during the last week of February 2019 (Economic Times 27 February 2019) breaking into the elite club of the world and this will have huge implications for India's data security and data sovereignty, besides the positive economic implication.

This achievement coupled with our capabilities in software development can make us a serious contender to become a major player in 5G supply chain. However, given our very poor ranking in the ICT adaption as per the WEF 2018 Report, we need to adopt multi-pronged approach to exploit the existing band while working hard to become a serious contender in the 5G band. A few suggestions in this regard are:-

- Exploit 4G and 4G LTE regime to boost our activities in governance, economics, and public outreach. This will take our economic growth to the next level. Our productivity and profitability will become similar to that of the developed nations. At a conservative estimate fivefold increase in productivity and profits in whatever activity we enable by the high speed ICT bandwidth.
- Optimize the use of 4G in network-centric operation in all our national security organizations. Since Armed Forces are way ahead in this field compared to other organizations such as police, BSF, CRPF, etc. the lead role can be taken up by the defence services. This will help improve our internal and external security profiles.
- Align with South Korea (Samsung already has a big footprint here), Japan, Finland and other trusted countries including the US for research and development in 5G technology and infra at appropriate levels. We should plan to join the global supply chain at high value level (chips, software, RF equipment, devices) in the next three to five years.
- Start transforming our organizations and work culture to optimize performance in network-centric ecosystem (get out of siloes, collaborate, share information, focus on goals, be flexible with rules, emphasize team achievements as against hoisting individual champions, and so on).
- Formulate a vision to be leaders in technology and knowledge in the next five years by increasing our investments in merit-generating ventures—education, skills, research etc.)
- Avoid falling head-over-heels in accepting 5G rollout sponsored by the Chinese companies. Global experience suggests that Chinese government as also their companies

have never been trustworthy. It is not unrestricted war that Chinese follow. They are unrestricted in almost all activities which they undertake for their own national benefits. Bulk of the 5G technologies arrived in China through computer network exploitation (CNE) or in plain simple words stealing.

★★★

Current IW theories and Impact on India

Literature Review (Think tanks, military scholars)

An impressive beginning, miles to go

THE INDIAN MILITARY establishment did study the 'First Gulf War' 1991 with considerable interest. While the Chinese and Russians started ways and means to evolve a military system which could counter the exceptionally advanced and also expensive American military technology with low cost but effective options, the Indians on their part started strengthening their cyber security, EW systems and modelled some of the units and formations to fight IW. An IW brigade was raised based on the EW Group with three units. Additional capability of fighting psychological operations, perception management and to some extent network-centric war were provided to the IW brigade.

However, the initiative fizzled out after some time. The IW brigade concept was discontinued. Instead the corps, command, and army headquarters were enabled with some staff in the form of IW cell or IW directorate. These cells initially attempted to address issues pertaining to perception management, psychological operations, and network-centric operations. Later the tech-heavy, network-centric part was discontinued. Thus at present at the tactical, operational, and strategic level, the dominant components are psychological-operations, perception management, and some efforts at cyber security with no synchronized operationalization of comprehensive cyber power. On 12 April 2019, a Task Force Report, 'Credible Cyber Deterrence in Armed Forces of India' was presented to the Indian Raksha Mantri (Defence Minister)[10]. From what the Raksha Mantri spoke on the event, it appeared that the Indian government has a positive outlook on the Task Report on raising a suitable organization to garner cyber power. We have discussed this in the section on cyber war.

A comparatively authentic reflection of Indian thought process on IW during the first decade after the Gulf War in 1991 can be gleaned from the Kargil Review Committee Report by Sage Publication. The report is relevant for this study for four reasons. To start with, this was the first Indo-Pak conventional war after Iraq War of 1991. Second, by this time IW was already a hot topic in Indian Armed Forces. The author was in Army War College during this period and was tasked to conduct research on IW sponsored by Army War College under their Chair of Excellence Program. Thirdly, Late K Subramanian—one of the most reputed experts on National Security—was the Chairman of the Committee, which prepared the report. Lastly the Pakistan sponsored proxy war was at its zenith.

The Indian Government edited the Kargil Report which has been published by Sage Publication. Some information considered classified has been deleted. However, the report does provide very valuable insight. It brings out (though indirectly) that India as a nation especially her security establishment has been learning the same lessons over and over again. Nothing much had changed on the strategic approach to national security. The report emphasizes that the civil-military relations

10 https://www.vifindia.org/sites/default/files/Credible-Cyber-Deterrence-in-Armed-Forces-of-India_0.pdf,Accessed 22 May 2019

in India during the time were characterized by massive disconnect and excessive civilian domination over the military. This is an important finding in the context of IW since war in the information age requires complete involvement of the government including the people in all the three stages—conflict prevention without compromise, conflict conduct at swift pace, and conflict termination at favourable terms which can result in long periods of peace.

However, there have been many changes at the three service organizational levels after Kargil, which enhance the war-fighting capability of Indian Armed Forces in the Information Age. The Defence Intelligence Agency has been established as recommended by the Committee. The Integrated Defence Staff (IDS) was established on October 2001. There has been some forward movement in Border Management System. Communication and sensor integration has been strengthened in the entire state of Jammu and Kashmir. Good 'all weather' roads have connected the entire region. The logistics in the area is much better now than what it was in 1999. The Armed Forces have structured cyber security agencies.

IW Doctrines by Indian Navy and Indian Air Force

The Indian Navy and Indian Air Force did make their IW doctrines and published these within their organizations sometimes around 1999 and 2001. Both these doctrines were generally in tune with what the Americans had 'discovered' in 1991 war and promulgated in their concepts on IW. It is very difficult to identify any resultant change in the force structure, capability or the strategic approach to war fighting, which was based on these new doctrines.

In 2005, the tri-service organization also brought in their doctrine applicable to all the three services. Some tweaking of organizations—in terms of creating new staff appointments—has been done at the levels of Corps Headquarters and above. The Army War College started a course on IW in their Senior Command Wing. The course dealt with perception management and other issues, which did not involve any IW technology.

Analysis of Indian Army Doctrine 2004

This doctrine has an elaborate section on IW. It says, 'IW will form a key component of our war-fighting doctrine. The excellent support base and infrastructure in information technology that is available in the country should be optimally exploited.' The doctrine declares that we are in a network-centric environment and hence the emphasis must shift to IW.

Some of the other issues raised in the document which are relevant to our study include increased battlefield transparency, situational awareness, enhanced degradation capability, reduced reaction time, and enlarged battle area. In very generic terms the doctrine refers to Revolution in Military Affairs (RMA). It also refers to 'moving from EW to C2W due to increased dependence on modern communication systems.'

It may not be prudent to question what the doctrine suggests. Obviously since the then chief signed it, the issues must have been thoroughly deliberated. We can look at the impact of the doctrine—What happened to the culture, force structure, weapons systems and surveillance and various concepts of networks critical for network-centric war.

First having very rightly identified the network-centric environment, following actions should have been taken:-

- Reduce the number and sizes of various headquarters since the network technologies and systems provide more than desired capability to get situational awareness and help in decision making and command and control. This did not happen. Headquarters remained oversized. A large number of headquarters which should have been redundant in such an environment still exist. Though, there are some measures underway to address this issue now in 2019 after fifteen years of this doctrine being made public.
- The doctrine mentions increased battlefield transparency. This is a function of Battlefield Surveillance System (BSS).

This critical system (BSS) is still a distant dream till as late as 2019—more than one and a half decades from the date the doctrine was made public.

- Other components of the system which ensure reduced reaction time, enhance degradation capabilities, enlarge battle area are included in Command Information Decision Support System (CIDSS) which encompasses tactical command control communication and information systems, BSS, Artillery Combat Command and Control Systems (ACCCS) as also systems integrating air defence, electronic warfare. As of now none of these systems are operationalized. The fate of these projects is same as that of the BSS.
- As regards moving from EW to C2W, the concept may entail grouping the other components of C2W (physical destruction through anti-radiation precision weapons, HERF, LASER weapons, and other EMP weapons). This has not been done. Ideally computer network weapons need to be grouped with the EW systems as has been done by the Chinese. This would have been more cost effective and realistic.

In short, during the period from formulation of doctrine to operationalization it has remained open-ended. It is still work-in-progress or work abandoned. Compare this with the operationalization of AirLand Battle theory and later enhancing the same to IW theories and operationalizing these between 1982 to 1991 as discussed earlier. Hence, in the absence of any tangible effect of the doctrine on strategies and operations, it just remains a document for discussion for over fifteen years.

Reflection on Joint Armed Forces Doctrine (2017) in the context of India's approach to IW

The Joint Armed Forces Doctrine-2017 (Indian tri-service HQ–Integrated Defence Staff abbreviated as IDS) lays out the doctrine in six chapters covering national security perspective, spectrum of conflict, military instrument of power, higher defence organization, integrated and joint structure, technological orchestration and capability development respectively. The document describes the doctrine in one of the appendices as, 'guide to action'. This signifies its importance towards operationalization. Each chapter is contributed by very senior officers known for their high level of performance and popularity as 'scholar soldiers'. The doctrine is based on a number of very important documents given in the reference. Hence there appears to be fair amount of research undertaken by the contributors.

There are some refreshing aspects in the document. It talks of national values, national aim, national interests' national security objectives and focuses on the well-being of 'our vast population' as part of national security perspective in the first chapter. While describing the core values, the doctrine draws from the preamble of the Indian constitution. Thus suggesting that sovereignty, socialism, secularism, democracy, republican character, justice, liberty, equality, fraternity, human dignity, unity and integrity etc. are our core national values. The words used look good and it is a safe and easy bet to consider these as core values. However, these core values do not stand objective scrutiny. Firstly, core values must be widely shared among all the citizens across geographical regions in the country. Everyone must understand what these core values mean to her/him. A very miniscule number of people would have read the preamble and lesser number would have understood the same. Hence the nation does not know that these are the core values. We may say they ought to know. Not necessarily. This brings us to the second observation on the core values. Thus socialism which is listed as the core value is an afterthought. It was included in 1976, that too in the preamble, without any definition. The constituent assembly that framed the constitution did not find it appropriate to tie up the nation with socialism. Third, many of the core values are not 'visible' in the governance and functioning of the nation. 'Justice' which is our core value should translate into expeditious justice to all in a transparent manner to the rich and the poor. Hence a common citizen would not identify justice as a core value. Similarly, other core values can be tested from what one can see and smell in India. A brief analysis of the Indian constitution by Subhash Kashyap is given in Appendix C.

The doctrine very rightly broadens the ambit of national security by including politico-diplomatic structure, water, economy, energy, education, technology, cyber and space as the key elements. As regards the conflict environment, the doctrine observes that we are in the fifth generation war. Elaborating this, it adds that hybrid war, economic war, etc. are the fifth generation war. This appears to be a case of using semantics. Such kinds of wars did exist during 300 BC.

The doctrine describes national power as comprising of military, economy, science and technology, leadership, national character, education and influence. However, there is a need to elaborate what we actually mean by these terms. Terms like leadership, economy, national character are not self-explanatory. As regards the components of national power, the doctrine includes economy, governance, knowledge and information, military, human capital, geography and natural resources, national will and leadership, internal security, science and technology and foreign policy. This is a very comprehensive approach. The seven pillars we have identified in the study include all these components.

Special Forces have been very rightly identified as the key elements of modern wars. However, the roles envisaged for the Special Forces in the doctrine are far below their desired capabilities. Highly trained infantry, capable of undertaking operations in network-centric approach, should be able to strike deep and sustain itself behind the enemy lines for reasonable time in support of offensive or defensive operations.

As regards the Higher Defence Organization—Department of Defence, Department of Defence Production, DRDO, and

Department of Ex-Serviceman Welfare have been identified. Since no comments are made on the efficiency of these organizations, it is perhaps assumed that all is well with the Higher Defence Organization. We need to undertake deep reforms in this area. All these organizations have performed much below the expectations and investments made in these areas. The Department of Defence (who are responsible for defence of India) has not shown any understanding of national security and military strategy. This is quite evident from their performance in all our conflicts with Pakistan and China. Defence production has a productivity level equivalent to one-fifth of international standards. Given our import bills for the past five years, the defence production department should be either disbanded or privatized. Post 1962, there had been a massive drive to create indigenous production facilities for weapon systems and military research. As the public sector defence production and defence research organization expanded their tentacles, the import bill (on weapons and military systems) started increasing. In 2017 India claimed top honours among weapon importing nations for five consecutive years!! On the contrary China and Pakistan both reduced their import of weapons and weapon systems over the last ten years both in absolute and percentage terms. Thus indigenization as a national goal existed on paper for a long time without decreasing the import content!

The DRDO capabilities can only be enhanced by making its functioning more professional and accountable.

Economy, science and technology, leadership, character, education and influence (diplomacy) create national power besides the military. This is a welcome change and important statement from IW perspective. One of the threats mentioned in the doctrine is cyber threat. Dealing with this threat in cyberspace is considered as operational level strategy as per the doctrine. The wealth generation capability of cyberspace is very rightly recognized. However, even in 2017, the tri-service thought process ignored the need for creating some kind of offensive or deterrent cyber power as was done by the Chinese.

Creation of necessary knowledge base and research and development facilities is visualized as part of the doctrine. Indian National Defence University (INDU) is being set up as a fully autonomous institution to be constituted under an Act of Parliament. The aim of INDU is to inculcate and promote co-ordination and interaction not just among the three services but also between them and other agencies of the government like civil bureaucracy, paramilitary agencies and intelligence agencies.

It would develop and propagate higher education in defence studies, defence management, defence technology, defence acquisition/ procurements, and promote policy-oriented research on all aspects related to national security. It would impart education to authorities/ leadership related with the business of national security, create synergy between academic community and government functionaries and encourage awareness of national security issues by reaching out to scholars and the audience beyond the official machinery.

Overall the doctrine touches upon most of the major issues albeit in a very officious and perfunctory manner. At most places there is visible effort to skirt contentious issues. Ideally a frank and realistic discussion based on our past experience and well-known weaknesses should have been more appropriate. This can be undertaken in other military writings.

Military Scholars on IW in the Indian Context

There are a number of think tank organizations working on issues related to national security as also on information war. Officers from the three services and also independent academicians write books, briefs, and articles on the subject. It may be very relevant to scan the trends in these writings. Though at the outset it can be said that bulk of the work is in complete agreement and at times propagation of what the western authors have already said.

Dr RC Mishra, an IPS cadre police officer, has addressed the issue on *Information Warfare and Cyber Security* (2003) Authors Press.

He has also quoted foreign authors on the subject. His emphasis remains on media and cyber security. Since social media was not on the horizon in 2003—at least in India—Dr Mishra has visualized its impact on information warfare. Surprisingly Dr Mishra has not emphasized the internal security aspect of IW and hence preparing the Indian Police force to deal with this vital threat.

Wing Commander MK Sharma, an aeronautical engineer in the Indian Air Force who has written a book, *Cyber Warfare: Power of Unseen (Knowledge World),* writing on behalf of Center for Air Power Studies, New Delhi in 2012 has reflected on China's numerical superiority in research output but the quality has been rather poor. In fact, almost all Chinese writings on IW reflect the US concepts.

The subject has also been covered in the government sponsored think tank, 'Institute of Defence Studies and Analysis (IDSA)', New Delhi in their report, 'IDSA Task Force Report: India's Cyber Security Challenge', 2012. Interestingly in the report, 'cyber security' and 'cyber war' appear to be equated with 'information war'. The report maintains that as India progresses, its reliance on the Internet will increase at a rapid pace. Globalization and governance require a wired society. Along with this India's vulnerability to the threats of IW will become greater.

The report paints a hypothetical situation (expected on a future date–30 June 2020) in which the telephone networks, SCADA systems of the Power Grid, ATC Management, Railway Traffic Control, financial services network, health services network, safety system network of chemical plants, and GPS system being used by a tri-service exercise collapse. The satellites go out of control network, pipelines in the oil refinery explode and obnoxious, poisonous gases from chemical plants leak as the safety network is hacked by the adversary. There appears to be an attempt to get 'inspired' from *Cyber War* by Richard Clarke.

Col Sanjeev Relia of Corps of Signals in his doctoral studies with the USI New Delhi has written on *Cyber Warfare and its*

Implications on National Security (Vij Books India Private Limited (2015). The book gives an excellent account of rapid improvement of telecommunication networks in India as also enhanced public investment in the ICT sector. He has also covered the evolution of modern systems in US, Russia, China, and Israel.

In order to get some 'in person' view from someone who has seen the functioning of the Indian tri-service organization as also the decision-making process at the Army Headquarters in India, I spent some time with Lt General Katoch on 13 December 2018. General Katoch brought out some very pertinent issues in the context of IW as it relates to Indian conditions. He emphasized that SF are strategic assets and in the context of IW these forces need to be used for long-term strategic roles such as indoctrination in the enemy held regions, training of forces friendly to us in the regions dominated by the adversary, collecting strategic intelligence in conjunction with other agencies operating abroad.

SF is also most suitable for psychological operations and perception management in the target regions. These forces have flexible organizations as also unconventional methods of operations. They operate in small teams and deliver much lethal or effective punch as compared to other conventional forces. This needs to be considered while raising, training, and tasking these forces.

Assessment

On the positive side India, especially the Indian Armed Forces, took serious note of events in the Gulf. Serious efforts were made to formalize the concepts and theories on IW. The two smaller services—the Indian Navy and the Indian Air Force—did come up with their IW doctrines in reasonable time frame. The Indian Army restructured some of their units and formations to suit Information Age war. The training establishments too commenced with designing new training and structures for IW. The Armed Forces became more alive to the need for cyber security.

As regards the slacks or major shortcomings in coming to grip with the new phenomena, following issues emerge as the critical steps yet to be taken:-

- There appeared to be near total lack of adapting to the specific requirements to India's national security environment. Those in position of making policies for IW perhaps ignored that India does not match the scales and audacity so common for United States.
- Preparing or theorizing for IW remained a purely military endeavour. The nation or the political leadership did not initiate any discernible action to prepare the country for this new age warfare.
- Even in the military, the views on IW were not widely shared and debated so that adequate consensus could be created to ensure smooth operationalization. Hence after raising the IW brigade and IW subgroups, the new formation and the new IW unit went back to their original roles and compositions. The network-centric war initially included in the conceptual format was later dropped. The initiatives were not pursued with the type of intensity essential for managing such a vital change. It was a case of one step forward and many steps back.
- Though the American writings very clearly mention cognitive levels of IW, the role of political and military leadership, linkages between culture and organization structure, the national value systems and so on; in the IW conflict spectrum we in India ignored most of the intangible factors in IW. The Indian thrust was more on technology or the psychological components. Though fortunately, the tri-service doctrine does make very elaborate mention of economic preparation and use of cyberspace for generating wealth there is no road map on how the IW conflict spectrum will be defined from the competition to conflict stage.

- The Indian effort in preparing for the cyber war focused only on the narrow confines of cyber security. Thus completely ignoring the cyber deterrent or cyber power.

Having seen the way in which the national security scholars were engaging with the subject, it may be relevant to look at our performance as a military organization.

★★★

India's Major Military Conflicts and IW Theories

India won all her wars except the one in 1962: True, as per conventional wisdom; need scrutiny under IW Paradigm

India's Military Experience through the Prism of IW

When India woke to freedom on the fateful midnight, 'when the world was asleep' the turmoil of the last great war was still unfolding. Our distant global environment as also our immediate neighbours were all raring for a fight. Within the next two and half decades—1947 to 1971—we were involved in six military conflicts with our immediate neighbours. First war with Pakistan in 1948, border skirmish at Barahoti with the Chinese, loss of Aksai Chin 1957 (without a fight!!), first war with China in 1962, second war with Pakistan 1965, conflict with China in 1967 at Nathu La, third war with Pakistan in 1971.

The period from 1971 to 2008 was another phase of conflicts primarily with Pakistan. Bit surprising since this decade followed our much touted victory in 1971. Major military events during this period include our Sri Lankan experience (1987 to 1990), major insurgency that broke out in J&K since 1990 and is still continuing, our mobilization in Operation Parakram (without achieving any results) in 2001, attack on Taj Hotel Mumbai in 2008. How have we fared in all these conflicts and wars?

Deciding on the Performance Parameters in these Military Engagements

What should be the performance parameters of victory or defeat or relative measures of success/failure in the above events? If the parameters are—territory captured as against territory lost, enemy soldiers killed against own military casualty, enemy major weapon systems destroyed against loss of own such systems, prisoners of war captured against own troops captured by the enemy—then, except for the loss of Aksai Chin (accepting defeat without even fighting) and war with China in 1962 we can claim legitimate victory in all other military engagements. But then war is not another sporting event. Much more is at stake than bragging rights for victory. Meaningful success of war is depicted by the relative state of peace and prosperity—ideally for all the warring factions, once the din of the battlefields has gone silent. At least the victor must enjoy better state of peace and prosperity for a long time. The European nations have not fought among themselves after 1945. They have done much better for themselves—economically and in human indices—after the Second World War. Also we need to dissuade ourselves that wars or military conflicts are the exclusive domains of Armed Forces. Nations fight wars. Armed forces are but one component of the national power utilized in wars for a brief part of the entire conflict spectrum With this as the background, we will look at some examples post 1991 till 2008 and then post 2014 to 2019 to compare two distinct styles of functioning in the IW era. The reason for picking up post 1991 period is obvious.

India's Military conflicts, Post 1991

1999 Kargil War

Background

Kargil and Dras sectors are part of the state of Jammu and Kashmir that has been the cause of all wars between India and Pakistan except for the 1971 operation for liberation of East Pakistan. The area lies in the extreme cold region (temperatures going down to minus 40 degrees Celsius. Also the heights range from 14,000 feet to almost 18,000 feet at places.

For obvious reasons the heights are not occupied in any strength. During the period preceding the Kargil War, a number of heights along sizeable region were not occupied since the Indian military thought that the Pakistanis will never be able to occupy these heights and sustain themselves. The Indian Armed forces were expected to dominate the area by surveillance. Out of the two brigades deployed in the entire region one was pulled out for task in the Srinagar valley. Thus for the entire stretch only one brigade was deployed (121 Infantry Brigade).

Taking advantage of the thin deployment in the region, Pakistan commenced occupying these heights stealthily through continuous infiltration first by the ISI trained mujahideen and later by regular troops of Northern Light Infantry. This continued for more than a year till the Indian Army came to know of the intrusion through the local shepherds who reported seeing heavy equipment (artillery guns) being deployed in the region.

Decision-making process before commencement

General VP Malik, the then COAS has given a detailed account of deficiencies of strategic decision-making process pertaining to national security issues. However, as regards the top political decision on Kargil intrusion, General Malik accepts that once the Cabinet Committee on Security (CCS) met, they gave the Armed Forces complete freedom to conduct operation with only one caveat. Indian forces will not cross the Line of Control with Pakistan during operations to evict the Pakistani intruders. For our case this part will suffice. The Indian Army got the first information of Pakistani intrusion on 03 May 1999 from Tashi Namgyal, a local shepherd.[11]

11 (https://www.indiatoday.in/india/story/kargil-war-meet-shepherd-warned-army-1572296-2019-07-22. Accessed 10 May 2019.)

How did the Indian troops react? A patrol was sent to verify the information. Five Indian soldiers were captured and tortured to death. On 26 May 1999, the IAF was launched into operations. IAF lost two fighter aircrafts and a combat helicopter. Four air crew were killed. One fighter pilot was captured. On 06 June 1999, a major army offensive was launched.[12] If we go through the state of affairs on the Indian side in Kargil from 03 to 26 May 1999, it was a state of utter confusion. The formations deployed in the region had no clue about what they were up against. Hence the unnecessary casualties to both for the IAF and the Indian Army.

Conduct of War in Brief

When the Indian Army commenced operations to evict the Pakistani intruders, an approximate area of 1500 square kilometres was under Pakistani occupation. The actual Pakistani deployment in Kargil is not very clear. However, it is likely that more than two-battalion sized force did occupy the area intruded by Pakistanis. India had to mobilize more than two divisions to evict the intruders from the area. The conflict started in mid-May and was over by 26 July 1999.

Military Result

India recovered all the territory captured, which Pakistan had occupied through prolonged intrusion. This was considered as Indian victory. The Indian Air Force was also used. India lost 527 soldiers including loss of three combat aircraft. Pakistan lost 357 to 453 troops including Mujahideen.

Political Outcome

Politically it did not make any difference to Pakistan. The people who planned and executed the Kargil war for Pakistan remained in

12 https://www.news18.com/news/india/kargil-vijay-diwas-2019-timeline-of-the-1999-operation-vijay-2246563.html. (Accessed 10 May 2019)

power. Pakistan continued with her policy to inflict damage to India through proxy war. The Pakistani Prime Minister who headed the government during the war was overthrown in a military coup by the general who had planned and executed the Kargil War.

Impact

While operationalizing the intrusion, Pakistan had assumed that if India starts war to evict the intrusion, the international community will intervene within two to three days fearing a nuclear flash point. This did not happen. International support was firmly with India. Pakistan realized that in a future military conflict with India she cannot rely on international support any more. However, for continuing with the proxy war in the Srinagar valley, Pakistan felt no resistance from any international quarter. Indian security forces continued suffering heavy casualties in Srinagar valley from Pakistan-sponsored terrorism.

Indian political leadership displayed resolute will to contest loss of territory. Nevertheless, India still remained a soft state who could be troubled by countries much smaller and weaker than her. In the context of IW this is a big drawback. The first battle to be won in IW is the battle of perception management. India lost that battle.

Communication system, higher defence management, and tri service coordination improved post Kargil but these attributes were not tested subsequently.

IW-related Issues

People and Leadership: Political leadership did support the military brass in Kargil operations but limiting the place and depth of counter strike exposed our limitations as a nation. The people identified themselves with the cause and supported the Armed Forces including those in the war zone.

Economic War: Pakistan did not suffer any major economic loss which could have prevented her from pursuing her anti-India activities. This was proved in 2001 during the militant attack on the Indian parliament and its aftermath.

Knowledge and Technology: Not tested.

Internal Security: Post Kargil, the internal security infrastructure in the region did improve. However, the overall situation in the country remained the same.

Armed Forces

- Information gathering and processing this into intelligence by the Indian Army were exceptionally poor. This smacked of gross negligence bordering on professional dishonesty. The then Chief Minister (Dr Farooq Abdullah) was more aware and concerned of the intrusion than the army leadership responsible for the zone. The then defence minister, Mr George Fernandes was appalled by the fact that an intrusion of this scale into such a sensitive area was first reported by the local shepherds!
- Looking at the sequence of events, sending a patrol first to ascertain the actual intrusion thus resulting in a loss of five men, involving IAF in an unplanned manner and with inadequate strength and again suffering casualty, indicates very lopsided response to such a grave situation.
- The fact that Kargil happened eight years after the 'First Information War' in the Gulf and the Indian Army was found in an information void due to its own failing, reflects on its poor learning curve. The IAF and the Indian Navy had also formulated their IW doctrines. In light of this environmental factor our performance in Kargil is much below par. In Kargil we should have been able to fight a network-centric war and use IW formation had we learnt the right lessons from the 1991 Gulf War.
- We lost the perception management battle. Pakistan as

also the rest of the international community found us wanting in taking bold offensive action in the face of such treachery.

- This was the first time the Indian media telecast the happenings in the battlefield to the drawing rooms of the Indian citizens. This did generate favourable public response for the military. However, some of the media coverage was not in the interest of the operational security for the ongoing tactical battle. We need to learn how to use media in a manner which boosts own morale without giving away sensitive operational information. Also bulk of the coverage was by mainstream media based in New Delhi. These correspondents, who later became celebrities, got special treatment while the local media was neglected. Keeping in view the overall impact on the population in the region as also in rest of the country, there is a need to empower the local media who cover the event in a manner which is understood by the local population. In insurgency-prone areas local population is extremely important for the purpose of perception management and psychological hardening.
- Nevertheless, the media coverage of Kargil war did bring the region to national focus. As against just 300 tourists visiting Kargil in 2000 just after the war was over, today more than a million people visit the place, especially the war memorial. The old habit of neglecting own territory since 'not even a blade of grass grows in the place' (reference to Aksai Chin in 1957 in the Indian parliament by Nehru) is firmly overcome. Development of communications and other infrastructure in Kargil is also commendable. The government today has undertaken much needed initiative of developing the border areas. This is a very effective step in perception

management of the local population (who bear the brunt of conflicts along the unsettled borders). It also sends the right signals across the Line of Control.

Cyberspace: This was not used to any noticeable degree both during and after the conflict.

International Relations: India managed the international relations well to the extent that none of the major powers (US, Russia, China) were inclined to intervene. The Pakistani bogey of nuclear flash point was called. However, beyond this nothing changed for Pakistan. She continued to get economic and military support from both the US and China. It was 9/11 that changed the equation, two years after Kargil.

In essence, the Kargil war highlighted our inability to learn both as a nation as also as professional Armed Forces. There is no excuse for not planning for such a contingency, not knowing about the intrusion in time and then failing to initiate operations in a manner that we do not lose troops unnecessarily.

2001 Operation Parakram

Background

On the heels of Kargil came the daring militant attack on the Indian Parliament on 13 December 2001. Nine Indians died in the attack—six police personnel, two parliament security staff and a gardener.

Decision-making Process

Speaking to Outlook Magazine (2 March 2009) Jaswant Singh, the Indian Minister of External Affairs, said that he would not defend operation Parakram. He added that when the decision was taken he was abroad. Gen Padmanabhan, the Chief of Army Staff (COAS) during operation Parakram felt that the nation had no coherent policy for retaliatory action against such a serious terrorist attack. As per him, air strike on selected targets in Pakistan—as suggested by the media— would have escalated the situation to an unacceptable level for India. He also argues that more than one month was taken to mobilize the three strike corps to their launch pads. The holding corps did not have the capability to launch a pre-emptive cold start strike. However, (as per the then Chief) even if pre-emptive strikes were launched in January 2002 (when the three strike corps were ready in their respective launch pads), India would have dealt a crippling blow to Pakistan. But as per Padmanabhan, the political leadership did not have the will to go to war.

This reflects overall confusion and a predominantly defensive approach. First, the foreign minister is a member of the cabinet committee on security. A major decision for full-scale mobilization and perhaps war should have involved him in the process. Second, the minister (with an armoured corps background) appears to be against offensive action. As regards the chief's statement, all holding corps do have capability to strike though with limited capabilities. Their action would have achieved surprise and hence paved the way for full components of the three strike corps. Thus any action after say 20 to 26 December 2001 by the holding corps would have given an opportunity to the strike corps to exploit the success gained by them due to total surprise. Pakistan was not prepared at all from 15 December 2001 to as late as middle of January 2002. Apparently few in the political leadership clearly understood at that time the military options available, just how long they would take to execute, and what their potential consequences could be. Besides, the Army did not seem to have planned and prepared for a short, sharp conflict with Pakistan, suggesting the lessons of the Kargil war remained unlearned.

Conduct

India mobilized her Armed Forces along the entire Indo-Pak borders along with the Navy and the Indian Air force. Even mines were laid as per the existing operational plan. Nevertheless, no operations were launched. The troops returned to their peace-time locations after almost a year.

Military Result

The mobilization came to an end in October 2002. An expenditure of Rs 8000 crore was incurred with a loss of 176 lives (while laying mines on own side).

Political Outcome

Did this mobilization deter Pakistan? Not really. Cross-border terrorism continued. In May 2002, the terrorists attacked the Indian cantonment in Kaluchak (Jammu). The massive effort achieved very little. Except for Pakistani President's reluctant speech on national television that Pakistan will not allow any terrorist attacks from the Pakistani soil, nothing much came out. The promise made in the speech was soon broken!!

Impact

Mobilization in operation Parakram did not have any impact on Pakistan. It diluted the credibility of Indian conventional deterrent. Also it exposed India's excessive fear of the Pakistani nuclear threat. The Army displayed lack of offensive spirit and innovative thinking in such a situation.

IW-related Issues

People and the Leadership: The political leadership as also the people were not clear about the overall objectives of this unprecedented mobilization. The Army (as per the admission of the then Chief) did not have any political mandate for tactical or strategic objectives in Pakistan after the mobilization. The window of opportunity closed in latter part of January 2002.

Economy: India did incur a cost of Rs 8000 crore. However, Pakistan did not suffer any major economic loss that could have crippled her proxy war in India. On the contrary Pakistan resumed her proxy war in India with the same and at times renewed vigour.

Knowledge and Technology: Not tested

Internal Security: Remained critical. Security forces continued to suffer heavy losses in the valley. Seven years after Parakram, Pakistan-backed terrorists inflicted maximum damage in one attack on 26 November 2008 at the Taj Hotel in Mumbai.

Armed Forces

- **Absence of innovative approach and bold offensive action:** Close decision cycle loops are essential in IW approach to war fighting. This requires timely collection, collation of information, converting the information so collected into intelligence (available courses of action), and selection of appropriate course before the enemy acts to neutralize our tactical advantage. This requires accurate situational awareness, innovative action plan, and above all offensive spirit. All this was lacking across political and military leadership.
- **Poor logistics in stage managing the strike formations in relevant areas:** General planning parameters for stage management of strike corps to their respective launch pads entail that if full support from the railways (rolling stock and tracks) and adequate road capacities are made available, these offensive formations would be poised to be launched within six to eight days of commencement of stage management. The fact that it took more than a month to achieve this stage indicates poor logistics.
- **Lack of doctrine for operations under different contingencies:** In 2001 the army and even the Armed Forces had no doctrine whatsoever. This was a serious flaw. The first doctrine came up in 2004. Even this doctrine does not mention any plans for operations in different contingencies. We now have a tri-services

doctrine published in 2017. It does not indicate any pre-emptive offensive action in case a predesignated red line is crossed. In the absence of such clear objectives, general mobilization of Armed Forces is wasteful.

★★★

Paradigm Shift in Myanmar, Uri and Balakot

Raid on the NSCN (K) and Kanglei Yawol Kanna Lup (KYKL) Camps in Myanmar

Background

Insurgency in Nagaland and Manipur—two of the states in the extreme North East of India bordering Myanmar—is more than seven decades old. The National Council of Nagaland (Khaplang) NSCN(K) and Kanglei Yawol Kanna Lup (KYKL) are two of the prominent insurgent groups fighting for liberation of Nagaland from the Indian jurisdiction. On 4 June 2015, this group ambushed one of the infantry battalions' column in Manipur and killed eighteen soldiers.

Preparation

The planning for the revenge attack was initiated soon after the above mentioned ambush. It was found that NSCN (K) and KYKL groups were responsible for the ambush.The operation was to be monitored by the top echelon of the Indian Government. This included the then Defence Minister–Late Manohar Parrikar, Home Minister–Rajnath Singh, National Security Adviser–AjitDoval, and Army Chief–General Dalbir Singh.

Indian Army's spectacular surgical strike in association with the Air Force inside Myanmar's boundary was a national statement for paradigm shift. It was for the first time that Indian defence forces carried out an offensive inside a neighbouring nation's territory without going into very detailed formalities of seeking permission.

Execution

21 Para commando (SF) was tasked to conduct the raid on two camps which were located around ten to fifteen kilometres inside the Myanmar territory. Though some media reports claim the MI 7 helicopters of the IAF supported the operation, in all probability the raid was conducted in a conventional manner by moving through the thick jungle during night and destroying the militant camps from some stand-off distance without getting involved in any hand-to-hand fight. The Indian agencies announced the raid after the SF teams returned safely. No account of casualty inflicted on the militants was given by the government sources. Media reports later estimated around fifty to hundred militants killed.

Impact

The NSCN was stunned since though operations had been conducted by the Indian troops in the Myanmar territory earlier all those were in conjunction with the Myanmar military and this level of surprise was never achieved. This was also a case of maximum casualty to the militant cadres.

Relevance in IW

People and Political Leadership: It was a signal to the militants' groups communicating a new resolve of the government indicating that the Indian military will seek and destroy militants in Myanmar territory. The signal went to China as also Pakistan since both these countries are known to support militancy in all north-east states of India since 1960. Perhaps this was a rehearsal for something bigger. It did send following signals:-

- Early signs of political will to go proactive.
- Synergy among the political and military leadership.

Economic War: Increased the cost of war for the militants in the Northeast. There was a marked reduction in the immediate aftermath of this surgical strike.

Knowledge and Technology: Not tested.

Internal Security: It did improve substantially in the region. However, it is far from being neutralized.

Armed Forces

This attack by infiltration is well within the capability of a regular infantry battalion. Using SF for such tasks amounts to employing a highly superior force for an ordinary operation.

Accurate intelligence and surveillance over the target during the planning and execution stages:-

- **Precise decision making and execution**. The objectives were clear and manageable. Execution was precise. There was no collateral damage.
- **Offensive spirit in military operation.** This was in full view as also the proactive approach of the political leadership.
- **Focused logistics**. Yes, but the scale was small.
- **Boosted morale of owntroops.**—It helped In psychological optimism among own troops and psychological deterrent over the insurgents.
- **Political conditioning of Myanmar**. This operation did help condition Myanmar's response and future expectations.
- **Psychological operations and perception management.** The success was not fully exploited in creating psychological impact. Many media houses including The Diplomat doubted that the Indian Army had actually conducted the raid.

Cyberspace: Not tested

International Relations: India was able to convince Myanmar to cooperate in her quest for cross-border surgical strike. There were a series of joint operations in the region after this surgical strike.

Surgical strikes in PoK in retaliation to terrorists attack on Indian infantry battalion in Uri (2016)

Background

The Kashmir dispute has been a constant feature in Indo-Pak relations since 1947. Post 1990, Pakistan stepped up proxy war in Kashmir at a very large scale. On 18 September 2016, four to six Pakistan-backed terrorists of Lashkar-e-Taiba launched a daring raid on the Indian troops in Uri close to Indo-Pak border near Muzaffarabad killing around twenty Indian troops. All the terrorists involved in the raid were killed.

The Indian Defence Minister, Late Shri Manohar Parrikar was convinced that this loss needed to be avenged in a bold and befitting manner. The Indian Prime Minister, the Home Minister, and the National Security Adviser came on board for precision strike in Pakistan occupied camps to avenge the terrorists' act in Uri.

Execution

On 29 September 2016, at midnight, a team of twenty-five commandos from 4 and 9 Para Commando (SF) along with Ghatak Platoons of 6 BIHAR and 10 DOGRAS (the battalions that had suffered casualties on 18 September) were dropped across the Line of Control LoC to attack six camps in PoK stretching from Poonch to Uri Sector.

All these camps were under technical and human surveillance from the time the decision for the precision attack was taken. The troops launched for the surgical strike knew the terrain and were equipped with surveillance equipment for real time information sharing. They had night vision capabilities, data links to receive inputs from airborne and space-borne surveillance systems.

The entire move and operation was also monitored by the assets with the NTRO and ISRO. The live feed was given to the Chief of Army Staff and the NSA in their respective operations rooms. The Northern Command was at full alert to launch conventional operations should the contingency arise. The three services were also in alert mode on some pretext or the other.

The surgical strike troops reached the target by early hours of the morning between 2 and 3 am. They launched surprise stand-off attack on the camps. Exfiltration started around 4:30 am in the morning. By 6 am all troops were safely on own side of the LoC. There was just one mine injury.

The strike managed to kill between thirty-eight to fifty terrorists and two Pakistani Army soldiers.

Impact

Pakistan's political leadership was placed in a bind. They tried their best to deny that any such attack had happened. The Indian political leaders in the opposition also got rattled. They realized that the success of this attack would make the ruling party very popular. It was hard for them to let the ruling party reap the benefits of this move. This exposed the fragile commitment of Indian political system towards national security. On the other hand, the ruling political party did make it a case of political one-upmanship both for the internal and external audience.

Militarily, the precise nature of the strike—strictly against the terrorists—sent a clear message to the international community as also to Pakistan. The presence of terrorists in PoK and Pakistani support to these elements was demonstrated very unambiguously. Though this fact is well known to the international community, its reemphasis hurt Pakistan internationally.

Again going by the depth of strikes in Pakistan Occupied Kashmir (PoK), employing SF was a case of using much superior force for a routine task. However, Pakistan's threshold was tested and the bluff of heavy retaliation by Pakistan was called. Uri was calibrated at higher level than Myanmar. In the immediate aftermath of the strike there was marginal reduction in terrorists' activity but the overall tempo of the proxy war remained unchanged.

IW Relevance

Active involvement of top political leadership and clarity of objective: As in the case of raid in Myanmar there was a clear objective and complete involvement of the top echelons of decision makers at political and military levels.

Economic war: No major impact on Pakistan.

Technology and knowledge: Not tested.

Internal security: Marginal improvement in the immediate aftermath of the surgical strike. However, Pakistan was able to rev up the tempo after a month.

Coordination and cooperation at larger scale: The operation was at a larger scale since instead of just two camps in friendly Myanmar the SF were to engage six camps in PoK where the enemy threat was much more pronounced. Failure in accomplishing the mission or even a few casualties to own troops would have made huge adverse impact politically as also internationally. Hence the stakes were very high.

Armed Forces

It was flawless execution by highly trained SF troops.

- **Synergy at much higher level:** There was a risk of local conflagration if surprise was lost and the Pakistanis retaliated. To cater for this contingency, the entire Northern Command as also formations in other sensitive regions were kept at high alert. This required large-scale preparation, coordination, and additional challenges in keeping the surprise element intact.
- **Integration of surveillance resources:** Not only the army assets but national assets for real time surveillance were integrated into the effort. The inputs received by the technical and human intelligence sources were made available to the strike elements in real time through various surveillance centres.

- o **Network-centric execution:** The surveillance and decision support networks did come into play. The teams were helped by the national assets thus ensuring concentration of impact. Also the damage assessment was done by the same network which did profile the success of the mission

Cyberspace: The military cyberspace was very effectively utilized to coordinate this operation which was launched at a much larger frontage though the depth of penetration was shallow.

International Relations: Pakistan was in a bind and hence refused to accept that the strike was actually launched. The international community stood firmly with India. Even the Organization of Islamic Community did not extend any meaningful support.

Air Strike on Balakot, February 2019

Background

On 14 February 2019, Pakistan-supported terrorist group attacked CRPF convoy comprising of troops (returning home from operational area) at Pulwama on the Banihal–Jammu Road. More than forty CRPF troops were killed in this Fidayeen attack. Jaish-e-Muhammad based in Pakistan with training and indoctrination facilities in Balakot, Sawai Nallah, and Bahawalpur in Pakistan took responsibility for this suicide attack.

General elections were due from mid-April 2019. This heavy loss of lives of security forces happened just two months from the commencement of voting for the general election. For the government these were testing times since the opposition could highlight this as a major weakness of the ruling party. It was easy to influence public opinion against the government. The Indian Prime Minister made a very terse statement that the terrorists have made a very grave error and will pay for it. His focus in this and all subsequent statements was on 'terrorists'. The words he used repeatedly were, 'perpetrators of this crime will not be spared.' The die was cast.

Preparation

It is now apparent that consultations with the concerned agencies, which included the IB, R&AW, and the three services commenced soon after the attack. Two decisions were taken during the early consultations. First, that the retaliatory action was a certainty. Second, the retaliation will be precise and against the terrorists who conducted the suicide attack.

As per intelligence agencies out of a total of fifteen camps in Pakistan, there were three camps run by the concerned terrorist group—Jaish-e-Muhammad (JeM):-

- Bahawalpur in Pakistani Punjab.
- Sawai Nallah near Muzaffarabad (PoK).
- Balakot in the Khyber Pakhtunkhwa province (KPK).

The first two targets were discarded since these were close to congested civilian localities and probability of collateral damage was very high. One of the sites also had a mosque close by. On the contrary the Balakot camp was on a secluded hill far removed from the civilian population. This camp was being constantly monitored by the Indian intelligence agencies and high resolution satellite imagery and other aerial photographs were available in great details.

Pakistan was certain that the scale of retaliation would be big. They perhaps anticipated ground attacks anywhere along their borders with India. Hence their troops were on high alert. On the contrary after initial discussions, the Cabinet Committee on Security (ministers of defence, foreign affairs, home, finance along with the national security advisor) under the Prime Minister had decided on precision air strike at Balakot in consultation with the three service chiefs. The air chief was informed and he was in direct communication with the Prime Minister.

The objective and the terms of reference were very clear to everyone involved. The top echelon in the services as also the government maintained complete secrecy. All activities were conducted as routine without any cancellation including the farewell party and the like.

The date of the strike was chosen in such a manner that the air show scheduled during the period was allowed to get over. The routine air fire power at the Pokhran ranges was conducted a few days before the strike. The aircrafts to be used in the strike also participated. Multiple air bases were selected from where the strike elements would take off. Twelve Mirage 2000 were to take off from Gwalior in central India. Four Sukhoi 30s were to take off from Bareilly in Uttar Pradesh. One each Israeli (AWAC aircraft Phalcon, Airborne Early Warning (AE&W) Indigenous Netra and Ilyushin 76s (IL76s) for mid-air refuelling took off from Agra/Delhi.

All these aircrafts were to fly over Delhi hence the ATC at Delhi was asked to provide a dark corridor window. The Mirage kept a low flight path to avoid early detection from the Pakistani RADARS. All other aircrafts were at high flight path. As the strike force approached the Pakistani RADAR ranges, the high flight path aircrafts were detected first.

These aircrafts turned towards Bahawalpur. Thus confirming Pakistani apprehension that the JeM camp at Bahawalpur would be attacked. A contingent of twelve Pakistani F16 took off to intercept this group heading towards Bahawalpur. Once this happened the actual strike force of twelve Mirages came up on the Pakistani RADARs. However, by this time the interceptors that could interfere with the Mirages were more than 150 kilometres away. The decoys (SU 30s) turned towards Indian airspace and came in close vicinity of the strike element.

The Mirages had a few minutes over the targets to lock in and release their precision-guided munitions on the six targets selected. Five of the targets received extremely precise hits by the SPICE munitions. The bombs pierced a small hole in the roofs of their respective targets and exploded inside the rooms with full impact making survival of any inmates impossible. The sixth target could not be hit since during the short time window of strike the pilot could not lock on to the target. Having accomplished the mission, the strike force turned homewards. By 3:30 am they landed at their respective bases—mission accomplished.

Early morning at around 5 am, Pakistan acknowledged that 'IAF had dropped some bombs in the jungle near Balakot uprooting some trees.'

Nevertheless, within twenty-four hours of the Indian strike, the Pakistan Air Force (PAF) scrambled to retaliate. IAF checked the incursion by PAF and both sides lost one aircraft each. Indian pilot who bailed out and landed in PoK was returned to India within sixty hours. Reportedly inhabitants of PoK killed the unfortunate Pakistani pilot who also landed in PoK since he was mistaken as Indian!

However, beyond the operational details something more significant happened when these decisions were taken and implemented:-

- The scale and risks were extremely high, hence the three services were on full alert for conventional war. The Prime Minister had met the three service chiefs himself in the presence of the NSA.
- Fourteen out of fifteen members of the United Nations Council on Security (UNCS) were with India during the Balakot strike. After the strike even China, the all-weather Pakistani ally, did not support Pakistan.
- Finally, on 01 May 2019, the UNSC including China declared Jaish Chief, Azhar Mahmood as a global terrorist. China was made to succumb to international pressure and jettison Pakistan.
- Though the Balakot strike was localized, preparations were made for full spectrum conflict. Complete synergy, collaboration, cooperation, and flow of information horizontally and vertically in the context of operations were ensured.

IW Relevance

People and the Leadership: The events preceding the Balakot strike had galvanized the people in supporting a befitting reply to Pakistani terror attacks. The nation could have accepted even a full-scale war with Pakistan. The situation was thus markedly different than that which prevailed in December 2001. The political leadership managed to be very astute, decisive, and displayed exceptional brilliance in calibrating the response. Besides, the decision cycle loop was short. Within a week of the Pulwama attack on the CRPF convoy, the strike was launched. The complete sequence of decision making was timely and well deliberated. Everybody who was responsible was onboard and all concerned ensured that complete secrecy was maintained. This ensures reasonable surprise though Pakistan was expecting big retaliation.

Economic War: Balakot increased the cost of proxy war for Pakistan manifold. Besides imposing the cost of military preparation for any future misadventure, the economic cost by way of disrupting the air service, revenue from the air flights through her air space hurt Pakistan during a period when her economy was going through the worst period.

Technology and Knowledge: India used her indigenous satellites for intelligence gathering, precision guidance, and knowledge sharing to near perfection. Innovative use of technology was made in 'deception' operations. The use of weapons and ammunition was well thought off. A combination of technological and human innovation ensured perfect score in this strike.

Internal Security: Balakot did deliver a mortal blow to the Pakistani support base for the terrorists. This was the first time that the Indian Armed Forces made the terrorists insecure in Pakistani hinterland. There has been remarkable decrease in the morale and the intensity of Pakistani proxy war in Kashmir post Balakot.

Armed Forces

Tri-service synergy: Though it was the IAF which launched a 'visible' operation which stunned Pakistan, the Army and the Navy were fully mobilized and kept the Pakistani establishment guessing and terrorized. This helped the IAF spring a complete surprise and prevented the Pakistanis from launching any counter strike using their army or navy. This synergy also checkmated any likely escalation by the Pakistanis. Network-centric war was displayed by the Indian Armed Forces for the first time. This included:-

- Concentration of impact at the point of decision by networking of widely dispersed forces in a very fast time frame.
- Enhancing the surveillance and target acquisition capabilities of the Platforms (Mirage 2000 and Su 30s) with the inputs from satellite and other sensors used for the purpose.
- Real-time guidance provided by the networked ground stations to the strike force as also during the air combat the next day when own sorties were guided by the ground based and airborne systems.
- Precision targeting, no collateral damage. The attack was so precise that even the buildings where the terrorists targeted remained intact except for a small hole in their respective roofs through which the spice missiles penetrated. The militants inside these buildings suffered the maximum damage. Approximately 300 odd terrorists in the buildings perished. It sent a clear message to Pakistan as also the international community that India's targets were the terrorists and not the ordinary citizens of Pakistan. Even the civilian infrastructure was not touched.

Perception management of the adversary as also the international community: The scale and depth of penetration in Pakistan forced her to accept that the strike did take place. The Pakistan Air Force retaliatory strike the next day did some damage control for Pakistan but the bar for continuing terrorism in J&K was raised by successful Balakot strike. The international community too realized India's new proactive posture and accepted the same without any protest. This was a major victory. China—the all-weather friend to Pakistan—

refrained from any adverse comment against India. De facto the international community accepted India's right to initiate any aggressive action to deter Pakistan from continuing with the proxy war in J&K.

Focused logistics: Though the point of impact was small, the logistics for the air operations involved major effort in terms of time, space, and stealth. It is here that the planning and execution achieved stunning results.

Cyberspace: The military cyberspace was fully exploited in:-

- Vectoring the strike, deception, and logistic forces.
- The strike elements received real time information from the ground-based and airborne systems through the military cyberspace.
- Even during the air-to-air combat the next day, the own intercepting aircrafts were fully guided by the airborne and ground stations.

International Relations: India emerged as a nation that could assert her right to be aggressive in self-defence. This was a major achievement in terms of scaling up the international approval for such retaliatory actions.

So far in the study we have not addressed the most critical components of IW—the political leadership and the macro economy in India. An objective assessment of these components is most essential for identifying the starting points for strategic options.

★★★

Netwar—Political and Economic War in Indian Context

India's Political Decision Making and Strategies for IW

Sound political decision making and implementation within tight time schedule are critical components of IW

What impact political decision making has on a nation's IW capabilities?

POLITICAL DECISION MAKING is the most relevant and most ignored aspect in almost all military writings on IW. There appears to be some possible reasons for this trend. First, when we talk of 'war' non-military aspect is excluded. We think of war in terms of soldiers, guns, ships, fighter aircrafts and the like. There is a tendency to divorce military and non-military factors. Second, we form opinions on what we see and not what has been the cause of 'what we see'. Thus the political leadership, economic strength or lack of it, people's perception that are the causes of the effect (war) generally remain hidden behind the noise of victory celebration or mourning after the defeat. Third, bulk of the writings on IW are centred on technologies. It is either cyber war hence related technologies or it is AI, big data, communications, IT enabled logistics as these relate to fighting wars. Very seldom we look at the pioneering use of these technologies in the business world. Lastly, there are hardly any debates in the academic and business world on the causes, dynamics and impacts of war on the national well-being. The citizen-centric discussion on war had been missing especially in India till we found very clear and unambiguous mention of centrality of human capital in 'Joint Doctrine Indian Armed Forces–2017'. As we have seen earlier, the joint doctrine expanded the ambit of national security to leadership, politics, economics, etc. It also recognized the importance of national power with various non-military components.

In our discussion on CNP, we had a glimpse of political decision making and its impact on national security (US, Israel, China, Pakistan) as also overall competitiveness. All these countries have been in some war or the other right from 1948. The first three countries synergized their national resources for continuing their aggressive military activities with those of citizen-centric growth trajectories. The last one (Pakistan) went too far with aggressive military adventurism and ignored her citizens. The effects on all the four nations are too vivid to ignore. Important lesson in the context of IW is that political leadership and political economy cannot be ignored in IW.

Again while the tangible resources mentioned in CNP do matter, the intangible factors of state that make major difference to the inherent power of the state are, state-society relationship, what the people think of themselves and the nation, and how the political class takes decisions. We will focus our attention on the decision-making process of the political class.

The way decisions are taken at the highest levels in the political leadership is the most critical intangible factor. Because in IW concept 'decision' lies at the critical juncture of OODA value chain. Unless 'observation' and 'orientation' crystalize into decisions, no action can be taken. Decisions not only depend on the information which triggers 'observation' and 'orientation' but to a very large extent depend on the character or 'being' of the decision maker. The value system, self-belief or the lack of it, sincerity of purpose, moral courage, faith in the people, impact the decision-making process.

It is this character which decides what the leader observes, to what goals the leadership orients, the type of decisions taken and the resoluteness of execution of the plan once the decisions are taken. A leadership which is timid, conceited, self-serving, disconnected from the realities and people will take decisions differently compared to a fearless, honest, sincere, selfless, and connected leadership notwithstanding the same set of information and threat environment. Also the former type of low self-esteem leadership will be loath to learn from their mistakes and instead get involved in cover-up activities. While courageous leaders will be fast learners from their own as well as others' mistakes. Even in the CNP context, as per Ashley Tellis, it is not the tangible assets that a nation has but the capability to use these assets that decides the national power. Thus political leadership—responsible for enabling and exploiting the resources—occupies central stage. To start with let us recount the academic framework of decision making as also leadership dialectics.

Academic framework of decision making (Decision Science as discussed in Operations Research)

Decision science identifies three types of environments for decision making. First, when the future state of nature is known. This is the most helpful environment. The decision makers should be able to work out the payoffs and penalties from their decisions with accuracy. Hence, there should not be any reason to go wrong here. Second, when the probabilities of future state of nature are known. Here also the decision makers should generally hit the high payoff buttons in each of their decisions. In the third type of environment, the decision maker does not know even the probability of future state of nature. This is the most difficult type of environment for making decisions. Here the decision makers make guesses. These guesses are based on the character or the personality of the decision maker. For our purpose we will assume that all political decisions of strategic nature belong to this environment of complete uncertainty about the future state of nature. It is here that the leadership assumes the future state as per their attitude or in our case the character of the leadership.

Theoretically, there are four types of leadership decisions in complete uncertainty of the future state of nature:-

- Criterion of Optimism.
- Criterion of Pessimism.
- Criterion of equal likelihood.
- Criterion of Realism.

For our discussion we will apply the first two criteria—that of optimism and pessimism. A leadership which is optimistic about the future state of nature will assume that the best case situation will prevail. They will select the maximum (from the payoff matrix) from the 'maximum gains' and hence the criterion is called as maximax. Having taken such a decision, they will follow a strategic 'stretch' approach to use their resources to get more from less. Such an approach creates super achievers in the nation and societies. This is what Israel does in peace and war; Japan does in business competitiveness. To a very large extent the American decision makers too are always sure of their success. It is not necessary that optimistic attitude in itself will pay high dividends. It can boomerang. As it did for Pakistan time and again, for Iraq in 1991 and for China in 1979 against Vietnam. Having taken a decision under the 'maximax' attitude the strategic approach must adopt 'stretch' mode for planning and utilization of resources. To that extent execution must be of a very high standard.

A pessimistic leadership will anticipate the worst state of nature and will select maximum of the minimum gains and hence the criterion is called as maximin. The strategic 'fit' approach is selected here. More often than not the leadership underestimates their resources. In a simpler way we can term these two approaches as 'bold' and 'cautious.' Sometimes too cautious approach entails grossly suboptimal use of resources. Such a situation creates organizational slack. Such leaders are not able to exploit the inherent talent of their people. Such organizations head towards inefficiency in creating and exploiting resources.

In the context of political leadership, we need to differentiate between output and outcome. The process output is of immediate nature. It is the immediate result the decision offers to the decision maker. Whereas outcome defines the long-term implication of the result from the decision. In simpler way output is in terms of production whereas outcome is in terms of impact of that production. As an example, a rigorous academic environment produces high quality academicians at the cost of numbers. This is output of the process involving academic rigor. The outcome of this approach is highly competent innovative culture, globally acclaimed reputation in quality, attracting committed and best in class students, high degree of societal acceptance and so on. It is but natural to expect the political leadership to strive for outcome and not for output.

Leadership: An Academic Framework

Having identified two types of approaches in decision making—optimistic and pessimistic—in relation to political decision making, it may be prudent to look at a more general and academic framework of 'leadership'. We find some interesting aspects when we try to develop an academic framework on leadership. Please refer Appendix A.

India's political leadership since 1946: National Security

The discussion that follows now is not a critique of the political leadership since 1946. However, the approach to decision making and its impact on the collective national psyche over the last seven decades is definitely relevant since that will describe the assets or liabilities we as a nation have today when we choose any strategy. Having formulated a common platform and framework for expectations from the highest political leadership, we may now look at the way our political leadership at the highest level has behaved with regard to strengthening the national security capabilities and related environment.

The first test given to the Indian leadership was about a year before India—and also Pakistan—became independent countries. In July 1946, the Cabinet Mission Plan approved a united India endowed with the powers of defence, foreign affairs, communication and to raise finance. Under the central government of united India, six Hindu majority provinces and six Muslim provinces were to be formed as per Syed Umar Hayat in his article, *The Direct Action Day: Myth and Reality*.

With this as the background, what were the decision alternatives with the political leadership which came into power in India on 15 August 1947:-

- Accept Cabinet Mission Plan and work for harmonious coexistence of Hindu and Muslim majority states under unified India. Visualize a future state that the two major religious communities will learn to cooperate and collaborate.
- Reject the Cabinet Mission Plan and ignore Jinnah's threat of direct action. This decision would envision a future state which believes that the violence due to the direct action by Jinnah would be far less compared to the violence if the country is partitioned based on religious beliefs.
- Reject Cabinet Mission Plan and accept partition. This decision will be based on the future state of nature where accepting partition would give least dividend at minimal risk.

The Indian leadership took the last option. This is minimin criterion (minimize losses and accept minimum payoff) under pessimism. What the Indian leadership thought in 1946 was that the two communities will never learn to live together (lack of faith in the people). They also thought that 50 percent of provinces with Hindu dominance and the other half as Muslim dominance can lead to two sets of provinces that will fight with each other in future (again pessimism and lack of self-belief). The result of this process was accepting the least risky option (as it appeared in 1946!). The output was partition of India. What was the outcome? Major General Lachhman Singh in his book, *Missed Opportunities: Indo-Pak War 1965* describes the situation around partition of India in the chapter, 'A Subcontinent Divides'—'Of the 14 million people that migrated half a million were killed.' This is the heaviest price India (and also Pakistan) paid for a decision taken under pessimism and fear.

Compare this with what Abraham Lincoln decided in 1861. Also compare this with the decision taken by Mao of China during his thirty-year struggle as also of Israeli leadership post 1948.

The second test of strategic leadership, which was to have a very long-term impact on independent India, was during the first war with Pakistan over Kashmir. Please refer to references in the endnotes for accessing the details of this war. As war entered a decisive phase in 1949 after almost year-long bitter fighting, the political decision makers had the following options:-

- Re-enforce the success gained by the Indian Armed forces in Jammu and Kashmir by inducting additional forces and declare to the world that India is determined to capture the entire territory which legitimately belongs to her. The future state of nature which the political leadership would have to envision with this decision being, 'the adverse international reaction if any can be managed and our forces are capable of achieving the objective.'
- Accept ceasefire and accept UN intervention. The future state envisioned while taking this decision is, 'As a new nation we will not be able to withstand international pressure and our Armed Forces are not likely to achieve the objective in the given time frame.'

The political leadership of the time took the second alternative. The output of this decision was immediate end of hostilities and cessation of violence and loss of lives on both sides for the time being. What was the outcome?

A UN sponsored resolution of Kashmir remains a pipedream. India later rejected the UN intervention. Post 1948, India and Pakistan fought three more wars and a bitter proxy war continues since 1988. India has already lost more than 14,000 security personnel between 1988 to 2019 and more than 50,000 civilians have died in Jammu and Kashmir during this period. These figures do not include the casualties in 1965 and 1999. Also, this does not include loss of lives and property in other parts of India inflicted by Pakistan-sponsored terrorists. Compare the Indian action with the Chinese response in Korea in 1951 against the US—a major superpower at that time with nuclear weapons. China, in 1951, did not have nuclear weapons but the leadership had courage and national pride.

Our decision making generally has been to avoid war at 'all costs'. One of the reasons especially in 1949 could have been that the world had witnessed a long and terrible world war from 1939 to 1945. Everyone was fed up with loss of lives and destruction of property. Hence the political leadership chose to end war early. Well the assumption that everyone was fed up of war in 1948 is not supported by facts. Bitter war was raging in Middle East between Israel and Arab states. In China, Mao's offensive was in the final stages. The Korean War became a multinational conflict from 1951 to 1954. Millions of soldiers and dozens of nations were still fighting. Also the long cold war had just begun. To terminate war early due to abhorrence for bloodshed is a novel thought. But did we succeed in avoiding bloodshed by this approach to decision making?

It may be revealing to analyse the casualties (South Asia Terrorist Portal) of security forces and those of terrorists from 1988 to 2019 (the present phase of terrorism in J&K started in 1988 and continues till date notwithstanding all our gestures of peace and goodwill). The casualties suffered by the security forces since 1988 to as late as 2007 was much higher than those suffered by the terrorists. The biggest margin is around 1996 when 1333 security personnel were martyred as against 376 terrorists killed. It is only after 2008 that security forces gained ascendency in terms of comparative casualties.

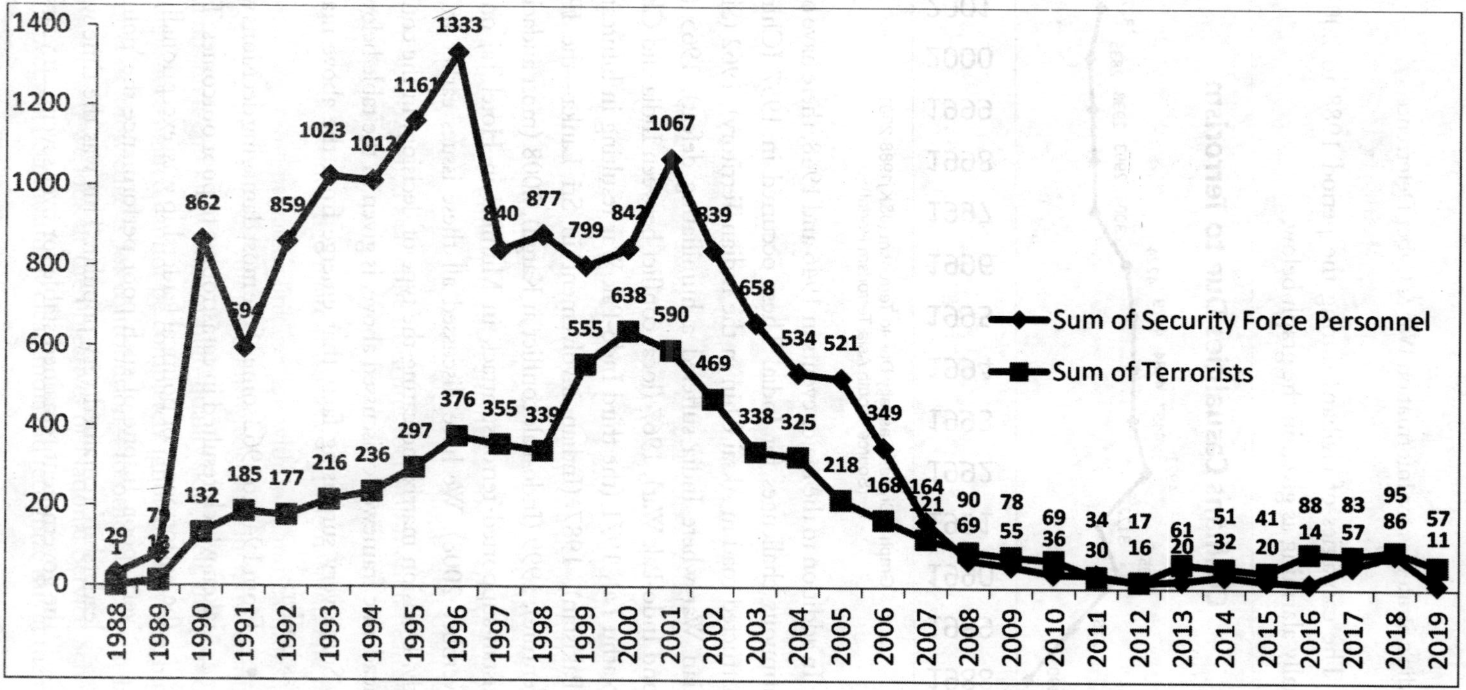

Graph 1. Comparison Casualty figures (J&K) Security Forces and Terrorists1988-2019 (Source: South Asia Terrorism Portal)

The casualties of civilians during the period 1988 to 2001 is equally alarming as given in the graph below.

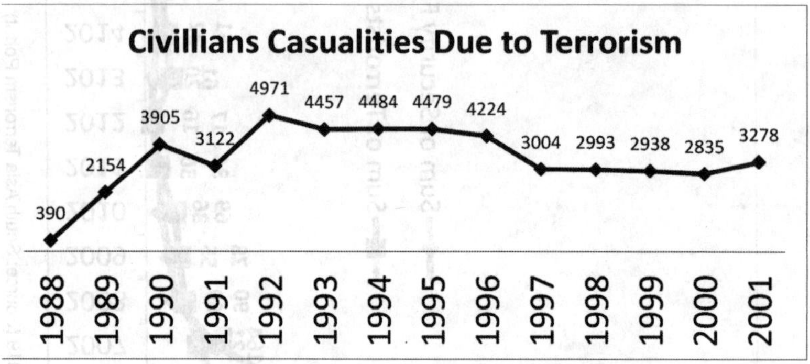

Graph 2 Civilian Casualty Due to Terrorism (J&K)1988-2001
(Source: South Asia Terrorism Portal)

In addition to the major events in 1946 and 1948, there have been continuous challenges for India. These occurred in 1957 (Chinese constructed road in Aksai Chin in the Indian Territory), 1962 (Sino-Indian War where India suffered a humiliating defeat), 1965 (the second Indo-Pak War), 1967 (local conflict between India and China at Nathu La), 1971 (the third Indo-Pak War resulting in bifurcation of Pakistan), 1987 (Indian involvement in Sri Lanka—the IPKF adventure), 1999 (Indo-Pak conflict at Kargil), 2008 (most audacious Pakistan-supported terrorist attack in Mumbai in Hotel Taj on 26 November 2008). We have discussed all these issues earlier in the study. Decision matrix indicating the type of decision, in the context of academic framework discussed above, is given in the table below.

Some very surprising facts that emerge from the above matrix are as under:-

- From 1946 to 1962 some of the most damaging decisions were taken which resulted in catastrophic to poor outcomes. Thus the performance of political leadership was 'exceptionally' to 'very' poor. Inspite of such poor performance the 'political leadership' remained very popular. This was the time when the government remained stable for over seventeen years!

- In 1987 though the decision was taken in the optimistic frame of mind the execution and hence the performance turned out to be catastrophic. Here again the political leadership did not suffer in popularity and hence remained stable.

Table 1. Decision Matrix National Security Since 1946

Time line	Optimistic/ Pessimistic	Output	Outcome	Performance	Popularity
1946	Pessimistic	Poor	Catastrophic	Exceptionally poor	High
1948	Pessimistic	Poor	Poor	Poor	High
1957	Pessimistic	Poor	Poor	Poor	High
1962	Pessimistic	Poor	Very poor	Exceptionally poor	Somewhat dented but remained unchallenged
1965	Optimistic	Good	Very good	Very good	High
1967	Pessimistic by political leadership, optimistic by the mid-level military leadership	Good	Very good	Good	High
1971	Optimistic	Outstanding	Poor	Good	High
1987	Optimistic	Poor	Very poor	Catastrophic	No change
1999	Balanced	Good	Good	Average	High
2008	Pessimistic	Poor	Poor	Poor	High, the government won another term to rule the country

Why is it that 'popularity' or the stability of the government in India is not correiated to performance in the domain of national security? There can be several reasons:-

- National security may not be an emotive issue with the people in general.

- The concerned government creates a halo effect around their select leaders with the help of pliable media and other tools of propaganda.
- People in general have come to accept that India is a soft state and we are not capable of doing better than what the leadership did in the given circumstances.

★★★

Political Economy and Fault Lines

Political leadership and macro economy

We examined political decision making in the context of national security. Another major component of IW is 'economic war'. As per the American authors, the method of conducting economic war is through 'sanctions' and 'blockades'. In the Indian context both these methods may not be relevant. On the contrary we need to build up economic strength and resilience to ensure that external threats do not affect our military preparation and economic growth while at the same time we ensure the well-being and economic productivity of our citizens at desired levels. It is in this context we will examine the way our political economy evolved over the last seven decades. Why is this relevant for the study? This analysis will help us identify our current starting point.

A brief acquaintance with the political economy first. Adam Smith in *The Wealth of Nations* (1740) identifies the people to state relationship in economic activities. Primarily there are two approaches by which the state can play its role. It can follow a strict 'command and control' approach in which bulk of the macro and micro economic decisions are taken by the state. People do as they are commanded and their activities are strictly controlled by state machinery. Alternatively, the state can choose to create an enabling ecosystem and lay down self-check based, broad policy guidelines and make the people free to choose economic activities within the ethical and societal norms. The state provides spiritual leadership (not connected with religion) with minimal intrusion into the affairs of the people within a very broad, shared framework. These are two extremes. Between these two extremes there are a number of alternatives. People need to learn to compete in a fair and level field within the country as also globally.

The concept of wealth creation, balanced distribution between the state and the people is further extended by Amartya Sen in his work, *The Idea of Justice*. The book focuses on economic activities as a means to ensure social justice. Sen makes a very novel observation on the relevance of wealth as a means to generate capabilities. Further, he describes that the extent of capabilities that wealth can generate depends on a number of human and environmental factors. In his view poverty is seen as deprivation of capability (to lead a happy life). Thus depending solely on income levels as a means of Human Development Index is erroneous.

The 'World Economic Forum (WEF) 2018' equivalence to Sen's ideas can be 'human capital'. By 'human capital' the WEF implies the skill sets, innovation and creativity of people, productive interaction, health and happiness, belief in the government and institutions and so on. In the context of information war, as it is understood today, the psychological orientation of people, internal harmony, insulation against psychological operations of the adversaries and lobbies sprung by hostile nations and groups become important aspects linking national security and political economy of the state. It may be relevant to scan the approach that we followed during the last seventy years of our independence and the impact it has had on the people in the context of national security.

In the context of national security and Information Warfare we need to go to the cognitive levels of people with regard to their loyalty to the state while carrying out economic activities. These include paying taxes, not indulging in any economically profitable activity that impacts national security etc. It is in this context that we will browse India's macro-economic journey, which reveals the decision-making ecosystems through the last seventy years.

As in the case of national security, for the political economy also we will formulate a framework for evaluation. The decision making can be optimistic or pessimistic. Leadership can be judged as transformative or transactional. Thereafter we will look at the immediate output in terms of GDP growth rate and poverty alleviation; and outcome will be in terms of global competitiveness:-

- Optimistic political economy approach will be based on faith in the capability of people and hence characterized by openness, free economy, minimal regulations, and encouragement to competition. The opposite of all these ie. closed economy, creating license permit environment, and excessive regulation will represent pessimism.
- Transformational political leadership in the economic sense would entail nudging the people to be honest in economic and financial dealings, pay taxes without hiding income, follow business ethics and compete based on merit and excellence. In our case this will be reflected by reduction on subsidy and quotas and pure welfare schemes which are fashionably dubbed as pro poor economy. The pro poor economy that has been going on for better part of the last seventy years has created more poverty and corruption. Though it is important to lift all the people above the abject poverty that most Indians lived in till very recently, there should be shift towards pro merit and pro wealth creation economy.
- The immediate output will be measured in terms of growth rate of GDP and alleviation of poverty.
- The outcome will be measured in terms of sustained improvement in global competitiveness.

The Wasted Years 1950 to 1980

Between 1950 and 1980, India's growth rate averaged around 3.5 percent per annum and this was at a time when the developing world, including Sub-Saharan Africa and other least-developed countries, showed a growth rate of 5.2 percent per annum. An important assumption in the choice of post-independence development strategy was the generation of wealth through high level of public sector investments.

The wealth so generated would then percolate to remove poverty. However, this did not happen, and the public sector—instead of being a generator of wealth for the community's good—became, over time, a consumer of community's savings. This reversal of roles had become evident by the early seventies, and the process reached its culmination by the early eighties. By then, the government began to borrow not only to meet its own revenue expenditure but also to finance public sector deficits and investments. During 1960-1975, total public sector borrowings averaged 4.4 percent of GDP. These increased to 6 percent of GDP by 1980-81.

Substantial Growth by ProfligateSpending Leading to Economic Disaster: 1980-90

In 1980, first attempts were made to open up the economy and also embrace IT. The GDP growth rate jumped to 5.6 percent, which by Indian standards was good though the world around us was growing at a much faster pace. However, during this period, the government spending was profligate and large-scale revenue deficit was created. Besides the public sector became more inefficient. The public sector drained out 9 percent of the GDP by 1989-90. Thus, the public sector, which was supposed to generate resources for the growth of the rest of the economy, gradually became a net drain on the society as a whole. This was the time that India went to IMF to save herself from the foreign debt payment default. IMF did help but forced India to liberalize. It was a very fortunate intervention for the Indian economy.

Dealing with Poverty

Almost half of the Indian population was below the poverty line in 1950. The poverty levels increased during the next twenty years till 1970-71. Poverty levels started decreasing from 1973-74 and thereafter continued to decrease. Please see graph below:

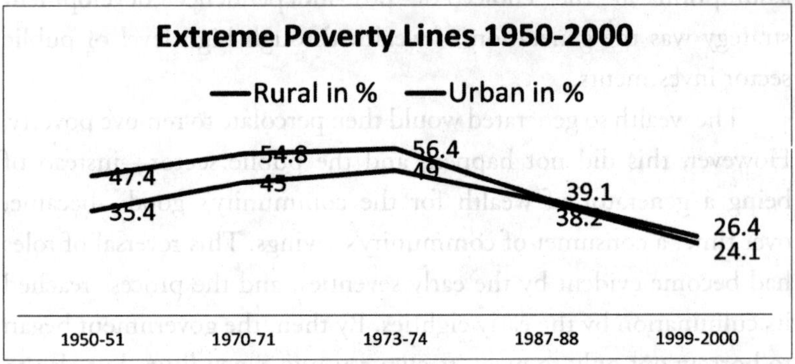

What we need to note is that the benchmark for below poverty line subsistence is extremely low for India given the international standards both in terms of purchasing power parity and capability in terms of Amartya Sen's theory. Some of India's continuing issues pertaining to efficiency and corrupt practices are:-

- Fairly developed banking sector but plagued by scams and scandals.
- Slow transformation of India's labour force from agriculture to industry and services.
- Poor performance in infrastructure build up—power, roads, railways, telecom, water, sanitation.
- Rent seeking political favouritism.
- Subsidism.
- Bureaucratic culture.
- Poor quality primary education and lack of proper skills.
- Poor health care.
- Antiquated laws and regulations.

Consolidation post Liberalization, 1991 to 2004

Post liberalization the Indian economy looked up. The Indian economy started growing at 6 to 7%. By 2004-05 the growth rate was almost close to 8 and 9%. However, the share of agriculture in economy started going down since no new technology was used in the agricultural sector after the green revolution of 1960s.

The work force in farming and agriculture remained high whereas the gross product from agriculture decreased. This increased the poverty levels among the farmers. There was immediate requirement of infusing technologies, better managerial practices, regulatory regime to incentivizing the farmers for global competition and improvements in infrastructure. Though during the last few years before 2004 the infrastructure improvements picked up and a good road map to growth was laid. The poverty level continued to decrease. The percentage of people below the poverty line was about 20 percent by 2005-06.

Period of Growth along with Global Liquidity Boom Followed by Low Growth, High Inflation Scams and Governance by Proxy: 2004 to 2014

During the period 2004 to 2014, India had a stable government at the Centre. The first term of this government from 2004 to 2009 showed robust growth along with the global boom. The second term from 2009 to 2014 was marked by high interest rates, stagnating high deficit, weak currency, loss of accountability and highest levels of scam unprecedented in the history of India's independence. Some economists and political scientists call this period as the lost decade. If this be so, then India lost five decades in her growth journey. First four decades since independence and later the period from 2004 to 2014. The relevant data is given below:

Steadying the ship: The World Bodies Recognize India's Economic Growth (2014-2018)

This is an interesting period in India's economic journey. For the first time

Table 2. GDP Growth Rates and Inflation 2004-05 to 13-14

Year	GDP Growth Rate in %	Inflation
2004-05	7	6.48
2005-06	9.5	4.47
2006-07	9.6	6.59
2007-08	9.3	4.73
2008-09	6.7	8.05
2009-10	8.6	3.81
2010-11	8.9	9.56
2011-12	6.7	8.94
2012-13	4.5	7.35
2013-14	4.9	6.06

(Source: Economic Surveys)

the high GDP growth rate was accompanied by manageable inflation rates. For India's standards it was lowest inflation rate over a reasonably sustained period of time. During this period, global slowdown due to economic setback of 2008 still continued. Most of the BRIC nations (Brazil, Russia, India, China) slowed down in comparison to India. Even China's growth for the first time was below that of India. Oil prices were low in the beginning then climbed up in 2017 and towards the end of 2018 again started going down. Nevertheless, the Indian growth kept a steady upward trend as the fastest growing economy in the world. Thus the Indian economy displayed resilience.

Table 3. GDP Growth Rates, Inflation, Fiscal Deficit and FDI 2014 to 2018 Economic Surveys

Year	GDP Growth Rate%	Inflation	Fiscal Deficit as % of GDP	FDI Billion dollars
2014	7.4	5.8	4.4	22
2015	8.2	3.6	4.1	31
2016	7.1	4.5	3.9	36
2017	6.7	3.6	3.5	36
2018	7.3	4.7	3.5	29

This was also the period when the Indian performance was repeatedly lauded by the world bodies like the World Bank,

International Monetary Fund (IMF) and the World Economic Forum (WEF). Even the rating agencies upgraded confidence in the Indian economy. Another feature of growth with less inflation during this period has been implementation of reforms to remove the major systemic weaknesses. Thus:-

- The banking sector went through major churning to get rid of NPAs and streamline the governance so that such NPAs do not come up again.
- Major initiatives were launched for skilling India's labour force. However, this aspect is still work-in-progress. The outcome is not seen at a recognizable level.
- There has been remarkable growth in road network, railways, in-land water transport. But the most spectacular jump has been in the sanitation sector. From less than 40 percent of the population getting access to proper sanitation the figure jumped to more than 97 percent in just fifty months since May 2014. Also the power sector has been spectacular in growth during the period.
- Political favouritism has been negligible, but subsidies are still very large. However, all these subsidies are going straight to the beneficiary through transparent online systems hence the pilferage has been arrested.
- Bureaucratic culture still persists though there are repeated and genuine efforts by the government to break the inertia and accelerate decision making as also execution.
- Revenue from direct and indirect taxes has increased. From 3.79 crore tax payers in 2013-14 the number of tax payers in 2017-18 is 6.84 crore. With demonetization and GST, the Indian economy has become more formal and transparent.
- Health care has received a big boost with government intervention for providing free health care to the poor through the Ayushman Bharat Scheme.

Keeping in view the change of guard or inflexion points in the macro-economic factors—decision to output, outcome, performance and popularity of the government—is tabulated below. Pessimistic decision making indicates excessive controls by the government and regulated economic regime. Optimistic decision making indicates creating an enabling environment by granting independence to people in economic activities and reposing faith in the business community.

Table 4. Decision Matrix Performance and Popularity Matrix 1947 to 2014

Time Line	Pessimistic/ optimistic	Output	Outcome	Performance	Popularity
1947-1964	Pessimistic	Extremely Poor	Catastrophic	Very Poor	High
1964-1973	Pessimistic	Extremely Poor	Catastrophic	Very Poor	High
1973-1980	Pessimistic	Poor	Poor	Poor	High
1980-1990	Pessimistic	Poor	Poor	Poor	Average
1990-2004	Optimistic	Good	Good	Good	Average
2004-2009	Optimistic	Good	Good	Good	High
2009-2014	Optimistic	Poor	Poor	Average	Low
2014-2019	Optimistic	High	High	High	High

Assessment

The above matrix brings out some important facts relevant to the study:-

- **No correlation between performance and popularity of political leadership:**
  - o In spite of very poor performance on the economic front from 1947 to 1973 and catastrophic outcomes, the political leadership remained very popular and the government enjoyed stability.
  - o Though the poverty figures started declining from 1974,

the economic performance in terms of growth remained poor. Again this did not affect the electorate since the political leadership remained popular and stable.

- The above phenomenon reflects the type of democratic awareness and the political manipulation during the period from 1947 to 1990.
- From 1990 to 2004 India registered steady economic growth. But this did not reflect on the stability of the Government. There were four changes in the government. These periods include 1991-96, followed by a brief period of thirteen days when the government was toppled. For the next two years a minority government ruled at the centre. From 1999 to 2004 was another full-term government. Apparently economic growth was not an emotive factor for elections of government at the centre during the period.
- From 2004 to 2014 the Indian government was stable. However, after registering good growth during the first five years the economic growth was again plagued by very high corruption and high rates of inflation. In 2014, the government at the centre changed. Perhaps indicating some correlation between performance and popularity.
- During the period 2014-18, the decision making was optimistic since many path-breaking bold decisions were taken which were also transformational in nature. The government remained very popular and was returned to power with a bigger mandate in 2019 May. This augurs well for the people and the leaders' synergy.

In view of the above data and facts we need to factor in following aspects to make the Indian economy resilient in the context of IW:-

- **Organizations and institutions for contribution and values not for creating jobs:** We have shown fundamental weakness in terms of creating and nurturing institutions and organizations. As a concept institutions or organizations are not established to create jobs. They are established for creating values and wealth. Institutions are value based and organizations are expected to be productive and self-sustaining. Jobs are by products. Our investment in public sector is much higher compared to the return we get. Overall public sector spending is a net drain on the economy. The public sector organizations are seen as organizations offering highly secure jobs with very little accountability. This practice must be discontinued.

- **Misconception about the bureaucracy:** There is a tendency to blame the bureaucracy for every shortcoming or inefficiency that we see in the Indian economy or administration. In general perception, bureaucracy is equated to IAS or IFS cadre or government employees selected through the Union Public Service Commission. Bureaucracy as per the classical theory denotes rigid structure, fixed jurisdiction, impersonal rules and mundane routine. The functional aspects are specialization, structure, predictability, stability, rationality and democracy. The dysfunctional aspects are rigidity, displacement of objectives, compartmentalization, empire building, and red-tape culture. In the ICT era, bureaucracy is not the preferred organization at operational and functional levels. The emphasis today is on goal-based organization compared to rule-based organization.
- **Need to move from transactional to transformational approach:** Our policies on human capital are based on transactional approach as compared to transformational culture. We appear to believe that more pay, excessive job security, and a generally condescending approach towards a public servant or an employee will enhance productivity and value addition. While attractive compensation and perks are

important elements, these are not known to create better work culture and productivity. Cadre upgradation in various government departments including the Armed Forces, the system of Non Functional Upgrades (NFU), protecting grossly inefficient public sector units, and sustaining bloating bureaucracy do not augur well for the overall efficiency of governance. We need to adopt transformational approach discussed in the leadership brief in Appendix A in all institutions and organizations. This is a huge task in itself given the inertia in the minds of concerned personnel.

- **Need very high calibre leaders to adopt transformational approach:** Transformational approach can only be adopted by leaders who are capable—leaders who can inspire, motivate, strategize and who stimulate achievements. We have a massive shortage of good leaders at all levels. This includes the Armed Forces. Good leaders come up when the ecosystem is appropriately designed to recognize and nurture them.
- **Very long decision cycle loops (procrastination):** Besides low productivity and stupendous inefficiencies, we also suffer from monumental procrastination. In the first place, at almost all levels, the decision-making process is excruciatingly slow. To add to this critical flaw especially in the knowledge era, operationalization of decisions taken is extremely slow. It takes years to take decisions and decades to implement these. In more alert and alive nations decisions are taken in days and implemented in a month or a year. We need to formulate a mechanism to correct this huge strategic flaw.
- **Pessimistic approach to decision-making creating organizational slacks:** Our decision-making has generally betrayed pessimism and risk aversion. Even when outcomes of decisions are known with certainty, we take decisions with less than optimal payoff. This weakness in decision-making cannot be explained except for the fact that the decision

makers may not be loyal to the organizations or people. When the outcomes are known with reasonably accurate probability we take the least risky decisions and hence forego higher payoff. In uncertain ecosystems, our decision makers have shown ranked pessimism. Their decisions are governed by their inherent fears and lack of bold approach. Incidentally bulk of our people at the lower rungs are bold and have good risk appetite. Our decision making must reflect this inherent optimism among the people.

- **Too much on subsidies and doles (Non Merit Investment):** Our economic policies have been generally based on subsidies and doles with an eye on winning elections. Our leaders not only failed to stop corrupt practices but they institutionalized corruption. More than quarter million (three lakh) companies were declared fake by the government in the process to cleanse the system very recently. These companies were involved in fictitious money transactions to hide corruption and bribe money. Tens of thousands of directors were removed. The banking sector inefficiencies displayed the policy of crony capitalism and patronage to loyal and corrupt people, and family members by some of the political parties. There is a need to institutionalize transparent processes and practices at the earliest. Though it is important for the leadership to lift people from abject poverty through subsidies and if required occasional doles, the period of subsidies must be short.

World Economic Forum (WEF) 2018 Report on National Security and IW

In order to get a sense of what the relevant global bodies feel of India's progress during the years 2014-15 to 2018-19, it may be prudent to scan the reports of WEF, which reflect the competitiveness of a nation in global community of more than 140 nations. In the context of IW, our ranking and global perception in economic systems and robustness provide us resilience, international support and hence higher capability to withstand economic warfare—a component of IW.

The WEF Report of 2018 is based on changed format and parameters. The reasons for the change in the approach to analysing the competitiveness of nations are due to the changing nature of global macro economy in the wake of 2008 economic meltdown, spread of terrorism in the world, and dramatic growth in Information and Communication Technologies (ICT) adaption in all economic and human activities. For our purpose—specific to national security and information war—the WEF observations on terrorism and ICT adaption will be helpful.

The report observes that financial crises can have long-lasting effect on productivity. Prolonged periods of underinvestment can lower the long-term growth trajectory. Though the effects of meltdown (post 2008) are now being steadily overcome, the ecosystem for global economy and competitiveness has changed. This changed environment is being called as the Fourth Industrial Revolution or 4IR in the WEF report. The basic tenets of 4IR entail enhanced emphasis on human capital, innovation, resilience and agility. Successful economies in the 4IR era need to:-

- Be resilient, building buffers and economic mechanisms to prevent financial crises or mass unemployment and to respond to external shocks. Resilience is a function of financial sector health and efficiency, macro-economic stability, and skills of human capital.
- Be agile, embracing change rather than resisting it. Companies, public policy-makers, and workers should be able to quickly adapt how they operate and to take advantage of the opportunities to produce goods or provide services in new ways. In the context of pillars of competitiveness (of WEF), agility is a function of competitiveness in the domestic markets, enhanced entrepreneurship among the

people, and risk taking or creative disturbance. It is also essential to reduce the level of bureaucratic interference and have lesser number of legal formalities. As an extension to this change in the non-military environment, the Armed Forces also need to be agile to the changing nature of security threats and future combat environment.

- Build an ecosystem of innovation. Incentivize innovators and innovations at all levels. All stakeholders contribute to create the best conditions for new ideas to emerge, to be financed and commercialized as new products and services. This critical trait in the society is directly related to ICT adaption for flow of ideas, market size (where India ranks very high), protection of property rights, and sound infrastructure to exploit the market size. Innovation is a powerful tool to manage change.
- Adopt a human-centric approach to economic development. This means recognizing that human capital is essential for generating prosperity and that any policy that adversely affects human factors' potential will reduce economic growth in the long run. As a consequence, policy-making will have to ensure that the speed of change and the introduction of new technologies ultimately translate into better living conditions. Healthy people in terms of physical, mental health and social wellbeing, coupled with labour market mobility in terms of rewards and respect for workers' rights along with collaboration, interaction and creativity are important aspects of competitiveness of human capital. Human capital is also strengthened by quality of education, which as per the WEF 2018 includes digital literacy, interpersonal skills, and ability to think critically and creatively.

Why is it important to take note of WEF 2018 tenets of the Fourth Industrial Revolution? It may not be difficult to build the logic to highlight the correlation and even causal relationship between 4IR and National Security/IW:-

- If the human capital, innovative capabilities and resultant payoffs, resilience and agility of a nation can be weakened, then it is possible to achieve victory over the adversary—even without fighting a war.
- In the information age there is ample scope to weaken these tenets of competitiveness of an adversary—using the IW concepts and techniques—without using any violent means. The major goals of netwar are based on these factors.
- The IW approach to disrupt the human capital, innovativeness, resilience, and agility of an adversary is extremely cost effective, innocuous, and devoid of collateral damage.

At this stage it may be prudent to get deeper into these tenets of the Fourth Industrial Revolution. The critical concepts of these tenets are entrepreneurial culture, disruptive ideas, multi-stakeholders, collaboration, critical thinking, meritocracy and social trust. The *twelve pillars* of global competitiveness as per the 4IR are spread over four major heads—enablers, human capital, markets, and innovation ecosystems. Individual pillars under each of these heads are as under:-

- Enablers. These are institutions, infrastructure, ICT adaption, macroeconomic factors.
- Human capital includes health, skills.
- Markets include product market, labour market, financial systems, market size.
- Innovation ecosystem includes business dynamism, innovation capability.

The basic tenets, critical concepts as also the pillars under each major heads as given above are inter-related. Neglecting one pillar or concept has adverse impact on a host of other parameters of competitiveness. Thus the concept of resilience is reflected in the financial system, which includes measures to minimize the risk of a financial meltdown and resources to adjust to external shocks. By the same token, the macroeconomic stability captures the extent to which a country's public sector can provide appropriate counter-cyclical measures and invest in projects that the private sector cannot finance. Similarly, skills capture workers' capacity to learn and adapt to changing circumstances.

The concept of agility is present in the domestic market competition and entrepreneurial culture because they imply greater capacity for 'creative destruction', allowing innovative companies to emerge against incumbents and rewarding a risk-taking attitude. In addition, the concept is present in the public-sector performance; lesser interventions by bureaucracy make it easier for businesses to reorganize and reinvent themselves when legal formalities are not taxing. Labour market flexibility implies agility through easier reallocation of talent across sectors and firms.

The innovation ecosystem encompasses all. Although business dynamism and innovation capability are the factors impacting innovation more directly, these need to be complemented by high levels of human capital (health, education, and skills); optimal allocation of skills (labour market functioning); and availability of venture capital and ad-hoc financial products (financial system development). Strong innovation ecosystem also presumes sound infrastructure, ICT readiness, and institutions that allow ideas to flow and protect property rights, and a large market size that incentivizes the generation of new ideas.

The human-centric approach to development is embodied by the health and skills factors, which together account for one-sixth of the total Global Competitive Index (GCI) score and take a broad approach to human capital: health is thought of as a state of complete physical, mental, and social well-being, not merely the absence of disease or disabilities. Education measures the skills humans need to thrive in the

4IR. The labour market includes measures of talent reward and respect of workers' rights, while the innovation capability includes measures that capture human collaboration, interaction, and creativity.

The best way to create an adverse impact on all these tenets with their wider ramifications in a democracy is to mislead the electorate in such a manner that they elect a corrupt, self-serving, timid, and indecisive government. An ecosystem of closed and controlled economy, rigid and corrupt bureaucracy, inept and unreliable police force, inefficient judiciary and rent-seeking economic growth are some of the factors which can easily retard the competitiveness of a nation in the era of 4IR. We will come back to this aspect later when we discuss the full conflict spectrum in IW. We may focus on those factors, which impact the national security more directly.

The most important pillar with respect to national security is 'institution'. For a clearer picture in the context of IW we will compare the rankings in 'institution' pillar of competence with those in terrorism, ICT adaption, ten years average of GDP growth, five years average of FDI, and Gini factor related to income inequality. The Gini factor of zero depicts completely equal distribution of wealth and factor of 100 depicts completely unequal distribution. Hence, higher Gini factor indicates more inequality. Please see table below:

Table 5. Broad Comparison in Economic and Security Related Factors

Country	Gini Factor	ICT Adaption	Institution	Terrorism	Ten years average GDP growth	Five years average FDI as percentage of GDP
China	42.2	26	65	111	7.9	1.2
India	35.1	117	47	137	6.8	1.7
Israel	41.4	39	26	117	3.4	3.7
Pakistan	33.5	127	109	140	3.6	.7
Russia	37.7	25	72	118	1.1	1.8
US	41.5	27	13	128	1.4	1.7

(Source: WEF 2018)

The Gini factor does indicate the level of income inequality but it is not indicative of growth and development of the country. As per the table above, the Chinese are the most unequal society (notwithstanding communism and relatively closed society), followed by the US (most open and developed nation), Israel, and India. The Pakistanis are the most equal society but least developed and poorest of the lot!

As against Gini factor, ICT adaption is an important factor of innovation, growth, and development. Surprisingly India has poor ICT adaption ranking in spite of vibrant IT industry. In institutional ranking India fairs better than China, Pakistan, and Russia. This is the first time since independence that India is pegged so high in the institutional ranking. The strength of institutes in a country has the strongest correlation with national security.

However, subfactors of 'Institute' pillar, which are more closely linked with national security include business costs of organized crime, homicide rate, terrorism incidence, reliability of police services, and social capital. A comparative table on these subfactors is given below:

Table 6. Comparison of Rankings in Security Specific Factors

Country	Business cost of organized crime	Homicide	Incidence of terrorism	Reliability of police	Social capital
China	65	15	111	63	125
India	90	75	137	60	78
Israel	60	45	117	42	41
Pakistan	121	84	140	100	105
Russia	78	117	118	88	117
US	53	92	128	19	9

(Source:World Economic Forum 2018)

In the US the social capital (collaboration) is exceptionally high so is the reliability of police. The business also suffers relatively far less from organized crime. These factors along with others propel her to the first place. All the countries listed above suffer from relatively high incidences of terrorism with Pakistan suffering the worst. At the same time, in global perception, Pakistan is the epicentre of all Islamic terrorists.

A major factor, which has immense bearing on IW as also on national growth, is the ICT adaption. It may be prudent to compare the selected countries against this subhead also.

The 2018 report of the WEF makes several positive references to India's improvement in global competitiveness. The most notable among these are spectacular improvement in institutions, ease of doing business, overall improvement in competitive index by five places in one year—by far the best by any country. To quote WEF, 'India is a remarkable example of a country that has been able to accelerate on the pathway of innovation where it now ranks 31st… this is particularly due to the quality of its research institutions.' The report also suggests that the innovative culture must spread beyond a few centres of excellence.

Table 7. ICT Adaption Ranking Comparison: World Economic Forum 2018

Countries	Mob subscribers per 100	Mob broaband per 100	Fixed broadband per 100	Fiber Internet subscriber per 100	Internet users % of population
China	94	45	36	7	82
India	111	116	107	97	103
Israel	47	21	31	93	31
Pakistan	126	119	109	99	126
Russia	11	51	46	12	49
US	61	9	19	40	40

In 2014, India attracted negative comments in the WEF report. Between 2010 and 2014 India dropped ten places in public institutions, twenty-three places in market competitiveness, and twenty places in labour market efficiency. The report also observed that very limited accessibility to sanitation by the Indian population (36 percent) hindered their social sustainability. India largely remains a poor country, which is developing with large disparities within the society. India's natural assets are also depleting. Fortunately, India has made remarkable progress in sanitation during the past five years with toilet facilities available to more than 97 percent of the population.

While we need to focus on reducing business cost of organized crime, incidents of terrorism and homicide; the most critical drawback in the context of IW preparedness is ICT adaption. As per the table above we lag in all parameters that comprise the ICT adaption competitiveness. India needs to establish a robust cyberspace business, governance, and such non-military uses and transform all the activities to exploit the cyberspace. The fear of cyber threats must be met proactively by investing in strengthening cyber security across the military and non-military cyberspace.

★★★

Strategies for India

Describing IW for strategy formulation

A critical and uphill task ahead

WE HAVE SEEN a number of ways IW has been defined and also described. All these definitions have their place and value for the purpose they have evolved. Some may be to arrive at various components of IW while some descriptions may be to identify technologies involved in IW. But none of those will meet the requirement of formulating comprehensive strategies for IW in specific context to India. Hence we need to describe IW in a more relevant and 'simple to understand' manner which helps us to develop strategies.

Firstly, IW is not about 'information'. It involves the decision-making capabilities from the available and acquired information. Secondly, for our purpose 'war' is what Clausewitz has defined. It involves the state, the people, and the Armed Forces.

It uses violence as a means and has a goal of reaching a better end state than what prevailed before the commencement of the war. Thirdly, in the twenty-first century, wars are not declared. It is part of a continuum which consists of given state of peace, emergence of some conflicting interests among nations, initial negotiation to resolve the conflict, and failure of resolution. This sequence is followed by escalating ladder of conflict spectrum to comprise of political and economic war along with netwar. Finally, active involvement of rival militaries heralding intense violence. As one of the adversaries gives up, the stage is set for new set of negotiations followed by new end state. The cycle goes on. A successful conflict termination heralds long periods of growth and peace. Premature or unwise termination results in wars in quick succession. In our case, we as a nation have been at war for better part of the seventy years that we have existed as a free nation. We have scanned the major, minor, and continuing conflicts involving high quantum of casualties to our citizens and Armed Forces.

With this as the background, formulating national strategies for IW will involve a series of 'decision cycles' at political, military, institutional, and societal levels for the purpose of achieving and sustaining desired end state. We have yet to achieve that state! The decision cycles involve identifying clear, unambiguous, and shared goals; acquiring and processing data in the context of the goals; processing the data through the value chain of information, intelligence; decision for selecting a given course of action; implementing the action plan by imposing desired control measures; studying the outcomes by gleaning feedback for continuous improvement across the entire value chain.

All the above activities are centred on the citizens. Hence our primary goal will be to enable and empower the citizens to be healthy (physically, mentally, and psychologically), productive, collaborative, creative, innovative, and conscious of their responsibilities towards the state and their rights. The spectrum for IW as described above will include periods of time during peace, undeclared hostilities below conventional war thresholds in terms of degree of violence, conventional war below the nuclear threshold, post-war conflict termination for a better end state, and sustaining the better end state for prolonged period. IW will also involve maintaining the geographical integrity of the state.

IW must ensure:-

- Comprehensive application across the entire set of domains—political, economic, military, institutional, and societal.
- Synchronization and prioritization of goals and implementation of resultant plans.
- Continuous adaption to changing environment and new technologies.

IW must desist and avoid:-

- Piecemeal application, since it will never be effective. The adversary will attack other echelons and make the limited application in one organization ineffective. We have seen this in 1971 when a comprehensive military victory failed to ensure sustained peace and growth.
- Contradiction of goals and their priorities. Contradicting goals by different organizations will neutralize each other's efforts.
- Sticking to rules and ignoring the principles. There are no rules in IW. It is as the Chinese term it, 'unrestricted war'. It will include everything from subversion, stealing information through cyberspace, misleading the adversary, lobbying, diluting the political and legal system, weakening the economic system, and so on. IW has goals; rules follow these goals and change as per the changing environment.

We have had a brief academic discussion on strategy formulation or the process of developing strategies. The most enduring feature of strategy development is discovering the core values and core purpose—in our case— of the nation. What are India's core values? What is the core purpose that we exist for as a nation? These never change. Everything that follows is subject to change with changing internal and external environment. Core values and core purpose are followed by vision, mission, goals, objectives, policies, rules, performance parameters, feedback channels, etc. The flexibility factor increases as we go down the value chain. Thus rules are the most flexible aspects and vision the least flexible component of strategy. Nevertheless, changes in rules is not for operational convenience but for alignment with the upstream value chain.

Core Values Vision and SWOT Analysis

What are core values? These values must be unambiguous that can translate into decisions without unnecessary pontifications and debates. These values need to be clear across the political and demographic canvas of the country. These need to be said in numerous different ways that can be understood across the length and breadth of the country. These should be stated in passionate, motivating manner with captivating imagination so that people identify themselves with these values. If we discover the right values that this nation has, the job of disseminating and making people understand these values will not be difficult. As we have discussed earlier, the preamble in the Indian Constitution does not give us our core values. We need to look at other sources with which the citizens are familiar. The past—which is cherished by the widest cross section of people beyond religion, region—which flows through the blood stream of all Indians.

Our history, for the purpose of our belief systems and values, includes the epics of those times. The stories of queens and kings that are part of Indian folklore will give a vivid picture. We need to identify stuff that the vast majority of Indians believe in and are proud of. Henry Kissinger in his book, *World Order*, has described the ecosystem of ancient India. He has very aptly quoted from *Bhagwat Gita* and Kautilya's *Arthashastra*. It is a very passionate and accurate description of the unique character India has, a culture and global movement, which influenced better part of civilized nations—without any violence and aggression—centuries ago. As per him,

India is the only nation or civilization which has assimilated global changes through many millennia without changing her core ideology. Let us look at some of the recent examples and suggestions:-

- When India proposed to the UN that 21 June be observed as 'International Day of Yoga' there was no country that opposed the proposal. We got 192 countries on board. Yoga started from India. Deeper meaning into Yoga (union with the universe) may bring out some of our core values.
- The UN observed that vegan eating habits are best suited for environmental sustenance. India has highest percentage of vegan population. In India, it is not linked with religion. Eating habits are linked with the inner struggle of each human being. Vegan food is considered to help the ecology as also gain mastery over desires so that the 'seekers' of truth and salvation are not disturbed in their path to salvation. United Nations Environment Program (UNEP)[13] recommends a meat and dairy-free diet. As an aside, International Cricket Council (ICC) has decided to use vegan cricket balls.
- Life was never considered dearer than principles. Indian traditions believe in rebirth. Indians were not known to care for life when it came to their honour or national pride. Our epics glorify honourable peace but not peace at the cost of national honour or at the cost of principles. 'Turning the other cheek,' has never been part of our core values. Vegan eating habits do not translate into non-violence in a just war.
- Strength of character, frugal habits, living in harmony with nature have been some of the traits that the civilization in this part of the world was known for.
- Indian products were valued world over till as late as the beginning of the seventeenth century much before the industrial revolution came.

---

13 https://www.theguardian.com/environment/2010/jun/02/un-report-meat-free-diet)(Accessed 10 August 2019.

We need to have a national security doctrine which must comprise of the following:-

- Clearly define our threat spectrum and root causes of continuing threats both internal and external. We need to remember that India was a unified entity from fourth century BC to second century BC, also from fourth century AD to seventh century AD. We disintegrated when central leadership was weak and due to internal threats abetted by external aggression. In view of the preceding discussions, our threats range from political, economic weaknesses to internal and external threats. Hence we need to get out of the mindset of looking at threats from the military point of view. Look at these from the citizens' point of view. This will give us a completely different range of concerns for national security. It will include excessive poverty, high rates of corruption, poor economic policies, regional and religious divides, poor and inept administration, inefficient judiciary and law enforcing agencies, high rates of drug addiction, and so on. As we go through this list we find that the role of military has shrunk considerably. This approach matches with the assessment made in the Joint Doctrine of Armed Forces discussed earlier.
- We should fix a time line by which these threats will be removed or marginalized. Bulk of planning and execution will have to be done outside the military domain.
- There must be clear demarcation of authority, responsibility, and accountability for internal and external threats. Ideally the Armed Forces must be dedicated towards meeting the external threats and police as also the paramilitary forces must cater for border management and internal threats. Internal threats also emanate from poor governance, bad economic policies, and weak institutions (judiciary, police, banking, administration).

- Our legal framework must very clearly and unambiguously state those activities that jeopardize national security. Stone pelting on security forces, making statements that foment mass hysteria against the nation or against any ethnic or religious groups are some of these activities. Democracies do have pressure groups and lobbies. Media—including the social media—does play positive as well as negative roles. The adversaries, which may include nation states or global bodies with vested interests will exploit the weaknesses in our institutions and internal environment to stoke dissent, create internal turbulence or an environment of despondency. This will have to be countered in a very subtle but effective manner. The social media today provides the opportunity for direct engagement with the citizens. Hence this informal media can be used to counter propaganda. It needs to be remembered that truth finally prevails.
- We as a nation must also understand that the personnel in the Armed Forces are professionals in their respective domains, which can be engaged in appropriate manner for appropriate tasks. Since they are designed to neutralize external threats, the level of violence and destructive power at their disposal will be very high. Hence as a rule Armed Forces must never be required to use force against the Indian citizens within the country. While using them against external threat, network-centric deployment and operations, precision targeting, concentration of effort as against concentration of forces, focused logistics, rapid engagement and disengagement, capability to work in small groups and teams, enhanced cognitive ability to withstand perception management by the adversary and tolerate battlespace stress, creating synergy through interoperability not only with the other services but also with requisite non-military organizations—are some of the key areas where the military needs to invest time and resources.

- Also when the Armed Forces are employed they must never be told how to operate. The role of the political leadership is to ensure that the Armed Forces are given the task and the wherewithal for accomplishing the task. The top echelon in the military leadership must be involved in the 'why' and 'what' of the task. Thereafter the 'how' can be discussed. There have been numerous occasions when the Armed Forces should not have been employed for the task they were forced to undertake. They should not have been given the operational parameters which ran counter to military wisdom. They should not have been stopped in their march to complete victory without any consultation. These are the issues that need to be ironed out to ensure synergy between the political leadership and the top military commanders.
- We must legislate the need for preparing an after-action report or war-history report bringing out all the factors truthfully and frankly for the citizens of the nation. These reports must be placed in the public domain within specified time. This will ensure that we do not learn the same lessons in every event. We need to give up our habit of learning the same lessons again and again.
- Should the conflict escalate to a level that necessitates employment of Armed Forces, clear goals and objectives must be set in conjunction with the government. Having achieved these goals, the Armed Forces must form part of the conflict termination negotiation.

Vision and Goals for IW-based National Security

Keeping in view the complete spectrum of IW, we will enunciate the major issues of vision statements under three heads. These can be debated. First part will involve insulating the nation against various threats to national security (political, economic, perception management, and so on) without compromising our national interests. Secondly, our vision for the capability of Armed Forces to neutralize external threats in the shortest possible time with minimal collateral damage. Finally, our vision for the next end state after conventional hostilities cease and negotiations commence. This part will address the aspects related to conflict termination.

Vision for insulating against IW threats

- India to be among the top twenty nations in terms of productivity and collaboration of human capital; reduced cost to business from crime, corruption and terrorism, ICT adaption, institutions, cyber security, transparency, innovation, creativity, research and development by 2030.
- Security forces other than the Armed Forces to conduct all anti-terrorist and anti-proxy wars, counter insurgency operations. The Armed Forces will not be required to use force against own citizens within the country.
- The extreme poverty levels to be completely eradicated and 100 percent of citizens liable to pay tax to pay full taxes in time by 2022.
- The farm sector productivity to be trebled in relation to levels prevailing in 2019 and no farmer committing suicide because of farm sector distress by 2022.

Vision for capability building for the armed forces

- The decision to appoint Chief of Defence Staff was announced on 15 August 2019. This is just a beginning to initiate a culture of inter-service and inter-organization cooperation and collaboration. One of the characteristics of information age society (hence by inference information age Armed Forces) is that there are no fixed organizations. The structure and operational dynamics of organizations change continuously as per the changing environments and roles. Hence there will be plenty of occasions when Armed

Forces will seek coordination with economists, psychologists, marketing experts, analysts, scientists, academic institutes, etc. as per the demand of the situation. The tendency to pretend that 'we know it all' needs to be curbed. The generalist culture does not work in the fast pace of knowledge world.

- The tri-services integration to be achieved down to operational level. In special operations, tri-services to develop the capability to function as combined teams for strategic goals by 2021.
- The Armed Forces to be equipped with modern weapon systems with more than 70 percent indigenous components by 2030.
- The budgeting system for defence expenditure to be based on desired capability. The overall capability to be formed through a group of programs, which should be executed through modern techniques of project management in 2020 budget. All rules that force surrendering the approved budget must be scrapped. Any surrender of budget must be approved by the Cabinet Committee on Security. Also the defence budget including the capabilities to be achieved, programs that form part of the capability must be presented to the Cabinet Committee on Security (CCS). Only CCS should have the authority to accept or reject any program/ capability. Those involved in the budgeting process must have sound knowledge of economics, econometrics, ICT enabled costing and procurement, analytics etc.
- India to maintain credible and demonstrated conventional deterrent. There must be a well-defined mechanism to operationalize this deterrent when a given threat threshold is crossed. There should be no doubt or ambiguity in the minds of political and military leadership of the target nation on the likely damage that will be caused to them

when they threaten Indian security. This should include cyber deterrent. While retaliating against major attacks on the Indian cyberspace, conventional forces should also be co-opted if required. Such a communication needs to be conveyed through IW doctrine by 2022.

- Indian Armed Forces to be in strategic alliance with friendly nations at regional and global levels to counter threats in her area of interest. This will be specifically important in the cyber war domain. Time line 2022.
- At organizational level, the Armed Forces to embrace transformational leadership approach promoting inspirational, selfless leaders at higher levels of command. The organizational dynamics to be so designed that self-centred, average and dysfunctional leaders do not reach the top. Armed forces to adopt a culture of continuously learning and adapting organization endowed with extremely developed cognitive ability, capable of exploiting modern technologies for war. Need to reduce hierarchies to maximum of four to five in the current structure and reduce the number of headquarters as also their size by a factor of three to ten. An ICT enabled armed force can free personnel from headquarters to field work. This should be done in phased manner by 2021. If we start establishing tri-service theatre commands with immediate effect—since the appointment of Chief of Defence Staff (CDS) has already been announced—then by 2022 we will have five theatre commands in place of thrice this number as of now. The aim of this exercise has more to do with bringing in efficiency as against the generally perceived aim of reducing cost.
- At strategic and operational levels, the Armed Forces must develop capability to exploit network-centric battlespace

with IW concepts of synergy, interoperability, cognitive ability, and leadership embedded at sub-unit levels in each arm and service. Time line 2022.

Vision for conflict termination

- As a part of national policy, India must not attack or threaten any nation. However, once threatened or likely to be attacked, India must have declared policy of pre-emptive action.
- The war objectives must be formulated in such a manner that after hostilities come to an end the state of peace must prevail for a minimum of the next five to six decades.
- India must make good all the economic damage caused to her due to the war imposed on her by the aggressor.
- The tri-service chief must always be part of the conflict-termination negotiations.

Having set the core ideology and the vision, we can formulate the IW strategies based on the seven pillars that we discussed right in the beginning. At the cost of repetition, the seven pillars that we identified are as under:-

- People and the Leaders.
- Vibrant Economy.
- Dynamic Knowledge and Technology Base.
- Robust Internal Security Apparatus.
- Armed Forces.
- Cyberspace.
- International Relations.

In order to derive relevant policies and approach routes for each of the pillars mentioned above it is important to know where we are today. This will indicate the quantum of efforts in order to strengthen the specific pillar to achieve overall desired capability. One of the management tools to do this is Strengths, Weaknesses, Opportunities, and Threats (SWOT) analysis.

The findings of the SWOT analysis will dictate our action plan based on the strategic approach we choose.

Strengths, Weaknesses, Opportunities, Threats (SWOT)

Strengths, weaknesses, opportunities, and threats will emanate from the issues that we have covered so far and the way the nation has performed during the last seven decades:-

Strengths (Internal factors under our control)

- **Sustained democracy:** This is our biggest and most acclaimed strength; also one of our core values. Except for a brief threat to democracy in 1975, when the then prime minister declared a state of emergency to suppress descent and opposition to her candidature, there has been generally smooth sailing for Indian democracy. Given the diversity and the complexity of India, the democracy in the country is very stable and in many cases has been exemplary.
- **People:** Looking at the way the Indian diaspora performs in most of the countries that they move/migrate to and also their performance at home against all odds, the Indian people are a national strength. They display:-
  - Great entrepreneurial capabilities
  - Are highly adaptable
  - Are Innovative, (proved in the 2018 WEF rating)
  - Live in complete harmony if not provoked by political propaganda and stimulus.
  - Highly, courageous and determined
  - Capable of sustained hard work under adverse conditions.
- **Geographic location:** Open seas on busy trade routes.

We can leverage this strength to strengthen alliance with major global powers in the West and the East.

- **Natural resources:** In terms of fertile land, water, green cover, and sustainable climate.
- **Historical linkages with regional and global powers:** India has ancient links with China, Thailand, Indonesia, Myanmar, and a number of countries in the Middle East. This can help us in deepening the people-to-people linkages and hence strengthen international relations.
- **Strategic Lmportance:** India has emerged as a counter balance to China and is now considered an important centre for anti-terror operations. Besides, as the fastest growing economy with an aspirational population, India is not only the biggest market after China but can be an attractive supply chain partner for most of the MNCs. If we decide to be a major player in 5G rollout as a countervailing force to China, we have the capability and alliance (US, Japan, South Korea, Finland) to do this.

Weaknesses (Internal factors under our control)

- **Political leadership:** Political manipulation and deeply entrenched feudal dynastic culture have generally characterized Indian political leadership. There have been cases when the leadership at the top did not get the elected representative as the chief executive of the nation. Bulk of the Indian political leaders have criminal background. Though India opted for democracy at the time of independence and sustained this form of governance for more than seventy years, her political leadership has generally been far below average when it came to performance both in economy and national security. They generally lacked vision, commitment, courage, honesty and have generally been tepid in the context of safeguarding the national security and economic interests of the country.

- **Bureaucracy:** Please refer to the way bureaucracy is defined in organizational structure (see glossary). Almost all public sector organizations and the higher echelons of military organization are bureaucratic in nature. Hence these are sluggish, loath to any change, unwilling and incapable of changes, self-serving, and corrupt. We inherited this bureaucracy from the British. Since there was not much change in the legal and administrative framework at the time of independence, our bureaucracy post-independence has not been people friendly and efficiency oriented. The so-called 'steel frame' has been unable to transform itself to the changing social and technological environment. Many of our administrative and social problems emanate from entrenched malpractices.
- **Historical backlog of poor governance:** Since 1947 we have taken a series of poor decisions that have landed us in very disadvantageous situations. This has also entrenched a culture of low efficiency and lack of national fervour. We have become accustomed and comfortable in our inabilities to strive for excellence. A large section of Indian intelligentsia considers the exceptionally poor performance as a function of environmental factors and the inherent constraints of free India in 1947. There is a tendency to ignore how other nations in the same situation around the same time did much better than us. This mindset is a serious weakness.
- **Poverty:** Our per capita income is very low. Though there has been significant improvement during the last five years we still rank much below China and most of the southeastern countries.
- **Inequality:** The Gini coefficient of .47 is not very

encouraging. We are not only a grossly unequal society but those of our citizens who are poor are far below the general poverty levels in other developing and developed nations. We need to achieve a lot to bring dignity of life to the poor in the country.

- **Lack of ICT adaption:** In spite of a vibrant IT industry, our ICT adaption is very low. During the last five years (2014-19), massive efforts have been made to enhance IT enabled services both in the public and private sectors. This has ensured major improvements in online transactions and ICT adaption. Nevertheless, keeping the calibre of our IT industry, we are yet to exploit the full potential of this major enabler.
- **Terrorism and internal turmoil:** We have comparatively high rates of terrorist activities and internal turmoil, which impacts security and increases the cost of business. Our progress in combating and eliminating terrorism has been the worst. The situation has deteriorated than what it was immediately after independence (1947 to 1955). This reflects very poorly on our political, administrative, and law-enforcing systems including the judiciary.
- **Disputed borders:** We have border disputes with two of our neighbours since independence. In spite of fighting five wars in seven decades we have not been able to resolve any of the border disputes. This costs us both in terms of national security and economy. Here again, the political leadership has displayed exceptionally poor level of understanding and decision making on important issues related to national security.
- **Illiteracy:** For the purpose of psychological preparation in IW, our current literacy rate and general awareness about national interests is low.
- **Transactional approach:** Our approach in adopting

efficiency enhancement measures has been transactional in all the cases. We tend to believe that increasing salary, giving huge perks and ignoring major lapses, and even allowing or ignoring corruption, will make the people and organizations better performers. Thus measures like cadre review in the Armed Forces (increasing the vacancies in higher ranks), fixing higher ratio of senior ranks in some parts of the Army (Infantry, Artillery), non functional financial upgradation (NFU) for almost all the government organizations except the Armed Forces, and so on were implemented from time to time. This might have fetched some additional votes for the concerned political parties but these measures have not improved performance of organizations that have benefitted from such favours. It is essential to address the issues related to hygiene factor for maintaining the desired satisfaction level but for making the organization aspire for delivering better services exceeding the aspirations of the citizens or making the Armed Forces as a feared fighting outfit (for the external adversary) at reasonable cost to the exchequer, a transformative and inspirational approach is required. In order to achieve this, the political leaders need to be far better than what they have been so far.

- **High import content in defence Procurement:** In spite of declared policy (since 1970) of keeping the import content as low as 30 percent, the percentage of indigenous defence production has deteriorated. The import content is in excess of 70 percent notwithstanding a large number of defence production establishments operating for the last four decades.
- **Armed Forces organizations and operational doctrine are dated:** The organizational structure, work culture, layers of hierarchies, strategic intent, and operational

doctrines resemble the World War II vintage ecosystem and dynamics. The Armed forces, have been very slow in identifying and adapting to changes in the likely combat environment.

Threats (External factor not under our control)

- **Hostile neighbours:** Both China and Pakistan have been openly hostile to Indian interests. They adopt an approach of joint opposition.
- **Internal political support to proxy wars and terrorism:** Ineffective, corrupt, and sluggish administrative, policing, judicial, and political systems have aided the adversary rather than strengthening own security forces in combating these conflicts. It is because of sheer dedication, risk tolerance, and sacrifice at the junior rungs of leadership that the situation has somehow been contained.
- **Demographic imbalances and inversion:** This has happened in the Kashmir valley and the North East (Tripura, Assam, West Bengal). Political establishments have allowed this to happen for political gains.
- **Global terrorism:** India is one of the main targets of global terrorism.

Opportunities (External factor not under our control)

- **Current international support:** Post 9/11 India's fight against terrorism got explicit global support. However, after proactive international outreach, from May 2014 the international support has transformed into very tangible actions by the international community. Most importantly changing trends in the Muslim countries of the Middle East, Saudi Arabia, UAE as also by Organization of Islamic Council (OIC) has made India a very influential country in the region as also globally.

Our western neighbour is completely isolated and on the east, China is much more circumspect than what she was earlier when weak governments ruled at the centre.

- **High percentage of young population:** This can be a great opportunity if harnessed well, else it can also be of immense negative impact.
- **Major improvements in critical pillars of competitiveness in 2018:** WEF Report. (WEF) The prominent among these pillars are institutional effectiveness, massive reduction in corruption, improvement in ease of doing business, innovation, research and development. This is a great opportunity on which we can build upon during the next ten to thirty days.
- **Drastic reduction in extreme poverty:** Even the World Economic Forum report lauded this improvement.
- **Reform orientation during last five years:** A number of reforms have been implemented through legislation as also through administrative actions. In our context, beginning of major reforms in the Armed Forces, choking flow of money to the organizations inimical to national interests, closing down around three lakh shell companies, eliminating hawala transactions, check on black money, increased online money transactions are some of the reforms that will strengthen the security infrastructure.
- **Proactive deterrence against terrorism:** The surgical strike in 2016 and the air strike on Balakot in 2019 have changed the security equation with the Western neighbour.
- **Steady economic growth with low inflation during the last five years:** Bold reforms, drastic reduction in corruption, transparency in governance, improvements in institutional strength, etc. have helped in steady

economic growth in spite of global headwinds and major efforts in cleansing the economic ecosystem. It is expected that once we learn to be honest in our business processes, start paying legitimate taxes, and pursue excellence, the growth will snowball into more than 10 percent per year.

Description of the SWOT matrix: Please refer to the pictorial description of the above factors in the figure below. The most important quadrant in the SWOT matrix is quadrant number 1 (right hand top) which depicts strengths and opportunities. Enhancing strengths and exploiting opportunities will entail acceleration towards goals with supporting tailwinds. However, the weaknesses given in the second quadrant (right hand bottom) will be acting as headwinds against the acceleration. The most prudent strategy will be to identify the weaknesses that are comparatively easy to remove. Following action plan needs to be initiated to use the SWOT matrix to address the seven pillars of IW:

- Focus on the strengths and opportunities quadrant. Enhance those strengths that are currently best aligned with the opportunities. Keep changing as the opportunities shift. But always work on own strengths.
- Take determined actions to remove weaknesses. This will accelerate the velocity of action in the first quadrant.
- Develop resilience against the threats. This in our case can be done by forging meaningful international alliances and initiating robust actions against internal threats.
- While countering threats exploit own strengths (see fourth quadrant) to gain momentum.

Strategies Based on the Seven Pillars of IW

Pillar 1. People and the Leadership

This is a vital domain in the IW spectrum. It is waged through various instruments generally (but not always) below overt violence.

Strengths

4.Threats	Strengths	1.Strengths	Opportunities
1. Hostile neighbours 2. Internal support to terrorism 3. Demographic imbalances 4. Global terrorism	1. Democracy 2. People 3. Geographic location 4. Natural resources 5. History 6. Strategic importance 7. Economy 8. GDP growth rate	1. Democracy 2. People 3. Geographic location 4. Natural resources 5. History 6. Strategic importance 7. Economy 8. GDP growth rate	1. Intl Support 2. Youth 3. WEF 2018 4. Drastic reduction in poverty 5. Reform orientation 6. Drastic reduction In corruption 7. International ranking

3. Threats	Weaknesses	2. Weaknesses	Opportunities
1. Hostile neighbours 2. Internal support to terrorism 3. Demographic imbalances 4. Global terrorism	1. Political leadership 2. Bucreaucracy 3. Hist backlog 4. Poverty 5. Inequality 6. ICT adoption 7. Terrorism and internal turmoil 8. Border dispute 9. Illiteracy 10. Transactional approach 11. Defence import 12. Org and modernization of security forces	1. Political leadership 2. Bucreaucracy 3. Hist backlog 4. Poverty 5. Inequality 6. ICT adoption 7. Terrorism and internal turmoil 8. Border dispute 9. Illiteracy 10. Transactional approach 11. Defence import 12. Org and modernization of security forces	1. International support 2. Youth 3. WEF 2018 4. Drastic reduction in poverty 5. Reform orientation 6. Drastic reduction in corruption 7. International ranking

Weaknesses

Figure 1. SWOT Matrix

- **Objectives:** The objective here is to change the political system or political behaviour of the adversary. In our context, the Chinese sustained manoeuvers to create an impression on the Indian leadership and political system to accept Chinese supremacy just after 1949, is an apt example. The Chinese not only succeeded in getting India to accept their suzerainty on Tibet but were also successful in neutralizing any diplomatic as well as military resistance to annexation of Aksai Chin.

- **Means:** The means used for political war comprise of all the components starting from netwar, international relations, economic war as also conventional operations. The US and UK use economic and military means to get the political systems of target countries to behave the way they desire. Pakistan has been very successful till very recently to use her religious alignment and international manoeuvring in keeping the Kashmir issue alive and tying a major part of Indian Armed Forces in counter-insurgency operations. However, after 9/11 (2001) and then 2014 the situation has started changing for the better (for India).
- **Defence against political war:** People are the most critical component in active defence against political war. As per the WEF 2018, people are described as the human capital of a nation. They insulate the nation against external and internal threats at three levels. First, through the individual to society and inter-societal relationship of collaboration and cooperation. Second, at the individual level through physical and mental and spiritual (integrity and ethics) health. Third, at economic level through productivity, innovation, and creativity, which provides economic resilience and agility. These are the areas where the political leadership must focus. It is very critical to enable and then empower the people in a democracy to secure them from external and internal turbulences. For this, leadership at the top must be transformational in nature. There may be definite need to support the less-privileged class through subsidies, grants, and other economic protection but all these should be temporary in nature. Political leadership need to resist from the temptation of transactional approach—giving unnecessary doles, freebies, subsidies, reservations, etc. on a permanent basis. Many nations have experienced economic

downturns due to this excessive state indulgence on their people for narrow and myopic political gains. We have covered the details of human capital while discussing WEF 2018 with specific reference to India. Some of the specific measures especially in the Indian context are:-

- Ensure nationwide acceptance of shared national ideology which intrinsically unites people against perception management and subversive activities by our known and likely adversaries including internal lobbies being supported by external help.
- Carefully monitor disruptive and destructive efforts by the adversary and pick up early signs. Act in time to avert the problem escalating to a level where resolution warrants huge efforts in time and resources. We need to remember that the problem in Kosovo did not crop up without warning. The early signals were transmitted almost eight years in advance. In our case, early signs of Pakistani aggression did become apparent in 1946 in Bengal. We had enough warning of Chinese annexation of Tibet as also Chinese designs in Aksai Chin. It was our failure to read the signals correctly and act in time that led us to the catastrophic predicament or prolonged struggle.
- Manage perception of own population by transparency in governance, information sharing, and participation by people in societal as also governance issues. We are very fortunate that democracy is one of our core values. Democracies are known to exhibit higher resilience over time as compared to totalitarian regimes. However, in the specific context of internal threats to India, fissiparous and divisive tendencies have been prevalent in India over several millennia. When the central leadership was strong, wise, and decisive, India remained a united

entity (for more than seven centuries—fourth to second century BC and fourth to seventh century AD). When divisiveness and lack of internal harmony prevailed, India disintegrated and even suffered long periods of military and political subjugation. Hence our political behaviour with external environment as also with own population must neutralize even remote probability of divisive tendencies. Even temporary concessions to any state of the Union must be curbed. The provision of separate status to any state outside the constitutional jurisdiction of India can be very dangerous. To that effect abrogation of temporary provisions of articles 370 and 35A of the constitutions (on 7 August 2019) is a step in the right direction.

- Maintain inter-religion and inter-region harmony while accepting and celebrating diversities. This is where individual to society and inter-society relations become so important in India.
- Include relevant aspects of national security in the educational system right from the early stage. Almost all the think tank organizations in India follow the military writings in the US and China. Surprisingly, a very obvious fact about the US and China remains unseen by our scholars following national security. A large number of their prestigious institutions have several courses on national security. In our education system, national security is either being completely ignored or worse, it gets a very lopsided and at times emotion-driven coverage. There is a need to include authentic and accurate facts about Indian past during school education. In the colleges very realistic approach to study of India's security in the context of global security environment must be debated and taught. The

scope of this endeavour is much larger than establishing National Defence University.

- Careful monitoring of social media. Almost all democracies are grappling with the problem of citizen privacy versus national security in the context of social media. Exceptionally fast pace of growth in technology, innovation in use of new technology, and growing clamour for privacy by the citizens adds to the governments' dilemma in ensuring national security and keeping the citizens satisfied about their privacy concerns. Given the level of harm the terror organizations or lobbies with vested interest can cause through social media, it is impossible for the government not to monitor social media. The US and most of the Western European countries have more access to social media interactions of their citizens than that of India. We need to have adequate legal protection for the security agencies to monitor social media for the sake of national security. The threat to national security through social media network emanate from some of the unique features of this new media. First, the ease of access. Reducing cost and increasing efficacy of smart phones makes a vast population connected to social media. Second, the ease of usage makes even an illiterate person with very average intelligence use some of the more popular applications—WhatsApp, Facebook, YouTube, and so on. Third, language is no barrier since available software makes use of almost all languages possible on this platform. Fourth, every individual user is enabled to generate any content—within a very wide scope—and upload on the platform. There is not much editing or scrutiny. These factors make the social media a powerful tool to spread information, disinformation, content capable to disrupt social harmony, fake news, corporate and official secrets. In India, since most political parties use social media to build up their public support, a huge amount of information on the media (since it is not scrutinized) contain half-truths, misleading facts, outright propaganda, lobbying, content supporting religious hatred, and paranoia. Given the type of ill-informed and emotionally charged population that uses and believes in every word on the social media, proper monitoring and sensitizing the users about the harmful impact of social media on national security becomes inevitable for the security agencies.

- Effective forensic means to identify internet crimes, fake news, propaganda, and subversion through cyberspace. This is where the organizations responsible for internal security as also the Armed Forces need to train and keep abreast of the latest techniques. Crimes in cyberspace have been increasing exponentially every day. These crimes span a wide range from innocuous personal pranks to terrorists-inspired activities including training, recruitment, psychological manoeuvring, perception management, spread of hatred, etc. Effective forensic means, which can counter the sophistication of the perpetrator of the crime are extremely essential.
- Effective legal system for quick retribution. Generally, a national security expert is amused when we link judicial system with national security. Nevertheless, the linkages are very strong. Look at some of the deficiencies of Indian judicial system. First, we have a very huge (mindboggling!) pendency of cases. If justice delayed is justice denied, then in case of India the poor cannot expect justice from the judicial system. Second, most reports on Indian judicial system accept that the system

is extremely corrupt. If this is true, then what justice can you accept from a corrupt system. Third, there is lack of transparency in selection of judges. Hence right people are not in the system. Fourth, the number of under-trial accused is very high. Most of these under-trial accused are poor citizens. Hence they cannot afford bail. Lastly, there is hardly any uninterrupted and transparent interaction between the poor masses and the judicial system. If we add all these factors then it is not difficult to visualize a vastly dissatisfied, disgruntled, and deprived population with sullen faces—easy prey for any anti-state perception management by a clever adversary. Add to this the business cost of high level of unhappiness. A very large number of clever and cunning people with willing support from our inimical neighbours can make a huge killing in this environment.

- Develop deterrence through counter espionage, counter subversion, and perception management. Given the multiplicity of societal goals, vested interests of various pressure groups and lobbies, and general diversity in terms of faiths, castes, and languages, perception management and social espionage is comparatively very easy in India. Thus countries hostile to our interests or even competitors will find it very easy to wage successful perception management operations using seemingly legal and benign ways. We need to develop an appropriate counter to this within the accepted international norms. Fortunately for us there are more serious fault-lines in society-state and inter-society relations in our hostile neighbourhood.

Pillar 2. Vibrant Economy

Objectives of economic war: During the era of mercantilism, the economic strength of a nation was primarily in the gold that the country had. Gold was also an asset to raise and maintain armies. However, the theories of mercantilism, balance of trade, and neo mercantilism have long been rendered obsolete with globalization and the advent of new theories such as absolute and comparative advantages. The global supply chains have made the world an intricately networked entity blurring the international boundaries. Nevertheless, national security aspects counter the international trade wisdom. International politics and international economy cross each other's trajectories and along these pathways economic wars are launched as part of IW.

The most recent examples of economic war involve the US and China as also the US sanctions against Iran. These examples also illustrate the ways to secure the nation against economic war and what not to do to ensure that own economy does not suffer from effects of economic war. The objectives of economic war can be in the seemingly innocuous domain of trade competition to open trade war. These objectives can even go to the extent of crippling the economic structure of the adversary by destroying their competitive edge in international products or services markets, forcing the adversary to downgrade their currency or even launching an open currency war.

What we are witnessing in Iran in 2019 is an all-out move—using diplomatic pressure, naval blockade, direct military threats—to bring Iran to her knees by making her absolutely helpless economically. We can also witness Pakistan's helplessness to India's proactive action in integrating Jammu and Kashmir with India by abrogating the temporary and contentious provisions of the Indian Constitution. Given the economic mess that Pakistan is in, now India can exercise a large number of options to settle the contentious issues with Pakistan on terms favourable to India. A long period of peace can then be expected—of course after initial period of bold action and perhaps limited period of overt and covert operations. The cost benefit ratio would suggest keeping the tempo on and if required increase it to a level that cannot be countered by Pakistan.

Means of waging economic war: Conflicts in this domain are part of a continuous process related to trade-based competitions. Some countries may follow the old approach of mercantilism to gain balance of trade advantages or resort to import substitutions, high tariff, quota systems or non-tariff methods for making imports impossible or extremely difficult. Under this seemingly benign approach, countries also follow dumping of their products in the target countries. Developed nations advance huge loans against import of their goods or services. In a more overt approach the following means may be adopted:-

- Blocking vital technologies.
- Blocking critical information related to niche products or services especially before these reach maturity stage.
- Indulge in cyber espionage to steal vital information (China has mastered this into a fine art).
- Operate through friendly NGOs to create legal hurdles for blocking sound economic policies in the garb of supporting pro poor economy. These moves reduce productivity, block innovations and creativity, and make the human capital inefficient in the target country. The most common of these techniques appear as 'stealing our jobs' and 'depriving the poor farmers of their land'.
- Promote insurgency, terrorism, and crime in general to increase the cost of business.
- Corrupt the political leadership to adopt policies beneficial to the proactive country against the target country.
- Creating huge scare in the cyberspace so that the target country hesitates to adapt business processes through ICT.

Securing against economic war: In the context of IW, inherent resilience in the economic growth and economic activities are extremely important. While we need to focus on sound headline indices such as GDP growth rate, inflation, interest rates, balance of payment, deficit as percentage of GDP in the national budget, per capita income, exchange rates and attractiveness of Indian currencies, ratings by international agencies on business and growth potential of the nation, there are other merit-related areas where India needs to orient her growth trajectory.

India needs to be part of the global supply chain for high-value products and services. This will entail institutional improvement, adoption of best practices, highly skilled and honest work force, labour mobility, efficient corporate conflict resolution in international and national transactions, capability to enforce contractual obligations in international business, international standards of logistics through all modes (road, surface, rail, air, mechanical handling at the ports, electronic data interchange (EDI) for funds transfer during import and export, and so on).

In view of the ubiquitous dependence on cyberspace for triggering and sustaining high rates of growth and inherent security concerns while exploiting the cyberspace, there is a need to make much higher investment in indigenous software and chip development (we have an excellent capability and opportunity in 5G rollout), and training and deployment of cyber security staff and experts.

In the context of SWOT matrix, recent reforms in the Indian economy since 2014, have placed the economy in the strength quadrant. The GDP growth rate too has been very good with controlled inflation and deficit. The fundamentals indicate economic security. However, to be competitive, especially in keeping with the national ambition, we need to prepare India as an alternative to China in global supply chain. This is a huge challenge. It is not easy. But in view of the continuity in political leadership and their optimistic approach to taking bold steps there is ample hope. The gains are exceptionally attractive and hence it is worth giving our best. Nevertheless, the 'people and the leadership' combination is the most critical pillar for resilient economy. Highly collaborative, innovative, creative and hence productive people led by selfless, wise, and decisive leadership that succeeds to create and maintain an ecosystem to enable people are two essential cornerstones of an economy resilient to the cyclic changes in global economy and orchestrated economic wars by the adversary.

Pillar 3. Knowledge and Technology

When we link knowledge and technology with IW in particular and national security in the information age in general, it is important to look at knowledge and technology a bit differently than what we are accustomed to. Firstly, knowledge does not exist in separate silos. It is the limitation of the average human mind that sees knowledge in different boxes as technical and non-technical and then into ever increasing specializations. Secondly, IW is not dependent entirely on 'technology'. A cursory look at artificial intelligence, big data, machine learning, deep learning (which are considered very important for IW) will reveal that all these specialized domains for IW draw heavily from all branches of knowledge that are generally considered non-technical. Thirdly, the core objective of all knowledge is to train the 'mind', attain equanimity and peace. Ethics and spiritualism (sans religion) play very important part in this. Look at the craving for Yoga across the globe. Also some of the most sought after disciplines in globally acclaimed academic institutes focus on mental health and ethics.

How does knowledge relate to society and the nation? The most myopic and most prevalent linkages are with jobs and earnings. If a degree or some skill gives you good knowledge and lucrative earnings, then it is high-end knowledge or high-quality skill. Well, this approach though short-sighted cannot be completely ignored. However, higher purpose of knowledge is for contribution—to others, society at large and nation. If we look at the objectives of National Service Scheme, this aspect will become amply clear. India did recognize this at the time of independence. Kothari commission did include this in the higher education system. Please refer to the policy guidelines on National Service Scheme.[14] But like so many other good things visualized at the time of independence this novel idea also was condemned to live on paper. With this as the backdrop we need to look at the linkages between knowledge and technology with IW.

Though the WEF 2018 has lauded the R&D achievements in the Indian institutes, it is limited to select premier organizations. On the whole the skills development and higher education sector in India are quite sluggish in view of the importance of technology and knowledge in IW. What we can learn from the US—pioneers in creating and operationalizing new knowledge and technologies—is the development of world-class institutes for creating knowledge and linking them up with the industries at global level. The state plays the role of facilitator and encourages excellence through competition. Premier academic institutes in the US are modelled to create jobs and not job seekers. The likes of Harvard, MIT, Stanford create great entrepreneurs (Bill Hewlett, David Packard, Michael Dell, Bill Gates, Paul Allen, and so on). Knowledge leaders in the world invest much higher percentage of their respective GDPs on R&D and other modes of creating and operationalizing knowledge compared to what we do. The World Bank data showing R&D expenditure as percentage of GDP by some select nations is given below:-

We can draw comfort from the fact that we spend more than double compared to Pakistan on R&D. What we need to realize is that given our size and legitimate national ambitions we must look at Republic of Korea, Japan, Israel, and China. All these nations started their respective journeys as independent countries around the same time (Korea-1954, Japan-1946 after near complete destruction in World War II, Isreal-1948, China-1949, India-1947). Another

14 https://mhrd.gov.in/nss-and-ncc-programmes-higher-educational-institutions.

Table 8. R&D Expenditure as percentage of GDP of Select Nations

Country	R&D Expenditure as % of GDP
China	2.01
Finland	2.75
Germany	2.94
India	0.62 (2015 figures)
Israel	4.25
Japan	3.14
Pakistan	0.25
R of Korea	4.23
Russia	1.10
Singapore	2.16
US	2.74

The data is for 2016 except for India.
Source:https://data.worldbank.org/indicator/gb.xpd.rsdv.gd.zs (World Bank Data UNESCO Institute of Statistics) Accessed 5 June 2019.

factor that emerges from the data above is the relative security of nations (both from internal and external threats) that spend higher percentages of GDP on R&D. These nations also have major components of their weapon systems manufactured indigenously. They are also net exporters of expensive weapon systems to countries that spend much less on R&D.

The modern weapon systems as also wealth-generating technologies and management processes are very complex and depend on niche technologies and management techniques. It takes much more time from idea to product and process. Also bulk of the production systems as also management tools involve large number of independent entities that have expertise in relevant fields. Hence for India it is very important to start investing in knowledge creation with a view to become part of the global supply chain at the higher ends of value chain.

While expenditure in absolute terms is an important factor, the way investments are utilized makes a huge difference. Thus Japan derives more than thrice from the same expenditure compared to the Americans and the West European countries. However, the conversion rate of ideas into products and services is fastest in the US. Both these factors are important. Somewhere these are also linked with government expenditure on education. If we look at the same set of countries and compare their expenditure on education as percentage of GDP, the figures will be revealing.

We need to consider some more facts to make sense of the data above:-

- Though China spends lesser percentage of GDP on education, the Chinese literacy rates, education system, including higher education are much higher than that of India.
- Similarly, Singapore, Japan, spend lesser percentage of GDP on education. Their education systems are the best in Asia.
- The US spends much higher percentage of GDP on education as well as on knowledge creation. She has been at the top of world ranking in almost all the indices.

Thus we need to increase our investment in R&D and education as also streamline the way the expenditure is incurred. There is another question related to investment in knowledge and technology.

Table 9. Expenditure on Education as percentage of GDP

Country	Expenditure on Education as % of GDP
China	1.99 (1999) Figures after 1999 not available in World Bank and UNESCO data
Finland	7.1 (2015)
Germany	4.8(2015)
India	3.8 (2013) India has been consistently spending less than 4% of GDP on education
Israel	5.9 (2015)
Japan	3.5 (2016)
Pakistan	2.8 (2017)
R of Korea	5.3 (2015)
Russia	3.8(2015)
Singapore	2.9 (2013)
US	5.0 (2014)

Note the Global Average is 4.1 period percent. Source https://data.worldbank.org/indicator/SE.XPD.TOTL.GD.ZS (Accessed 5 June 2019).

Should aspects of national security be included in the various levels of education? What do we include in school education that builds up a correct perspective of our national heritage? Do we establish academic institutes of higher learning in all streams that establish linkages between various subjects and national security? As an example while studying international relations, should the students be exposed to furthering national security objectives through international relations? Similarly, for economy, psychology, physics, and so on. Such practice is followed in the US. China has universities dealing with information war, military applications of science and technology. There are a number of books from Brassey's Publishing on military technology and warfare.

Pillar 4. Robust Internal Security

India's primary threat to national security emanates from internal turbulence. We may call it insurgency, terrorism, Pakistan-sponsored proxy war, and so on. Most internal security experts categorize these internal threats as proxy war in Kashmir, North East insurgency, left-wing insurgency, Naxalite insurgency, Khalistan terrorism, etc. Add to this the ISIS sponsored movement and we get a total of fifty-two global terrorists' groups targeting India. In terms of regional importance of the threat, South Asia ranks second after Middle East and North Africa in terms of least peaceful region. Specifically, in India more than half the Indian states are affected by the internal security threat. Around five years ago, 243 districts were affected by the Naxalite insurgency. Today that number is ninety-nine. India has been losing more citizens (security forces, civilians, insurgents, and home grown terrorists) due to this internal threat. 12,000 civilians and 300 security personnel died due to Naxalite insurgency between 1980 to 2018.[15]

668 security personnel, 2724 civilians, and 2870 extremists died

15 https://economictimes.indiatimes.com/news/defence/over-15000-killed-in-naxal-violence-since-1980-mha/articleshow/47664197.cms Accessed 7 June 2019.

between 2001 to 2006 due to North East insurgency—a conflict which has been going on since early 50s.[16]

3053 security forces, 9178 civilians, and 14,356 local and 2358 foreign terrorists died in J&K from 1990 to 2001.[17]

If we add up the figures from 2001 to 2019, the figure in case of J&K will be almost double of what has been given above. Add to this the loss of property, slowing down of economic activities and psychological impact, we have a huge problem at hand; and the most unfortunate as also dangerous fact is that we appear to have accepted this as 'business as usual'. Why have we not applied the theories of IW to our internal security threats? Our internal security apparatus does not seem to be discussing IW as this is being done in the Armed Forces. Perhaps one of the reasons could be, because the US did not coin the phrase in the context of internal security! But the US did completely revamp her intelligence network (post 9/11) that tracks their internal security threats. In our case efforts have just begun with the NSA being given the cabinet minister's rank with eighteen members under him including the three service chiefs, two chiefs of the intelligence agencies (IB and R&AW), five secretaries (defence, home, finance, revenue, space), Governor Reserve Bank of India (RBI) and Vice Chairman Niti Aayog.

In order to get a strategic perception about our internal security apparatus let us look at the bigger picture specific to India. First, public order and policing, as per the constitution, is a state subject. If the state does not want to share information, then centre cannot force the state to do so. In the Indian political system, there have

16 https://mdoner.gov.in/contentimages/files/ARC_7thReport_Ch12.pdf Accessed 7 June 2019.

17 https://mea.gov.in/in-focus-article.htm?18987/ Fact+Sheet+on+Jammu+amp+Kashmir) Accessed 7 June 2019.

been several cases where state chief ministers have been supportive of individuals and groups who belong to terrorists or insurgents' organizations. Prakash Singh, former DG BSF, DGP Assam and DGP UP writing in Times of India, 19 September 2019, 'Caught in a Time Warp' observed that only one Home Minister of India, Indrajit Gupta made sincere efforts to implement Police Reform (but could not do so). All others did not even try. As per him, the democratic structure itself will collapse if police are not able to take lawful action against certain category of criminals. Fortunately, some efforts appear on the horizon. One such being the decision to set up the first central university in Greater Noida, Uttar Pradesh which will conduct undergraduate and post graduate level courses on policing, internal security, cyber-crime and forensic science. The current Home Minister Shri Amit Shah too has commenced work on police as well as legal reforms so that conviction rates in India improve. The internal security situation is quite serious and complex. In India there have been cases where leaders of national political parties have been asking help from external enemy to help them win elections!! Second, intelligence sharing between the state and central police organization is on informal basis. If the state is governed by a party belonging to the opposition, then the state police confronts and harasses the central investigation agencies. Thirdly, the central intelligence agencies act as competitors and not collaborators. Fourthly, India has 180 police personnel per million people, as compared to 250 to 500 per million in the West. As per Ajai Sahni, Executive Director, Institute of Conflict Management, the police in India is third grade in terms of efficiency. Hence even first grade technology cannot be of any help. Fifthly, our judicial system—in the context of criminal justice—is extremely sluggish. Hence the approach to neutralize internal security threats is generally militaristic by using force and avoiding judicial dispensation. Since already clogged, the judicial system will be entirely ineffective to address the issue. Consequently, the security forces will get demoralized by witnessing their hard work and sacrifices go up in lengthy judicial procedures and pontification.

Objectives In the context of IW and the discussions above, following objectives emerge for strengthening this major pillar:-

- Eliminate terrorism in the country by a pre-decided timeline, say by 2022.
- Eliminate left-wing supported Naxalite insurgency from the remaining ninety districts by 2022.
- Resolve insurgency and militancy-related issues in the North East by 2022.

Strategic Approach

- Align the strategic approach to addressing the internal security threats to the core ideology. This ideology emanates from the well-being of the citizens and national integrity.
- Ensure decisive and strong central governance in the context of national security without allowing the states to go astray in the name of federalism. We need to remember that historically India has disintegrated under weak and indecisive central governance. It will be prudent to note here that getting majority vote in elections does not guarantee a strong and decisive central government. We have already seen that post-1947 India has suffered unprecedented losses in terms of economic disasters, loss of territory, and going down in global ranking with majority and stable governments at the centre. Some of the coalition governments have performed better in this respect. Hence numbers do not matter. Leaders do.
- Modernize the internal security apparatus without any delay. This involves modernizing the command structure, the individual service (State police, CID, CBI, CRPF, BSF, Assam Rifles, CISF, ITBP, SSB, and NSG), judicial system, administrative system, governance with specific emphasis on state-citizen relation. Implement the judicial, police, and administrative reforms immediately.

- Establish national internal security network that must include the surveillance or intelligence network, operational network, training and skills development network, secure database, decision support network, and fire support network in case of dealing with external groups along the coast or high-intensity militancy areas. These networks must use modern tools of artificial intelligence, big data, machine learning, etc. for accuracy and speed.
- Establish interoperability and collaboration nodes between the internal security apparatus and the Armed Forces. These nodes will ensure keeping the Armed Forces abreast of the important aspects of internal security so that in case they get involved in a situation or have to support some operations there is no loss of time in getting situational awareness.

Operational Dynamics In view of the need to modernize the police force, the Prime Minister, Shri Modi coined the acronym SMART for sensitive, mobile, alert, reliable, tech-savvy policemen. At the organizational level, the following sequence may be relevant:-

- Once the strategic intent is clear to all, we need to understand that goals are constant; rules change as per the environment.
- For our strategic goals, the sensors in the internal security network (surveillance network) collect information. The Kargil Review Committee had recommended strengthening the internal security network which resulted in establishing Multi Agency Centres (MAC) for the purpose of data fusion of inputs received from different intelligence sources. Besides the MAC, Subsidiary Multi Agency Centres (SMAC) were also established to make information collection more comprehensive. However, under the current centre-state relations many states do not send any information to the MACs or the SMACs. This issue is likely to be resolved once the police reforms are implemented.

- The processors and data storage devices process this information as per different operational requirements and store the same for point of use.
- The processed data thus becomes intelligence (gives decision alternatives).
- The decision support systems help in selecting one of the alternatives.
- Having selected the course of action, the action phase starts with all the control measures in place to ensure that the execution is as per the plan.
- The output of the action is fed to the feedback loop to modify the execution in case desired outputs are not being achieved.
- This cycle continues in a manner that actual output is similar to the desired output. A series of such processes over a period of time will take us to the outcome stage which can be compared with the strategic goal.

A detailed discussion on the Armed Forces—the fifth pillar of IW follows. Many of the recommendations for remodelling the Armed Forces may also be relevant for the internal security apparatus. These can be debated and adapted with suitable modification.

Pillar 5. Armed Forces

Though the involvement of the Armed Forces in IW is expected to be as the last resort and that too for a short part of the IW spectrum, its performance is most critical for the overall success of IW. Unlike the other pillars of IW, the Armed Forces do not have the luxury of coming out runners-up. Failure to win a war decisively inflicts exponentially large damage to the overall cause.

Besides, while launching the Armed Forces into an intense engagement with the adversary, all other pillars must be fully prepared and in support. This is one aspect which is ignored in bulk of writings on the 1991 Iraq War. When the US-led coalition forces went into the First Iraq War, all the pillars of IW were prepared at their best and ready for continuous support. All the Human Development Indices (HDIs) for the Americans as also the other partners were in the top bracket. The political leadership displayed good qualities and had the backing of their people. This took care of the first pillar. The US economy was the largest in the world—more than double of the next best in the race (China). Economies of other coalition partners were also in the top twenty brackets. In any case the entire war effort including the salaries of the fighting men and women were paid by countries like Japan and Saudi Arabia. None of the coalition partners had any disconcerting internal turmoil. They all were leaders in creation and operationalization of knowledge and were highly connected as also ICT enabled to fight network-centric war. In international relations the entire world including the Arab nations were with them.

All these factors must be more important to us than the type of aircrafts, tanks, ships, and the guns used by the coalition forces. We may not need some of those weapon systems (simply cannot afford the extravagant luxury) but we will definitely need a mature political leadership, good HDIs and economic strength, favourable internal security situation, and supportive international community for any conflict in the IW spectrum. How do we attain this level in the short, mid, and the long terms?

Setting the stage in specific context of India: Short Time

In the context of Indian Armed Forces, the backlog of historical events has created an exceptionally high friction. Excessive efforts in terms of capital and resources are being sucked in by continuing proxy war, insurgency, terrorism, and unresolved border disputes. The internal security agencies, governance and administration have generally been incapable and inefficient to neutralize this turbulence and maintain sustained peace and high level of citizen satisfaction.

This results in tying up of major resources of Armed Forces in doing somebody else's job. Hence, the first set of tasks for preparing the ground for Armed Forces as a critical pillar of IW are as under:-

- Apply concerted and synergistic efforts to neutralize the proxy war and terrorists' threats. This must involve the political leadership (both at the state and the central levels), administration, police, judiciary, civil society, media, and the Armed Forces.
- Preparation of Armed Forces for this task is quite different than that for conventional operations. Hence small team operations, precision targeting to minimize collateral damage, psychological operations, perception management in conjunction with the media, civil society, political leadership, internalizing and respecting the customs and traditions of the local population become important aspects for these operations.
- The SF must be employed in strategic role for operating deep inside the region where terrorists are trained before being launched. The SF will be required to function in non-traditional roles, undercover at times, in collaboration with other agencies such as Intelligence Bureau and Research and Analysis Wing.

Medium Term (Organizational transformation)

Organizational transformation is the most effective approach to address the dysfunctional issues related to an organization. The process involves first identifying the gaps between the ideal expectations against the performance and culture of the organization. Secondly, applying transformational leadership approach (discussed in Appendix A) to align the organizational dynamics in tune with the organizational goals and societal expectation. The process is based on hard facts sans emotion and assumed image of the organizations. To elucidate this point, consider the fact the CEO of General Electric while deciding to apply Six Sigma approach to the organization had observed that our 'quality stinks'. When he made this observation GE was global leader in market share and profit margins!

As national institutions, the British Army between the two great wars and the American Army after the Vietnam War were subjected to objective scrutiny. Norman Dixon (in *Psychology of Military Incompetence*) writing in the context of British Army after the First World War observed, 'military organizations make for military incompetence in two ways—directly by forcing members to act in a fashion that is not always conducive to military success and indirectly by attracting, selecting, and promoting a minority of people with particular defect of intellect and personality.' Post-Vietnam, a War College report (US Army) quoted by Gabriel A Richard and Savage L Paul in their book *Crisis in Command*, uncovered a recurring pattern of the 'ambitious, transitory commander—marginally skilled in the complexities of his duties, engulfed in producing transitory results, fearful of personal failure, too busy to talk with or listen to his subordinates, and determined to submit acceptably optimistic reports which reflect faultless completion of a variety of tasks at the expense of sweat and frustration of his subordinates.'

In the Indian context, a number of senior commanders have analysed the leadership and organizational issues in the Indian Army post-independence. Notable among these are Major General VK Singh in *Leadership in the Indian Army: Biographies of Twelve Soldiers*. Lieutenant General Harbaksh Singh, *War Dispatches: Indo-Pak Conflict 1965*, Henderson Brooks, *1962 Report*, Major General Samay Ram, *Stress Suicide and Fratricides in the Army: Crisis Within*. RK Anand in *Assault on Merit*. We can sum up their findings under role of higher military leadership in the context of IW.

The role of senior military leadership (Generalship) was envisaged by Norman Dixon (*On the Psychology of Military Incompetence*) even before the Second World War when IW as a phrase was not known. That role or capability fits in very well even today. Dixon says that,

'Senior commanders are expected to receive, process, and transmit information in a way that yields maximum gain for the minimum cost. Ideally in conformation with the directives with which he has been tasked/programmed.' This looks simple in ideal theoretical conditions if we assume that the top commanders in the Armed Forces operate in a very narrow range of domain with respect to the roles assigned to them. In other words, their job profiles and working ethos remove all irrelevant aspects which can blur the focus on the primary role of war fighting. Second requirement for optimal processing of information within reasonable time frame for arriving at accurate decision in relation to the assigned tasks is that the commanders can cope with 'system noise'. Dixon as well as other military scholars we have discussed earlier felt that by acquiring knowledge or information, the top commanders can reduce uncertainty in case the commander can control the 'system noise'. Thus two factors emerge during collecting, processing, and transmitting information (from the commanders to the command). Alignment with the task and elimination/reduction of system noise. We need to analyse these two factors in the context of Indian politico-military interface and experience.

In order to be objective in our analysis let us look at the facts first. Just after independence, the first prime minister of independent India was shown the Commander in Chief's (C in C) plan for force structuring of Indian Army in the context of external threats. Major General Rudra[18] was the person who was tasked to show the plan to the prime minister. After showing the paper to the prime minister, Rudra came out of the prime minister's office. This is what he said to his colleagues who wanted to know the prime minister's observation on the C in C's plan. 'The PM took one look at my paper and blew

18 Major General A Rudra by Major General DK Palit, quoted in, 1962: A View from the Other Side of the Hill, A USI Study Edited by Major General PJS Sandhu, Vij Books India Pvt Limited, New Delhi 2015, ISBN 9789384464769 Pp 240.

his top. "Rubbish, total rubbish!" he shouted. "We do not need a defence plan. Our policy is ahimsa (non-violence). We foresee no military threats. Scrap the Army! The police are good enough to meet our security needs."'

What relevance this incident has to our study? It describes an aspect of system noise. Political apathy to the legitimate security requirement impedes the decision-making process of military leaders. Sometimes even brilliant military commanders fall prey to this kind of system noise. Let us look at some examples.

Major General VK Singh in his book on leadership qualities of some of the best generals that India had at the time of Independence lauded Cariappa's role in keeping the army apolitical. This, as per VK Singh has been his greatest achievement. He firmly refused to take the Indian National Army (also known as Azad Hind Fauj) personnel back into the army since he thought that they would bring politics into the army. There was a lot of political pressure on him to do so. Nehru relented only when Cariappa threatened to resign.

Now compare this to his response when Nehru refused to allow him to send additional troops in J&K to recapture entire J&K from Pakistani occupation. This time Cariappa obeyed meekly. Induction of the patriotic INA personnel into Indian Army was a political decision over which Cariappa had no locus standi. Similarly, military operations in J&K was Cariappa's domain as the Army Commander where Nehru should not have intervened. Cariappa had other unpleasant brushes with Nehru. In May 1951, when he presented his plans to defend the Chinese borders more effectively in view of the envisaged Chinese threat he was told that it was not the C-in-C's business to tell the Prime Minister how to defend the country. A self-respecting C-in-C should have thrown his resignation on the arrogant Prime Minister. That did not happen. Later Cariappa rued his decision not to protest. He could have saved the country a big humiliation. (Pp 43 VK Singh). Again an effort to sustain and even magnify system noise for the top military leaders. In such ecosystem the top commanders will be found reluctant to use their superior military skills unless they are endowed with exceptional moral courage.

VK Singh in his book has also included Thakur Nathu Singh as one of the outstanding generals in 1947. Thakur Nathu Singh's reaction to Nehru's idea of retaining British officers (in the erstwhile British Indian Army) for a few years after independence on the plea that the Indian officers do not have enough experience, was, 'Officers sitting here have more than twenty-five years' service and are capable of holding senior appointments in the Armed Forces. As for experience if I may ask you, Sir what experience do you have to hold the post of Prime Minister?' (VK Singh Pp 78). Thakur Nathu Singh was the type of general who could have worked through the system noise. But unfortunately such generalship is rare.

In spite of being patriotic to the core, Nathu Singh did find British officers endowed with better qualities in some respects when compared to the Indian Officers. He had lamented that, 'I have not known a British officer who placed his own interest before the country's and I have hardly known any Indian officer who did not.' (VK Singh Pp 80)

Commenting on the way the senior commanders performed during the 1962 Sino-Indian war, the authors in the above mentioned USI Study observed that due to extreme political apathy the Armed Forces in general felt isolated. Except for someone like Lt General BM Kaul, who was close to Nehru and Krishna Menon (the then PM and Defence Minister respectively); other military commanders felt completely isolated. Hence, they did not exhibit any initiative and enthusiasm during the war. In other words, a resolute military leadership endowed with professional honesty and moral courage could have saved India from the humiliation of 1962 in spite of many political blunders before the onset of hostilities. Can we attribute low calibre generalship to system noise? Perhaps most of these generals thought that it was not their job to get involved in strategic aspects of national security. Though, it must be said that some of the generals during this war were professionally outstanding with regard to their knowledge on 'what needs to be done'. But they lacked the guts to do it.

The story of higher military leadership in 1965 is also not very encouraging in the context of the two IW related factors mentioned above. Lt Gen Harbaksh Singh, the Western Army Commander in 1965 responsible for defence of Punjab noticed a 'tendency among higher command to succumb to pressure of events and fall an easy prey to dark and gloomy apprehensions. In many situations lack of aggressive action resulted in failure to exploit many favourable situations.'[19]

In the 1965 Indo-Pak War, the political establishment was acutely aware of the general criticism of political blunders of 1962. Hence the Armed Forces were given a free hand to plan and execute the response to Pakistani aggression. Did things change? Let us have a look.

As per the military intelligence on 31 August 1965, the Pakistanis were expected to take at least three months to start their offensive against India. The Pakistanis attacked the next day! The then Chief of Army Staff, General JN Chaudhary—as per many military commentators and experts (Inder Malhotra, DK Palit)—had decided to fight along the Bias River when he came to know that Pakistani Army had three armoured divisions. This would have given away bulk of Punjab to the Pakistanis without any fight. The then Prime Minister Late Lal Bahadur Shastri rejected the plan to withdraw along River Bias. Lt General Harbaksh Singh, the Western Army Commander supported the prime minister. Harbaksh was a bold and committed general. The threat of three Pakistani armoured divisions did not impress him much as it did his Chief. Thus it was the Indian Prime Minister, supported by Harbaksh who saved Punjab in 1965. Many a time we debate that strategic military decisions must be left to the military commanders. This is what Late Lal Bahadur

19 War Dispatches: Indo-Pak Conflict 1965, Lt Gen Harbaksh Singh, Sona Printers New Delhi1991 ISBN 81-7062-117-8 Pp 194.

Shastri did by entrusting General JN Chaudhuri. But he had to overrule him when he found the Chief not up to the task. Hence in military leadership what uniform you wear does not matter. Who is in the uniform does matter.

Again in the famous battle across the Ichhogil Canal, only one of the three battalions could cross the water obstacle. The remaining two battalions were too cautious to advance to the water obstacle. The supporting armour did not venture across the bridgehead established by the battalion that had crossed the canal. The brigade commander and the division commander of the battalion that had crossed continued to drag their feet. It was the Army Commander who was pushing for offensive defence. This prompted Harbaksh to comment adversely on the senior commanders during 1965. Major General Lachhman Singh in his book, *Missed Opportunities,* has also commented adversely on the way the military leadership performed during this operation. Details of military operations (54 Infantry Brigade) for move across Ichhogil do not instil confidence in the capabilities of many commanding officers, brigade commanders, and even the divisional corps commanders. It was Harbaksh who saved the day for India. The then prime minister asked the then Chief, if India could continue her military operations for some more time to achieve decisive victory. He was informed by the Chief that, 'the Army has no ammunition to continue the operations.' the prime Minister was forced to accept the ceasefire offer made by the Pakistan president. Later it emerged that India still had about two weeks of ammunition to continue intense war! (Lachhman Singh in *Missed Opportunities*)

Major General VK Singh, in his book narrates how Manekshaw was told by the then prime minister and her cabinet ministers to commence operation in erstwhile East Pakistan (now Bangladesh) immediately (March 1971).The conversation (given in Sam Manekshaw's biography) reveals the cavalier way the Chief was ordered. Of course, Manekshaw did not agree and decided on his own timings and methods.

Major General Samay Ram, writing in 2011, on stress in the Indian Army found that the senior officers are, 'hierarchy, status, and privilege conscious. Always want good results, some greedy minds indulge in corrupt practice.'[20]

In post-independent India, the ability of military commanders to receive, process, and use information in consonance with the task has been seriously hampered due to a number of reasons. This problem of misalignment has been because of the type of political and military leaders. The advent of information age does not help the leadership if they lack the basics. The readers can infer from the above examples the realities of task alignment and system noise in the Indian context. What appear very evident from the above are the following:

- There has been lack of clarity on issues related to national security.
- The political and the military leaderships were seldom in synergy with each other.
- The military leadership did create and suffer from 'system noise'. This 'noise' comprised of:
    - Self-centred approach. Thakur Nathu Singh had predicted this in 1948.
    - Lack of moral courage to follow their professional counsel and tendency to succumb to political pressure. Incidentally in the Indian Military Academy one of the warriors' code is 'to speak the truth with bluntness'. The senior officers on most occasions defied this code. The warriors' codes are displayed in the cadet mess in the IMA.
    - Fear of the unknown. Magnifying the chances of failure and telescoping the probabilities of success. Hence

20 Stress Suicide and Fratricide in the Army: Crisis Within, Major General Samay Ram, Vij Books India Limited New Delhi 2011, ISBN 9789380177410 Pp 122-123

failure to display offensive spirit.

It may not be out of place here to recount some statistics from the performance of the German Army during the Second World War. Richard Gabriel and Paul L Savage writing in their book, *Crisis in Command* (1977), observed on the role of German generals in ensuring organizational cohesiveness in adverse situations. They said that, 'The average German officer's risk of being killed in action was far greater than his men. The risk of field-grade officers to get killed in action was even greater. Of 675 officers on the German list, 223 were killed (around 33 percent). Overall 30.8 percent German officers were killed as against 26.1 percent men. The Indian Army figures may not be very different except for the fact that in the German Army of Second World War a very large number officers killed in action were of senior ranks—brigadiers and above.

Coming back to our subject—the organizational aspects; the Americans besides critically examining the dysfunctional aspects of their army studied the Bekaa Valley and Golan Heights conflicts between Syria and Israel. Before the American forces were launched in Iraq in 1991, the new doctrines and resultant forces' capabilities were tested in Grenada and Panama. This is what we need to do for bringing in transformation of Armed Forces. Make a study of our organizational behaviour in the Armed Forces for the last decades. Identify the dysfunctional aspects. Thereafter commence with reforms in the structure, culture, weapon mix, network-centric orientation, and general ecosystem of Armed Forces. We need to remember the characteristics of ICT-enabled organizations.

Military Organizations in Knowledge Era

Military organization is an institution defined as a responsive adaptive group, which is a product of social needs and pressures. It is part of a large system, ie. community or the society and should be the forward looking, adaptive, and proactive part of the community. Institutions incorporate, foster, and protect normative relationships and action patterns and perform functions and services, which are valued in the environment. Thus institutions have values that extend beyond the role incumbents who may come and go. It is more enduring, has ability to adopt over time to changing needs and values. The internal structure embodies and protects commonly held values and norms of the society. Institutions influence the environment in a positive way. Military as an institution is characterized by sense of national integration, effectiveness in performing difficult and dangerous tasks, high sense of discipline and physical fitness, clean habits and ethos. While adapting to the ICT ecosystem as discussed earlier, the military needs to incorporate the following organizational culture to remain relevant and competent:-

- Stick to the goals and objectives. Rules keep evolving and changing. Hence from rules and SOP (Standard Operating Procedures) based organization, the military organization must transform to goals-driven organization where rules adapt to the changing environment.
- There are no fixed jobs and hence there are no permanent organizations. If the organization is not required, it must go. If 'band platoon' in an infantry battalion is not required today, then either the personnel in the platoon are skilled for something else or get disbanded. Similarly, all organizations need to be scrutinized. Similarly, if intelligence gathering is based on surveillance network, the people involved in the job must be trained to exploit the network and present intelligence to create accurate situational awareness related to terrain, enemy, own forces, as also logistics.
- Organizations are not created to provide jobs; these are created to add value or meet emergent requirements. Hence when an organization is raised, the value addition clause must be very clear in a reasonable time frame. If there is no value addition or contribution by the organization, the people in the organization must be reskilled and employed

in different relevant organizations.

- More the number of layers, less efficient the organization. By this norm itself the military organization does not lend itself to efficiency. Unnecessary layers create internal friction, delays, and demotivation for the talented pool of personnel.
- Wasteful activities, long waiting time, lack of clarity of tasks, ceremonials to pander to tall egos and whims are avoided in modern organizations. Every member's time is precious irrespective of the hierarchy at which the team member is working. Hence wasteful activities must be ruthlessly cut down.
- Develop the art of learning to learn. Knowledge era is characterized by fast pace of obsolescence. What the soldiers learn today may become irrelevant in the next two to three years. Hence the capability to unlearn and relearn must be inbuilt in the organization. There is definite need to incorporate online learning culture in the Armed Forces with linkages with institutions that produce the domain knowledge and skills.

Military organization in interaction with the technological, political and societal environment

A schematic arrangement given below depicts different levels of military organization surrounded by political, societal environment, and the technological environment:

In IW paradigm, the military exists as an extension of national capabilities. The technological capabilities, cyberspace, political leadership, efficiency of the bureaucracy, knowledge base etc. remain in support of the military at functional, tactical, operational, and strategic levels. This would involve structured arrangements for establishing the support linkages at every level. Thus, say at corps or even at brigade level, the formation headquarters must be able to tap on the requisite resources of non-military organization for training,

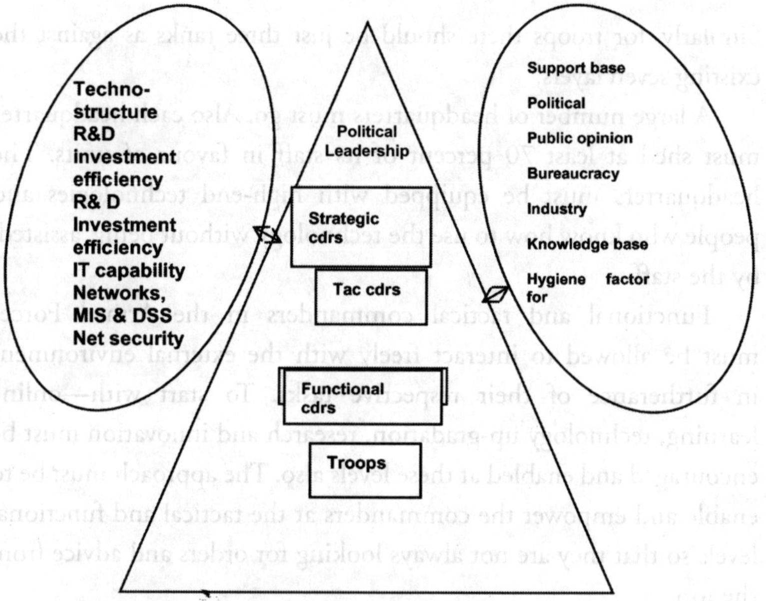

Figure 2:Military Organization as a subset of National Capability

knowledge sharing, focused research and innovation, technical trouble-shooting, and modification. In order to get maximum benefits from such linkages and ICT infrastructure, the internal structure of the military needs to be transformed.

Today the military hierarchy has around nine different ranks. Also there is very strong rank consciousness; hence a constant craving for the next rank. There are disproportionately large number of supervisors or staff appointments than 'hands-on' workers. There are redundant and overstaffed headquarters 'creating' work (more of it is 'paper work') for limited number of 'hands-on' working members. Efficient organizations have very few headquarters, which are very scantily staffed by highly efficient members who handle their work without much staff help by exploiting technology to the maximum.

They have three to five levels. It is only the bureaucracy and related organizations where the number of ranks, rank consciousness, protocols, and sense of entitlement are high. There is a need to rationalize the ranks structure from the existing nine to just four.

Similarly, for troops there should be just three ranks as against the existing seven layers.

A large number of headquarters must go. Also each headquarter must shed at least 70 percent of its staff in favour of units. The headquarters must be equipped with high-end technologies and people who know how to use the technology without being 'assisted' by the staff.

Functional and tactical commanders in the Armed Forces must be allowed to interact freely with the external environment in furtherance of their respective tasks. To start with—online learning, technology up-gradation, research and innovation must be encouraged and enabled at these levels also. The approach must be to enable and empower the commanders at the tactical and functional levels so that they are not always looking for orders and advice from the top.

The Armed Forces as a whole must be organized for knowledge management. It must be accepted by the security forces in general that a very high percentage of skills and knowledge critical for national security resides in organizations and institutions outside their closed and highly-guarded perimeters!

Organization and Management of Knowledge

The military organization suggested above must be tailored for effective knowledge management (KM). KM is a discipline that promotes a collaborative and integrated approach to the creation, capture, organization, access, and use of information assets of an organization. The means and techniques for KM available in the info age provide unprecedented capabilities in collecting, storing, manipulating, disseminating, and most importantly, exploiting knowledge. These means can be put to effective use for achieving military objectives by ensuring that contextual knowledge is available to the body of troops/commanders in right time (free flow) and right format (free form). An indirect payoff from effective KM is reduction in number of headquarters as also number of personnel in each headquarter. Please see figure for a possible 'Knowledge Flow' diagram:

Basic principles for application of Knowledge Management across the organization are as under:-

- The organization must follow system approach while dealing

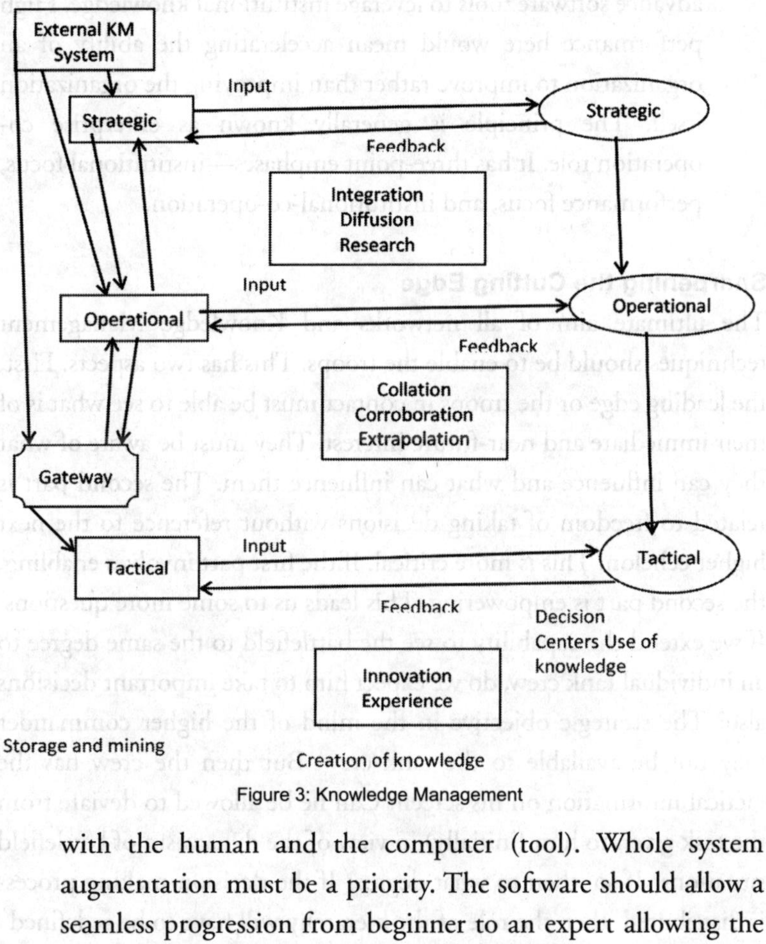

Figure 3: Knowledge Management

with the human and the computer (tool). Whole system augmentation must be a priority. The software should allow a seamless progression from beginner to an expert allowing the user to ultimately lose awareness of the tool and concentrate on the task.

- Address the human and computer system co-evolution. This

entails higher level of integration between the user and the technology. Instead of stepwise release of new version, there is a need to incorporate much more rapid iteration of software improvement. Remember only first-rate organizations can exploit first-rate technologies.

- We need to combine high-performance technology with advance software tools to leverage institutional knowledge. High performance here would mean accelerating the ability of an organization to improve rather than improving the organization itself. The principle is generally known as enterprise co-operation role. It has three-point emphases—institutional focus, performance focus, and institutional-co-operation.

Sharpening the Cutting Edge

The ultimate aim of all networks and Knowledge Management techniques should be to enable the troops. This has two aspects. First, the leading edge or the troops in contact must be able to see what is of their immediate and near-future interest. They must be aware of what they can influence and what can influence them. The second part is related to freedom of taking decisions without reference to the next higher echelon. This is more critical. If the first part involves enabling, the second part is empowering. This leads us to some more questions. If we extend the capability to see the battlefield to the same degree to an individual tank crew, do we expect him to take important decisions also? The strategic objective in the mind of the higher commander may not be available to the tank crew. But then the crew has the tactical information on his screen. Can he be allowed to deviate from the task given to him (initially) in view of the dynamism of battlefield situations? If so, then to what degree? If the decision-making process is distributed, then the role of the hierarchy will have to be redefined.

In the 1971 operations on the Western front such a situation arose, of course, without the help of modern systems. Commanding Officer Poona Horse (Lt Col Hanut, later Lt Gen Hanut) saw the

Pakistani tanks coming out of their hides—on feeling threatened—and moving across an area which as per the Indian Division in that area was heavily mined. On seeing free movement of Pakistani Armour, Hanut who was in contact, very correctly inferred that there were no mines in that area. He wanted to commence the advance without any elaborate bridgehead operations. He apprised the higher echelon and sought permission. The divisional Commander (Maj Gen Vaidya—later the Chief of Army Staff) declined. The operations got delayed for three days. The Pakistanis got enough time to occupy defences on River Basantar. A major opportunity was thus lost since the subordinate commanders though privy to better information and aware of the overall picture did not have the authority to act on the knowledge available with him. There are many cases in the history of Indian wars where the subordinate commanders were much better placed to take decisions but lacked the authority to do so.

With impressive IT capability of the Land Warrior system, diffusion of power—away from the highly centralized hierarchy—would become a possibility. How do we optimize this capability? An extreme level of diffusion of power may also lead to the phenomenon of self-organization. This poses a real threat to very large organizations like the Army that depend on strong hierarchical controls. The concept of self-organizing means that when the system components interact, they produce synergistic emergent properties not displayed by the individual components. The phenomenon has very high adaptive skill, ie., ability to learn from experience. The concepts of artificial intelligence (AI) are based on this phenomenon. It displays a life-like behaviour emanating from simple rules, unfolding from the bottom. A simplistic simile can be a school of fish or a swarm of bees. The school or the swarm goes through a variety of obstacles, changing channels and reorganizing their shapes frequently without any external control. This behaviour has been simulated in computer graphics based on simple rules such as of separation (do not get too close to any object including each other), alignment (matching the speed and direction of nearby companions), cohesion (head for the perceived centre of mass). Applying this to say a company or platoon of infantrymen, equipped with the Land Warrior system, we can devise rules for a swarming attack. As the information systems make the battlespace (relevant for small force levels—from a combat team to a combat command) reasonably clear for immediate time interval, the members in the team and command can create the synergy of say a football team (the coach just watches from the sidelines and can interfere in a very limited way when the game is on) or school of fish, or swarming bees without any interference from higher echelons.

It can be easily seen that with the convergence of surveillance, communication, precision movement, quick sensor-shooter decision system to control movement and weapon system, an organic swarming organization can be created. This organization will be extremely adaptive, will function without any external control and will have the capability to function in a chaotic combat environment with devastating accuracy. But then there are some inherent drawbacks. The organization has no central control. It is non-predictable, non-understandable and non-immediate. It suits the din of combat at company and squadron levels, which cannot be centrally controlled. It is not predicable and non-understandable. This perhaps gives us a clue of the organizational culture at battalion, company, and platoon, which we have briefly hinted above.

If we want to place anything bigger than the battalion in that situation, the program dynamics will be too complex and failure may entail bigger penalties. However, there will be payoffs in terms of impact of force application at a larger scale. This brings us to an important deduction with regard to organization structure. More number of small self-organizing and highly motivated organizations will be much more effective in the IW as against large organizations with long chains of hierarchies and excessive staff interface.

There is a general belief that IT-enabled organizations should adopt a network organizational structure. This needs to be closely scrutinized. Firstly, we need to be clear of the networked organization concept. In a networked organization, the horizontal component of information flow is more enhanced than the vertical component. Information flows horizontally in the organization with distributive decision-making authority. Hence, promoting delegation, decentralization, and knowledge sharing. The vertical linkages for policy guidelines and decision-making are less. The organization does not function on standard operating procedure, rulebooks, and strict boundaries of authorities and responsibilities. Instead the decision-making process is based on goals and objectives, hinged on dynamic knowledge base which continuously adapts to the changing environment.

In hierarchies, decision-making is centralized. The flow of information is either top down or bottom up. Whereas decision-making is more at the top, at lower levels control function tend to ensure that execution is as per the decision made at the top. It must be remembered that both the systems have their own set of advantages and disadvantages. In case of a network, the organization displays adaptability and resilience. These advantages occur due to dependence on a broader and dynamic knowledge base. Also the distributive decision-making minimizes probability of major errors. However, the vertical control lines are less and centralized control is lacking; thus, the organization is uncontrollable and runs a short-term risk of below-par performance.

Information Systems in a Network-centric Environment: The objectives of an information system in a network-centric environment are:-

- **Get the right information in right time:** This is achieved by the first component ie. sensors or the intelligence, surveillance, and reconnaissance system commonly known as ISR.
- **Right information reaches the right location/person in right time:** Here we deal with the communication system

which include processors, receptors, databases, transmitters (in the era of convergence this would mean networks), rules, and synergy.

- **Precision application of force/weapon system and feedback:** If we analyse this objective it takes us back to converged network (convergence of communication and IT/computers).

The three objectives discussed above form the first iteration of a dynamic cycle. This iteration is repeated till the overall objective/goal is achieved or target neutralized. The successive running of the iteration requires sensors to 'see' the effect of force/weapon application, pass the information back to the network for repeat, modify or call off further action/force applicable.

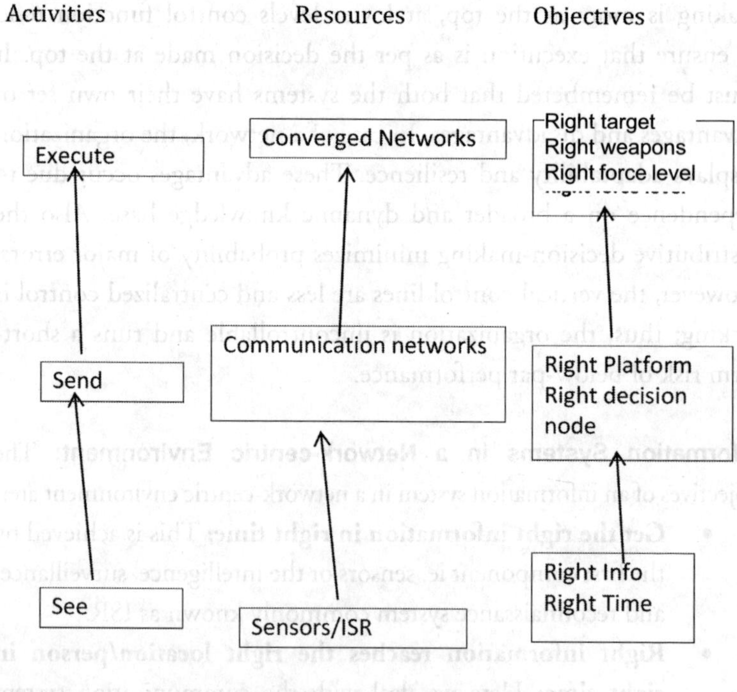

Figure 4: Objectives of Information System

Since war is always two sided, the adversary will attack the information system at the levels discussed above. Information assurance would involve neutralizing the adversary's efforts to degrade our functions mentioned above. This brings out two distinct functions in information domain—information assurance for own forces and information disruption for the adversary. Both these functions need detailed domain expertise in ICTs. The organization that undertakes these functions in the Indian Army is Corps of Signals. Its organization and functions need to be oriented to facilitate network-centric operations at tactical and operational levels. Consequently, the Corps needs to enhance its presence in the combat zone. Excessive attachment to the 'backbone' communication will keep them away from their legitimate and specialized military role which cannot be performed by non-military organizations.

Integrating the troops in contact with the command and control nodes in a network-centric operation. The primary role of command and control nodes is to generate an updated battlespace awareness and keep the forward elements updated with the combat environment and target information, in synch with the dynamics of battlespace. Thus, besides maintaining real-time enemy, own troops information, along with logistics, terrain, weather updates, the C2 nodes also prepare decision-support systems and knowledge-based expert systems. The information systems need to integrate sensors—where data is collected—with data integration/data fusion systems and the Decision Support System (DSS). Please see figure below:-

In the figure above the data is collected by the Electronic Warfare Systems (EWS), Remote Ground Sensors (RGS), troops in contact, satellites, and airborne systems. There may be a number of other sensors such as weapon locating or other RADARs. The data picked up by the sensors is integrated or diffused in data integration or data fusion systems. Data fusion converts the input received from sensors in a suitable representational form to save bandwidth. In data integration, the objective is synergistic use of information provided by the sensory devices to assist accomplishment of task by the system.

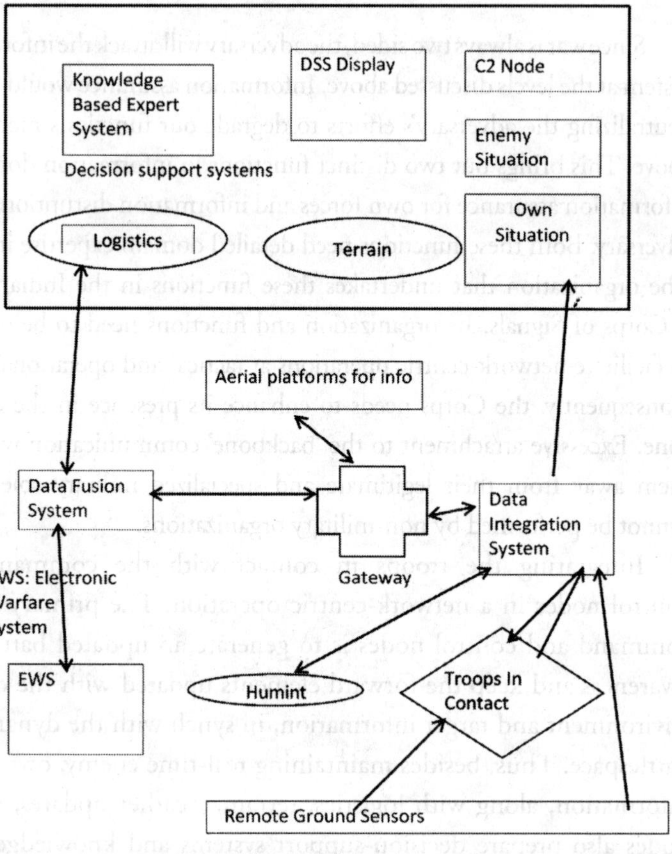

Figure 5: Integrating the Command and Control Nodes in the Combat Zone

Command and control (C2) are critical functions in IW. The C2 nodes shown in the figure above need to have complete situational awareness in terms of terrain, enemy, logistics, and other knowledge base. This helps the staff in the C2 nodes to take decisions either manually or through DSS. However, the capability of situational awareness needs to be available to the nodes at strategic, operational, and tactical levels. Relevant actionable information must also be available to the troops in contact. These troops should be able to 'pull' the desired information through various gateways, which have the authority to allow or deny information through automated controls. An integrated model of various C2 nodes at the three levels is given below:-

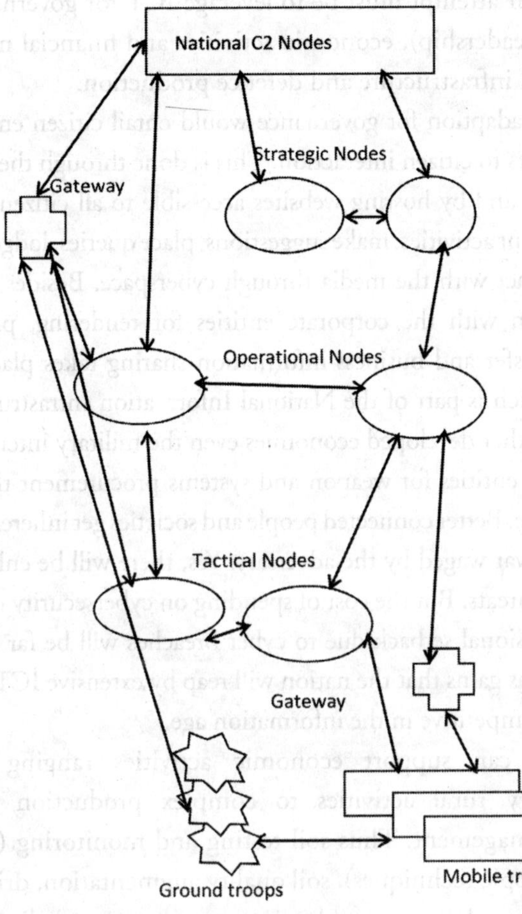

Figure 6: Distributed C2 Nodes

Pillar 6. ICT adaption

As we have seen earlier the ICT adaption, as per the WEF, is based on the number of broadband connections and the speeds available for Internet traffic. These parameters in the context of IW are too rudimentary to make any impact. To leverage ICT in IW, the exploitation needs to be on a wider expanse with deeper involvement in each sector to provide competitive advantage. All the other six pillars of IW envisaged by us need to be supported by the ICT.

Hence our attempt must be to leverage ICT for governance (people and the leadership), economic activities and financial management, industrial infrastructure and defence production.

ICT adaption for governance would entail citizen empowerment, and leaders to citizen interaction. This is done through the social media platforms and by hosting websites accessible to all citizens to monitor government activities, make suggestions, place queries, lodge complaints, and interact with the media through cyberspace. Besides, government interaction with the corporate entities for tendering, procurements, fund transfer and business-information sharing takes place exploiting ICTs, which is part of the National Information Infrastructure. In the US and other developed economies even the military interacts with the corporate entities for weapon and systems procurement through open cyberspace. Better connected people and societies get inherent protection from netwar waged by the adversary. Yes, there will be enhanced cyber security threats. But the cost of spending on cybersecurity measures and even occasional setback due to cyber breaches will be far less than the continuous gains that the nation will reap by extensive ICT adaption to remain competitive in the information age.

ICT can support economic activities ranging from very elementary rural activities to complex production and supply chain management. Thus soil testing and monitoring (soil sensors, spectroscopic techniques), soil quality augmentation, drip irrigation, environmental scan, production to consumers' links, demand forecast, export facilitation, electronic data interface (EDI) for expeditious payments, etc. are just some of the areas where ICT adaption can support the economic activities in the rural areas. As the scale and complexity of economic activity increases, ICT can be used for quality enhancement, monitoring the production or services processes for optimum operations, market scan for trend analysis, connecting with the customer for relationship management, skills development and training etc. One of the major hurdles for growth of the SMEs in India is availability of adequate working capital with the small entrepreneurs. These small enterprises generally play the role of suppliers to the bigger organizations in the supply chain. Dues to these suppliers are generally delayed without any reason. If the chain of supplies and the payment received is visible online the bigger enterprises will be forced to clear the dues in time. Besides it will help calculation and refund based on the GST documents.

Financial management in IW environment involves security of cyberspace used by the banking systems. This includes the banking and non-banking financial systems. Besides the transparency of banking activities, monitoring the legitimacy of transactions as per the regulatory authorities, verification of borrowers' credentials, project verification prior to lending, and tracking the loan recovery, etc. can be very effectively done by the ICT tools (digital communications, artificial intelligence, data processing and process specific software).

It needs to be understood that use of ICTs for all the activities related to—citizen to government, citizen to the society, and citizen to citizen raises the speed, efficiency, and accuracy by factors of ten to fifty. Similarly, in the manufacturing and service delivery sectors, use of cyberspace through AI and big data creates far more wealth (without cutting down on employment). There is a need that we create a more pervasive cyberspace and bring in behavioural changes among various organizations mentioned above to adapt to ICT for better efficiency. There is also a requirement of continuous skilling of people to undertake high-end tasks in this environment.

The biggest boost to industrial infrastructure is through ICT-enabled processes. As per the MoD Annual Report 2017-18, Department of Industrial Policy and Promotion (DIPP) has so far issued 343 industrial licenses (ILs) covering 206 companies till November 2017 for manufacture of a wide range of defence items to private companies. Sixty-nine licensed companies covering 112 industrial licenses have so far reported commencement of production. The MoD Report also claims initiating eProcurement, ePayment, eAuction, and complaints management through relevant portals. Devina Sengupta, in an article in Economic Times 31 August 2016[21] identifies additive manufacturing, advanced robotics, industrial internet of things (IIOT) and augmented reality to boost advanced manufacturing with consistent high quality. These ICT enablers can even help small enterprises which act as suppliers to the bigger companies involved in defence production. The entire ecosystem of defence production needs a group of tier one companies which are real big in size, knowledge base, quality, ethics and working capital. These tier one companies will then be fed by tier two to tier four companies as per their production facilities, size of operations, working capital, and quality of production. The four tiers will have to be integrated in a network to exchange design, development, innovation, supply of components and products, and payments in a transparent and regulated manner. If we recollect the birth of Internet, it all started from the American DARPA which used the internet (restricted in spread and scope during those days) to exchange research and development ideas and project management for defence production. Selected academic institutes in the US were also taken on board. This model can work for Indian defence production to enhance productivity, cope with rapid modernization, and enhance the 'make in India' component.

Prabhala and Chengappa writing in *The Hindu Business Line* (20 June 2018) elaborated on the government's ambitious plan (as per Defence Production Policy-DProP) for 2025 to achieve defence production worth Rs 1,70,000 crore. The defence export to reach Rs 35,000 crore. These activities will be supported by an investment of Rs 70,000 crore. The thrust will be to achieve global

21 https://economictimes.indiatimes.com/news/economy/indicators/80-of-indian-manufacturing-industry-to-adopt-the-advanced-trends-by-2020-tata-strategic-report/articleshow/53943260.cms (Accessed 10 September 2019).

leadership in artificial intelligence and cyberspace technologies.[22]

The increase in defence exports—to Rs 10,745 crore in 2018-19 from Rs 4,682 crore in 2017-18. The US is the major contributor to this export with a share of Rs 5000 crore. The increase in exports comes after recent changes in policy that have made it easier for companies to get official permissions.[23]

Pillar 7. International Relations

International relations, as a branch of political science, help us analyse and formulate foreign policy (first line of national defence) of a country. But what factors do we analyse? What is the edifice on which the foreign policy is formulated having analysed the international relations? These two questions lead us to a vastly multi-disciplinary field. As regards the first question, the factors comprise of almost all the subjects that affect mankind—from culture, philosophy, social science, psychology, economy, history, criminology to science and technology. The players who participate in international relations around these factors include the governments, non-government organizations, societies, intellectuals and academicians, international organizations, multinational companies, militaries, and (for the last few decades) the terrorist organizations. If this be so, then formulation of foreign policy in relation to India would be equally complex and critical at the same time.

Addressing the second question pertaining to the basis of foreign policy we need to know who we are (as a nation). Once we are clear about 'who we are' it is easy to answer, 'what we want' (from the foreign policy). At times it is also possible to answer the 'who-we-are' from, 'what-we-want'. The former American Secretary of Defence, Harold Brown, for example, includes the maintenance of

22 https://www.thehindubusinessline.com/opinion/how-to-fire-up-defence-production/article24211990.ece (Accessed 10 September 2019).

23 https://economictimes.indiatimes.com/news/defence/indias-defence-exports-more-than-double/articleshow/69835284.cms?from=mdr 4 Sep 2019 (accessed 10 September 2019).

'economic relations with the rest of the world on reasonable terms' in his conception of national security in the context of international relations.

In view of the above discussion, foreign policy (and hence international relations) needs to be closely linked with the overall strategy a nation follows. We have seen earlier that post-independent India did not have a very clear strategy of national security, economic growth, and even political activities. Consequently, we kept struggling with frequent crises trying to solve the same problem over and over again. We have had a reasonably detailed activities scan pertaining to political decision making and economic policies. A brief review of India's foreign policy in the context of strengthening national security will be in order.

Bulk of the literature—emanating from the writings of former foreign service bureaucrats and some Indian academicians—start the journey from August 1947. Hence non-alignment policy, enunciated by India's first Prime Minister Jawaharlal Nehru, governed the approach to our international relations. It is termed as moralistic or keeping equidistance from the two power centres – the US and erstwhile USSR (Indian foreign policy[24] and contemporary security challenges, Rohan Mukherjee). It does elaborate the period of idealism (1950s-60s), intermittent realism (70s-80s) and dawn of pragmatism (post 1990s). The approaches are also linked with India's national as well as regional security. However, the question as to 'who we are as a nation', remains unanswered. The paper also does not link up the outcomes from the foreign policy in the context of goals that were set—if at all any goals were set to be achieved by following any given foreign policy. In the Gateway House publication, 15 August 2016, *A Brief History of India's Foreign Policy*,[25] a similar

24 https://www.researchgate.net/publication/227734908_Indian_foreign_policy_and_contemporary_security_challenges (January 2011)

25 https://www.gatewayhouse.in/wp-content/uploads/2016/08/GH_History-of-Indias-Foreign-Policy.pdf (Accessed 10 September 2019)

approach is followed where India's foreign policy keeps shifting with time, with changing regional and global environment, in tune with the economic growth and regional security challenges (1948, 1962, 1965, 1971, and so on). Again the core of the foreign policy is missing in this paper since there was no core. The foreign policy of the world's most populous democracy floated on events. In a VIF publication, *India's Foreign Policy and National Security*, edited by CD Sahay, he has been more explicit in addressing the question 'why this policy'. He also linked it more directly to national security or the strategic approach to national security.[26] Quoting a Rand corporation report on the subject he says, 'India thinks defensively due to the geography and cultural belief systems, so India never had a strategic culture.' There is also the argument that India's scriptures prescribe Dharmayuddha, the ethics of war, so today's India is unable to master the war game.

A more extensive reference to India's core ideology in the context of foreign policy comes from an unlikely source—Henry Kissinger in his book, *World Order*—which we have quoted in the introduction to this book. It is very interesting to note Kissinger's insight into the 'essence' of India based specifically on Bhagwat Gita and Kautilya's Arthashastra. Some of his observations can be very valuable in discovering our core and formulating our vision both for foreign policy and nation building. As per his observations, the diversity of India defies definition. India's history traces man's continuous quest for reality. When India existed in a united form (much bigger than the current size)—from fourth to second centuries BC and fourth to seventh centuries AD, she generated vast cultural influence sans any invasion or violence. It spread to Myanmar (Burma), China, Indonesia, Sri Lanka (Ceylon), Thailand, and beyond. Even when

26 https://www.vifindia.org/book/2018/november/19/indias-foreign-policy-and-national-security-strategy (Accessed 12 September 2019).

conquered militarily by several tribes and invaders, India transcended the foreigners, treating their supreme ambition with equanimity—without fear, anger or hatred. The essence of India's spiritual pursuit and quest for the infinite continued unabated. Quoting from Bhagwat Gita, Kissinger identified the Indian faith in the fact that outward manifestations are illusory. These emanate from reality which is timeless and devoid of any differentiating manifestation. Thus establishing the oneness of the cosmic existence—not only of the humans or the living —but all that can be seen or felt and also that which cannot be seen and felt. Hence, in Bhagwat Gita, Lord Krishna urges the warrior prince Arjun to fight—as part of his duty or dharma—with equanimity (devoid of fear, excitement, and expectations for the outcome).

Kissinger also quotes Kautilya who postulated the theories of statecraft including foreign policy principles two thousand years before Clausewitz and Machiavelli. Thus as per Kissinger, Kautilya had envisaged the theories of balance of power—through the 'circle of states'—much before the Europeans translated these facts into theories. Kissinger found more ruthless competition in Arthashastra but all this ruthlessness was directed to uphold dharma.

Coming to the modern times post 1947—Kissinger found that Nehru decided to formulate Indian foreign policy which should be most advantageous to India. 'Whatever policy you may lay down, the art of conducting foreign affairs of a country lies in finding out what is most advantageous to the country.' This is how Kissinger quotes Nehru just after independence (pp 201 *World Order: The Multiplicity of Asia*).

Did we have foreign policy which helped our interests as a nation? Do we have one today? What are the basis of our foreign policy? Answers to these questions—based on the outcomes and even explicit admission by the people who are expected to know—are not very encouraging. We lacked the core and hence a clear vision and hence kept on blundering from one crisis to another learning the same lessons again. If we wish to develop a core ideology for our foreign policy then Kissinger's analysis appears an apt starting point; it is ironic but bulk of writings by our foreign policy experts ignore the question, 'who we are'. This question has been answered by Kissinger in the context of international relations.

Some of the tenets emerging from the above discussion, which can form part of our core ideology in foreign policy are as under:-

- 'Who we are?' can only be discovered if we go back to our actual history dating back thousands of years. It comes out from the epics and hymns well known in the folklore of India.
- Our intrinsic values transcend temporal manifestation and are very powerful to influence humanity across countries and continents without using any coercion.
- India's propensity for peace does not translate itself into passivism, timidity, and shunning violence at any cost. Our value systems very clearly advocate fighting a war—if necessary in the national interest—without fear, with resolute determination, and with full preparation.
- Our international relations draw strength from our economic might, military power, and wellbeing of citizens through good governance and selfless leadership.
- Our geographical location, history, and neighbourhood clearly extend our forward defences much beyond the geographical borders. In this context, domination of the sea routes, relations with littoral countries along the major routes, and expansionist activities of established adversaries become critical factors.
- In the context of IW, the global information environment connects the countries through multiple levels and with large basket of interests at each level. Hence we need to be constantly alert to safeguard our interests at each level. No country can afford to remain isolated from the international network.

- The global information environment also provides an effective tool for perception management in the international mindspace.

Objectives of IW through International Relations

- Isolate the adversary in international community. Ideal examples of isolation are Iran at present (2019), Pakistan since 2015, Iraq just before the First Gulf War. For a nation isolated in the international community, it becomes extremely difficult to survive for long. Her economy, psychological robustness of the citizens, cyberspace, and geographical integrity become vulnerable.
- Use political and economic leverage to run down the target nation in projecting her views to the international community.
- Gain trade related advantages.
- Create alliances for economic and security-related aspects.

Means used for exploiting International Relations in IW

- Military power.
- Cyber Power.
- Technological prowess.
- Economic Strength.
- Ideological and cultural similarities.
- Remaining in synch with the modern global environment.

If we consider the 1991 Iraq War as the First Information War, then it is impossible to miss the perfect international support and approval garnered by the US for the coalition forces. On the contrary Iraq was completely isolated. Even the Arab nations—for whom Iraq had jettisoned American support during the Arab-Israel conflicts—did not support their Arab brethren.

International Relations for IW

The lesson for us is that in our current and future struggle we need to form and sustain meaningful trustworthy alliances—the way we did in 1971 and also during the Kargil conflict of 1999. Besides, international relations will help in following spheres of IW-related activities:

- Countering cyber threats.
- Indigenization of weapons and embedded systems.
- Economic growth.
- Resilience against global economic downturns through balanced trade alliance (meeting our energy requirements, maintaining exports and FDI inflows).

How India has been able to isolate Pakistan in the global community that matters, is an ideal example of preparing the stage for an IW conflict where we can win without fighting. However, there is a word of caution. International communities side with the efficient and the strong. Weak and indecisive nations get exploited by the powerful international community. We did experience this in 1962 when our humiliating defeat (due to our own inefficiency and poor leadership) made us subject of international ridicule. In the 1965 war with Pakistan the international community was firmly on Pakistani side. Fortunately for us Pakistan failed to capitalize on that support. Hence first step towards ensuring strong and meaningful international relations is to become an economically and militarily strong nation.

★★★

Appendix A

An Academic Brief on Leadership

We find some interesting aspects while trying to develop an academic and perceptive framework on leadership. Consider Maharana Pratap, Queen of Jhansi, Lakshmi Bai, Siraj ud-Daulah, Subhash Chandra Bose. Then ask two questions. First 'what is the factor common to all these famous personalities from the Indian history?' Most likely the answers will range from great leaders, inspiring figures, pride of the nation, and so on. Now tell yourselves that all these personalities from the Indian past lost major wars in their lives. They are not victorious generals of the past. Now, check again whether you still consider them as great leaders. Chances are you will stick to your earlier perception.

An important deduction is that leadership is not only about the destination or the goal, it is as much about the journey or the process. Failure to achieve the goal does not take away the excellence of leadership. In fact, no leader howsoever great can guarantee victory. But belief in self and the team coupled with single-minded selfless pursuit of the common good creates the magnetism and the resultant faith in the leader.

To explain the above phenomena following theory can be considered. A leader's impact on the people she/he leads is based on four parts of his persona. Firstly, her/his basic character or being; secondly, leader's deeds; thirdly, what the leader sees in a situation or a leader's perception of the situation. Lastly, what the leader tells the team. The impact of these four parts is in decreasing order. Thus 'to be' the first part related to the inherent persona and character of the leader is the most potent dimension of leadership. 'To do' which means her/his actions come the next. 'To see' which depicts leader's perception of a given situation is the third aspect. Does he see opportunity and hope for his people or he sees opportunity for self or despondency. The last and the least important aspect of leadership is what the leader tells. 'To tell' or the speeches a leader makes are irrelevant if the other parts are hollow. Many great leaders in history across the globe were not outstanding speakers. Infact, Lincoln, Gandhi, and even Mandela were not known for making very impressive speeches. But what they spoke went straight to the hearts of their audience. Each word they spoke transformed and mesmerized their countrymen. This does not mean that great orators cannot be great leaders. The oratory skill in itself is no indication of a great leader.

As per the ancient Indian philosopher and statesman Kautilya, a leader must be free of lust, anger, greed, conceit, arrogance, and foolhardiness. As regards using cognitive abilities, Kautilya maintained that learning imparts discipline to only those who have mental faculties of—obedience to teacher, and desire and ability to learn. The leader should then have capacity to retain and understand what is learnt. When understanding is complete the leader will be able to reflect on it and then develop the ability to make inferences by deliberating on the knowledge acquired. Such a capability will remove bias and tendency to template. Leaders cannot be 'theory blind'.

The Chinese philosopher, Lao Tzu makes very important observations—with deep meaning—on leadership. He says that 'the key to good leadership is to facilitate others to accomplish their task not through coercion but via more subtle process of interpersonal influence. A leader is best, when people barely know he exists, not so good when people obey and acclaim him, worse when they despise him.' As per him, a good leader is one—who talks little; when his work is done, his aim fulfilled, they (his followers) will say, 'we did it ourselves'.

Harvard Business Review Publication of 1977 brings out Leadership and Management based on articulation, communication of clear vision, creating a sense of urgency to achieve the goals emanating from the vision, institutionalizing an approach or road map, removing constraints and obstacles, creating a culture of collaboration and cooperation to meet the challenges of rapid changes in the external environment.

Another—and more modern—approach to leadership enunciated by the Harvard academic circles is the five levels of leadership. In this the highest level, level five leadership focuses on enduring excellence of the nation or the organization. These leaders think beyond their self-interests and beyond a short-time horizon. Level five leaders set the path for many decades if not centuries of excellence of their nations. They are extremely humble and have steely determination to pursue their goal once they are convinced of the path. Just below level five are the level four leaders who are effective, competent, have good organizational skills, and stimulate the group to achieve high standards. What separates the level four from level five is the degree of selflessness and character. Where level five leaders inspire many generations ahead of themselves without promoting their own interests, level four leaders are self-centred and lack long-term vision. The rest of the levels of leadership pertain to competent manager, contributing team member, and capable individual.

Somewhat similar to the level five leadership is the concept of Transformational Leadership. With their charisma, idealized influence, inspirational motivation, intellectual stimulation, and individualized consideration, they bring out the best from the people. Generally, leaders establish a system of reward and penalty in relation to a single goal. These are transactional leaders. The transformational leaders on the other hand build up unique capabilities in individuals so that they achieve spectacular gains by themselves. Transformational leaders believe that each individual is a winner in her/his unique field. The leader in this case has four basic functions:-

- As a strategist, the leader has a clear vision (strategic thinker); functions in well-defined goals, objectives (structured deliverer); and has the functional accesses (tactical specialist).
- As an achiever, the leader inspires the team with the overall vision, displays resilience in execution, and is proactive in engaging with the environment.
- As an engager the transformational leadership model is based on support to the team, empowering the team with training and development, and using the charisma for relevant networking.
- With regard to facilitating the functions, the leader excels in collaboration, championing the altruistic courses and activities, and presenting a role model with his actions.

Eastern and Western Philosophies of Leadership

The Indian and the Chinese thoughts on leadership are based on the edifice of character of a different kind. It is not based on physical and moral courage but goes deeper at a level that transcends to metaphysical and at times spiritual levels. Thus freedom from lust, greed, anger as observed by Kautilya and leading while remaining invisible and allowing the team to think that they have done the task themselves, require an altogether different level of character which is more easily understood in the East. There is an element of mystique and spirituality associated with 'character' of a leader in the Indian context. Thus equanimity, focus on Karma (duty) and not on the rewards from Karma, pursuing for excellence in each endeavour, and remaining detached are some of the Indian values associated with the character of great leaders and kings.

The Western concept of character is more worldly and objective oriented. Character is derived from the Greek word 'arête' meaning virtue. This virtue is linked with not lying, cheating, stealing and other immoral behaviour. Character in the Western philosophies does not talk about detached pursuit of excellence without concern about the outcome. The Western thoughts on leadership as discussed in Harvard Business Review appear to be based on skills, knowledge, and attitude. However, as the leaders gain the capability of transforming their command or when they climb the ladder from level one to level five, there appears to be some semblance between the Eastern and the Western concepts of leadership. The military leaders of the West also emphasise strength of character in leadership.

Political Leadership: Desired Rubric

Based on the earlier discussion on the Eastern and Western thoughts on leadership and the peculiar environment of information age or the tenets of knowledge society, we may try to develop a rubric for benchmarking the top political leadership:-

- Since the political leadership—especially in a democracy like India—represents the people in the country, it should have unwavering faith in the roots of the nation. There cannot be any ambiguity on the historical legacy and proven capability of the people. India has been a global leader and the entire world used to seek knowledge and enlightenment from India in the not too distant past. We should not feel shy of our achievements some three centuries ago. Our history did not start from 1947 or even from 1600. The nation is much older than these timelines. The core ideology of the nation must be drawn from these roots. Vision, mission, and approach path follow.
- The leaders must have proven strength of character as

understood in the popular belief of the people. Given our ancestral belief system, the strength of character hinges on absence of lust and desire, absence of conceit and fear. The leaders should be selfless and always be concerned for the people and the nation.

- Political leadership must focus on enabling and empowering as against doling out favours, freebies, quotas, and controlling the distribution. They must emphasise on transforming the society through inspirational ecosystem, motivational leadership, strategic thinking, and creating an environment of rewarding achievers rather than supporting inefficiencies.
- The top leaders must be able to learn from the outcomes of their strategic approach and make bold course corrections. Once their approach has been proved wrong, they must show wisdom and flexibility to change the course.
- Keeping in view our immense diversity, the leaders must have tremendous influence to harmonise and create a collaborating society.
- Lastly, the leaders must combine humility with unwavering resolve to follow the correct path. Too many compromises for too long for whatsoever reasons are always counter-productive.

Essential Capabilities in Individuals in a Knowledge-driven Organization

Based on this peculiar environment of information age or the tenets of knowledge society, we may try to develop a rubric which captures the different levels of essentials among the people in a military organization. Essentially there are five segments in the rubric. These include learnability, creativity, collaborative skills, character, and leadership capabilities. Each of these can be defined as basic, advance, and maximum. We suggest the following gradation:-

- Learnability.
    - Basic: Capable of acquiring desired knowledge and skills under sustained and intensely monitored training environment.
    - Advance: Capable of upgrading own capability using online resources with periodic intervention by the trainers/educator.
    - Maximum: Identifies new skills and knowledge in the context of own role and trains herself/himself using appropriate online resources and experiential learning.
- Creativity.
    - Basic: Displays ingenuity, resourcefulness, and innovativeness in accomplishing the given task.
    - Advance: Offers original and workable ideas for transforming a process, product, or organization.
    - Max: Capable of visualizing the future vividly and accurately offers solutions to meet the future challenges.
- Collaboration.
    - Basic: Shares information within the team without undue emphasis to take individual credit.
    - Advance: Always willing to share ideas and information within larger organization for the overall excellence of the organization without any special efforts to claim credit.
    - Max: Consistent focus on excellence in process, product, and organization across different organizations and willing to apportion the credit to others.
- Character.
    - Basic: Fairly honest with integrity and loyalty to the immediate organisation
    - Advance: Devoid of greed, selfishness, self-aggrandisement. Always works for the organization. Has moral courage to speak her/his mind without fear

of adverse comment or career interest.
  - Max: Complete absence of lust, greed, conceit, arrogance, foolhardiness. Maintains balance and equanimity in success and failure.
- Leadership.
  - Basic: Competent in accomplishing own task and leading a small team in short-term definite task.
  - Advance: Competent to work through uncertainty, define own task in a given environment. Can effectively lead a large organization to achieve set goals during the next two to three years.
  - Maximum: Creates an empowered and self-sustaining organization with a culture of continued excellence much after the leader has left the organization. Such leaders set the tone for the next twenty to thirty years.

The Rubric is tabulated below:-

Learnability Max	Creativity Max	Collaboration Max	Character Max	Leadership Max
Learnability Advance	Creativity Advance	Collaboration Advance	Character Advance	Leadership Advance
Learnability Basic	Creativity Basic	Collaboration Basic	Character Basic	Leadership Basic

Appendix B

Russian Intervention in American Presidential Elections in 2016

Russian Cyber Operations in American Elections 2016. (Report prepared by CIA, FBI and the NSA)

'Russian efforts to influence the 2016 US presidential election represent the most recent expression of Moscow's longstanding desire to undermine the US-led liberal democratic order, but these activities demonstrated a significant escalation in directness, level of activity, and scope of effort compared to previous operations.'

Russian President, Vladimir Putin ordered an influence campaign in 2016 aimed at the US presidential election. Russia's goals were to undermine public faith in the US democratic process, denigrate Secretary Clinton, and harm her electability and potential presidency. We further assess that Putin and the Russian Government developed a clear preference for President-elect Trump.

- Putin and the Russian Government aspired to help President-elect Trump's election chances when possible by discrediting Secretary Clinton and publicly contrasting her unfavourably to him. All three agencies agree with this judgment. CIA and FBI have high confidence in this judgment; NSA has moderate confidence.

- Moscow's approach evolved over the course of the campaign based on Russia's understanding of the electoral prospects of the two main candidates. When it appeared to Moscow that Secretary Clinton was likely to win the election, the Russian influence campaign began to focus more on undermining her future presidency.
- Moscow's influence campaign followed a Russian messaging strategy that blends covert intelligence operations—such as cyber activity—with overt efforts by Russian Government agencies, state-funded media, third-party intermediaries, and paid social media users or 'trolls'. Russia, like its Soviet predecessor, has a history of conducting covert influence campaigns, focused on US presidential elections, that have used intelligence officers and agents and press placements to disparage candidates perceived as hostile to the Kremlin.
- Russia's intelligence services conducted cyber operations against targets associated with the 2016 US presidential election, including targets associated with both major US political parties.
- Russian military intelligence (General Staff Main Intelligence Directorate or GRU) used the Guccifer 2.0 persona and DCLeaks.com to release US victim data obtained in cyber operations publicly and in exclusives to media outlets and relayed material to WikiLeaks.
- Russian intelligence obtained and maintained access to elements of multiple US state or local electoral boards. Department of Homeland Security (DHS) assesses that the types of systems Russian actors targeted or compromised were not involved in vote tallying.
- Russia's state-run propaganda machine contributed to the

influence campaign by serving as a platform for Kremlin messaging to Russian and international audiences. Moscow will apply lessons learnt from its Putin-ordered campaign aimed at the US presidential election to future influence efforts worldwide, including against US allies and their election processes.

***

Appendix C

India's Core Values and the Constitution

Subhash C Kashyap in his book, *Our Constitution: An Introduction to India's Constitution and Constitutional Law* says:

- The founding fathers made it very clear that they are not writing on a clean slate…they would build on the existing structure and experience of institutions already established.
- Nearly 75 percent of the Constitution can be said to be a reproduction of the Government of India Act of 1935 with suitable adaption and modifications. The question is who was governing India in 1935.
- The concepts of Directive Principles were borrowed from Irish Constitution.
- The Bill of Rights enshrined in the US Constitution could be said to have inspired our Fundamental Rights.
- The Canadian Constitution inter alia influenced the federal structure.

- Parliamentary system with ministerial responsibilities came from the British Constitution.
- Parliamentary privileges came from the Australian Constitution.
- Emergency provisions were borrowed from the Constitution of the German Reich.

It is very difficult to fathom that any of our core values are similar to the value systems of the countries mentioned above. If we go through the speeches of various leaders in the constituent assembly, the emotions will not be very flattering.

In the context of IW, the constitution is irrelevant since it does not talk about any national security, vision, or policy. The Joint Doctrine of Indian Armed Forces 2017 admits, 'Even though we have no formally articulated National Security Policy and Strategy, it does not imply that they do not exist or are not sufficiently understood.' This appears to be a very tall claim. The doctrine further identifies the core values from the preamble of the Constitution: 'Our core National values are best reflected in the Preamble of our Constitution, which are; sovereignty, socialism, secularism, democracy, republican character, justice, liberty, equality, fraternity, human dignity, unity and integrity of our Nation, respect for our diversity, peaceful co-existence, pluralism, tolerance and international peace defined by a just international order.' Incidentally 'socialism' was added to the preamble in the forty-second amendment in 1976. It has not been defined in the constitution. The founding fathers did not want this term to be included. They found that this would restrict the governance of the country. Many of the terms listed above do not qualify to be the core values. While a large number of these core values have remained empty words. Our actions over the past decades do not reflect these values. In our country justice is inordinately delayed and hence denied. We have a collegium system of nominating top judges—the only of its kind in the world. At one time two houses of the parliament ruled its abolition with the required majority. The 'collegium' turned it down! Human dignity as reflected in human development index of the World Economic Forum is almost neglected. Most importantly in the context of decision making, so critical in IW, none of these core values help. The core values from the Constitution as listed in the doctrine are not supported by the way our political leadership has taken decisions over the last several decades. Neither do the outcomes of those decisions measure up to what was expected to be achieved by us in light of these core values.

***

Endnotes

Introduction and relevance of issues discussed

Collins Jim, *Built to Last*, Random House Business Books, 2005, ISBN 97818844135844

Collins Jim, *Good to Great,* Random House Business Books, 2001, ISBN 9780712676090

HBR's 10 Must Reads, *On Leadership*, Harvard Business Review Press, 2011, ISBN9781422157978

Hamel Gary, Prahalad CK, *Competing for the Future*, McGraw Hill Education (India) Private Limited, 1994, ISBN9780070486719

HBR'S 10 Must Reads, *On Managing People,* Harvard Business Review Press, 2011, ISBN 9781422158012

Kissinger Henry, *World Order,* Penguin Books, Published at 375 Hudson Street New York in 2015, ISBN 978-1-59420-614-6,

Evolution of IW Through an American Experience

Campen D Alan, '*The First Information War,* Bookmart Publishers (New Delhi) in Arrangement with Armed Forces Communications & Electronic 1992, Association Press USA, ISBN 81-87583-00-2

Sullivan Gordon R and Col James M Dubik, *War in the Information Age,* Strategic Studies Institute (US) 6 June 1994

Sullivan Gordon R and Lt Col Anthony M Corolles, *The Army in the Information Age,* Strategic Studies Institute (US) 31 March 1995

Owens A William US Navy, *The Emerging System of Systems,* Military Review 1995

Tonny Brems Knudsen and Carsten Bagge Laustsen (Editors), *Kosovo Between War and Peace: Nationalism, Peacebuilding and International Trusteeship*, Routledge Taylor and Francis Group 2006 ISBN 10: O-714-65598-8

Latawski Paul and Smith Martin A, *The Kosovo Crisis and the Evolution of Post-Cold War European Security*, Manchester University Press New York 2003 ISBN719059801

Wallace C Arnold (US Army), Manprint: Battle Command and Digitization, Military Review, May-June 1995

Gordon R Sullivan (US Army), Future Vision, Military Review, May-June 1999

Toffler Alvin and Toffler Heidi, *War and Anti-War: Survival at the Dawn of the 21st Century*, Little Brown and Company 1994

Gary Hamel, C K Prahalad, *Competing for the Future*, McGraw Hill Education Private Limited 2014, ISBN 9780040486713

Terri Terriff, 'The Past as Future: The US Army's Vision of Warfare in 21st Century' The Journal of Military and Strategic Studies, Volume 15, Issue 3, 2014

Denning Dorothy E, *Information Warfare and Security*, Georgetown University, ACM Press, (1999) ISBN 981-235-948—6

Judah Tim, Kosovo, *War and Revenge*, Yale University Press, New Haven 2000, ISBN O-300-08313-0

Building up and Operationalization Post Iraq Wars

Libicki Martin C, *What is Information Warfare?* Center for Advanced Concepts and Technology. Institute for National Strategic Studies. National Defence University. August 1995

Kahneman Daniel, *Thinking, Fast and Slow*, Penguin Random House 2011

Barnaby Frank, *The Automated Battlefield*, London Sidgwick and Jackson 1986.

Bruce W. Watson, Bruce George, Peter Tsouras, B. L. Cyr, *Military Lessons of Gulf War*, Published by Book Club Associates 1991.

Waltz Edward, *Information Warfare Principles and Operations*, Artech House, Boston, London 1998.

Mohammad Mahmoud, *A Theory of ISIS: Political Violence and Transformation of Global Order*, Pluto Press 2018 ISBN 9780745399096 (Stanford DTP)

Rasheed Adil (Dr), *ISIS: Race to Armageddon,* Vij Books India Private Limited, New Delhi 2015, ISBN 978-93-84464-77-6

Impact on China, Russia, Israel, Pakistan

Russian involvement in the US elections of 2016 (http://www.dni.gov/files/documents/ica_2017_pdf (Accessed 10 March 2019)

Gideon Avidor and Russell Fuller, *Information and Warfare: The Israeli Case* https://pdfs.semanticscholar.org/e7b1/8125b65c011d218027697a71181a4f02288a.pdf-2016 (Accessed 10 March 2019)

The 'Seventh Stage' Of Terrorism in China – Combating Terrorism... https://ctc.usma.edu/the-seventh-stage-of-terrorism-in-china/ (Accessed 10 March 2019)

'The Bajwa Doctrine: The Pakistani Military Has Done More than Enough,' Kamal Alam

Mansoor Ahmed, *Security Doctrines, Technologies and Escalation Ladders: A Pakistani Perspective*

Understanding information warfare and its relevance to Pakistan, www.issi.org.pk/wp-content/uploads/2014/06/1379480610_58047454.pdf (Accessed 10 March 2019)

Pakistan | Journal of Information Warfare https://www.jinfowar.com/tags/pakistan

Syed M Amir Husain, Pakistan needs an Information Warfare capability http://www.defencejournal.com/july98/pakneeds1.htm

Israel's National Security Towards the 21st Century https://books.google.co.in/books?isbn=1135280215 (Accessed 10 March 2019)

How Serious Is the Islamic State Threat to China? | The Diplomat https://thediplomat.com/2017/03/how-serious-is-the-islamic-state-threat-to-china/ (Accessed 12 March 2019)

The Geopolitics of Israel: Biblical and Modern. http://worldview.stratfor.com/article/geopolitics-Isreal-biblical-and-modern. (Accessed 12 March 2019)

South Asian Geopolitics Has Pakistan Lost its Plot? https://idsa.in/.../jds_11_4_2017_south-asian-geopolitics-has-pakistan-lost-its-plot. pdf
www.rand.org?content/dam/rand/pub/conf_proceedings J Mulvenon. (Accessed 12 March 2019)

Analysis of Epistemology

Toffler Alvin and Toffler Heidi, *War and Anti-War: Survival at the Dawn of the 21st Century*, Little Brown and Company 1994

Ventre Daniel, *Information Warfare*, ISTE Wiley 2016, ISBN 978-1-84821-660-0

Khanduri Chandra B, *Kautilya – On War: The Military Wisdom of Arthasastra*, Greenfields Publishers 2013, ISBN 978-93-81089-125

Murray Williamson and Major General Scales Robert H, '*The Iraq*

War: A Military History' The Belknap Press: An Imprint of Harvard University Press 2003 ISBN 0-674-01280 United States Armed Forces History 20th Century

Sharma R N and Sharma Y K, *Gulf War II* 2003, Shubhi Publication, ISBN 81-87226-85-4

Campen D Alan, *The First Information War,* Bookmart Publishers (New Delhi) in Arrangement with Armed Forces Communications & Electronic 1992, Association Press USA, ISBN 81-87583-00-2

Sun Tzu, *The Art of War*, translated from Chinese by Lionel Giles, MA (1910) Published in 2000, Allande Online Publishing, 2 Park House, 21st St Leonard Rd, ISBN 1 903328-03-09 (Accessed 12 March 2019) https://sites.ualberta.ca/~enoch/Readings/The_Art_Of_War.pdf

Comparison with 1st and 2nd wave wars

Rangarajan L N, *Kautilya: The Arthashastra,* Penguin Books New Delhi, 1990, ISBN 9780140446036

Shamasastry R, *Kautilya's Arthasastra,* Fifth Edition 1956, Raghubir Printing Press, Mysore, India

Kangle RP, *The Kautilya Arthasastra,* Part 2, Published by Motilal Banarsidass, New Delhi, 1972, ISBN 81-208-0040-0

Gautam Pradeep Kumar, Mishra Saurabh, Gupta Arvind *Indigenous Historical Knowledge: Kautilya and His Vocabulary*, IDSA, Pentagon Press, New Delhi, 2016, ISBN 978-81-8274-909-2

Khanduri Chandra B, *Kautilya – On War: The Military Wisdom of Arthasastra*, Greenfields Publishers 2013, ISBN 978-93-81089-125

Sun Tzu, *The Art of War*, translated from Chinese by Lionel Giles, MA (1910) Published in 2000 Allande Online Publishing, 2 Park House, 21st St Leonard Rd, ISBN 1 903328-03-09 (Accessed 12 March 2019) https://sites.ualberta.ca/~enoch/Readings/The_Art_Of_War.pdf

Griffith Samuel B, Sun Tzu, *The Art of War,* Clarendon Press: Oxford University Press 1963

Clausewitz Carl Von, *On War*, Browntone Books, March 2009, ISBN 9781434404961

Hart Liddell B, *Thoughts on War* (1943) Faber and Faber Ltd, 24 Russel Square, London

Comparison with the theories of CNP

http://www.indiandefencereview.com/news/as-india-consolidates-its-comprehensive-power/ (Accessed 2 April 2019)

Comprehensive National Power | ORF https://www.orfonline.org/research/comprehensive-national-power/ Manoj Joshi (Accessed 2 April 2019)

RANKED: The 25 most powerful nations on earth, https://www.businessinsider.in/RANKED-The-25-most-powerful-nations-on-earth/articleshow/64894895.cms (Accessed 2 April 2019)

AI, Communication and Big Data

Stuart Russell, Norvig Peter, *Artificial Intelligence: A Modern Approach*, Pearson, 9th Reprint (2003) ISBN 978-81-7758-367-0

Nilson Nils J, *Principles of Artificial Intelligence*, Tenth Reprint (2002), Narosa Publishing House ISBN 81-85198-29-2

Wooldridge Michael, *An Introduction to MultiAgent Systems*, John Wiley &Sons Ltd, 2009, ISBN 9780407519462

Laudon Kenneth C, Carol Guercio Traver, *E Commerce*, Pearson Education 2003 ISBN 81-297-0112-X

Ravindran, Phillips, Solberg, *Operations Research Principles and Practice*

Tanenbaum Andrew S, *Computer Networks,* Fourth Edition (2006) Pearson Education

Big Data: Understanding Big Data https://www.researchgate.net/publication/291229189_Big_Data_Understanding_Big_Data Kevin Taylor Sakyi, Aston University January 2016 (Accessed 15 April 2019)

Introduction to Big Data Xiaomeng Su, Institutt for informatikk og e-læring ved NTNU Learning material is developed for course IINI3012 Big Data

https://www.ntnu.no/iie/fag/big/lessons/lesson2.pdf (Accessed 15 April 2019)

Kothari C R, *Research Methodology: Methods and Techniques*, Second Edition, New Age International Publishers 2009, ISBN (13) 978-81-224-1522-3

Richard I Levin, David S Rubin, *Statistics for Management*, Seventh Edition 1997 Prentice Hall India ISBN 9788120312357

ICT Adaption

http://idea-space.eu:19001/up/319cc877736053b53fe46efc79a29be6.pdf Case study Zara. (Accessed 15 April 2019)

Dell Direct http://web.mit.edu/course/15/15.823/attach/Dell%20CASE.pdf http://citeseerx.ist.psu.edu/viewdoc/download?doi=10.1.1.86.3069&rep=rep1&type=pdf (Accessed 15 April 2019)

Li Fung
https://commons.clarku.edu/cgi/viewcontent.cgi?article=1030&context=mosakowski institute (Accessed 15 April 2019)

Tanenbaum Andrew S, *Computer Networks*, Eastern, Economy Edition, 1999.

G Winfield Treese & Lawrence Stewart C, *Designing Systems for Internet Commerce*, Low Priced Edition 1999

Glossary of Computer Security Terms NCSC-TG-404, nsa (Aqua Book) version 1, 1988.

CISCO IOS Network Security Techmedia, New Delhi, 1999

Pathak Ashok, 'Optimizing India's Defence Expenditure' VIF Brief 12 December 2018.

Chase Richard B, Shankar Ravi, Jacobs F Roberts, *Operations and Supply Chain Management*, McGraw Hill 2017 ISBN 13: 978-93-392-0410-5

Kubiak TM, Benbow Donald W, *The Certified Six Sigma Black Belt Handbook*, Pearson 2016 ISBN 978-81-371-2869-7

IW Defence

(Indian Express 23 August 18 quoting National Security Secretariat Report http://indianexpress.com.) (Accessed 5 May 2019)

Rid Thomas, *Cyber War Will Not Take Place*, C Hurst & Co Publishers 2013, ISBN: 978-1-84904-280-2

Clarke A Richard and Knake Robert K, *Cyber Warfare: The Next Threat to National Security and What to do About it,* Harper Collins Publishers, 10 East 53rd Street New York 10022, First Edition 2010 ISBN 978-0-06-196223-3

James A Green (Editor) *Cyber Warfare: A Multidisciplinary Analysis*, Routledge Taylor & Francis Group (2015) ISBN 978-1-138-79307-1

Institute of Defence Studies and Analysis (IDSA)Task Force Report March 2012, 'India's Cyber Security Challenge'

Rajiv Gupta (Home Secretary), while speaking at FICCI on 'Smart Policing Partnership with Corporate and Academia' (www.indiatoday.in 31 May 2018)

Cyber Deterrence

Dr VK Saraswat of NITI Aayog while briefing at the 'cyber security conclave' in Vigyan Bhawan on 29 October 2018, (https://niti.gov.in/writereaddata/files/document_publication/CyberSecurityConclaveAtVigyanBhavanDelhi_1.pdf) Cyber Security Innovations and Challenges 29 October 2018.

IDSA monograph series 55 of November 2016, 'The Social Media Challenge to National Security: Impact and Opportunities. A Conceptual Overview' by Shruti Pandalai ISBN 978-93-82-169-68-0. https://idsa.in/monograph/social-media-challenge-to-national-security

Fifth Generation Wireless Technology (5G) and its Impact on IW

Jan-Peter Kleinhans, *5G Vs National Security: A European Perspective* Feb 2019

Milo Medin and Gilman Louie, *The 5G Ecosystem: Risks &Opportunities* for DoD. Defence Innovation Board, 3 April 2019

The National Security Challenges of Fifth Generation (5G) Wireless Communications: Winning the Race to 5G, Securely, Intelligence and National Security Alliance, Cyber Council, June 2019.

Economics Times 27 Feb 2019. https://economictimes.indiatimes.com/tech/hardware/signalchip-launches-indias-first-indigenous-semiconductor-chips-for-4g-lte-5g-nrmodems/articleshow/68185877.cms (Accessed 5 August 2019)

http://www.pib.nic.in/Pressreleaseshare.aspx?PRID=1566475 Press Information Bureau Government of India Ministry of Communication 27 Feb 2019 (Accessed 5 August 2019).

National Digital Communication Policy 2018 http://dot.gov.in/sites/default/files/Final%20NDCP-2018.pdf?download=1(Accessed 5 August 2019)

Current IW Theories and Impact on India

Relia Sanjeev (Col-Corps of Signals), *Cyber Warfare: Its Implications on National Security*, Vij Books India Private Limited (2015). ISBN 978-93-84464-82-0

Mishra RC, *Information Warfare and Cyber Security*, Author's Press (2003). ISBN 81-7273-143-4

Sharma MK (Wing Commander), *Cyber Warfare: The Power of the Unseen*, World (2012) Centre for Air Power Studies

http://www.files.ethz.ch/isn/157030/India Indian Army Doctrine Issued by Headquarters (HQ) Army Training Command (ARTRAC) October 2004. (Accessed 5 August 2019)

http://www.ids.nic.in/dot/

JointDoctrineIndianArmedForces2017pdf Joint Doctrine Indian Armed Forces Issued by HQ, Integrated Defence Staff of the Ministry of Defence April 2017 (Accessed 5 August 2019)

Katoch PC and Datta Saikat, *India's Special Forces: History and Future of Special Forces*, Vij Books India Private Limited New Delhi 2013, ISBN 978-93-82573-97-5

From Surprise to Reckoning: The Kargil Review Committee Report, Sage Publications Private Limited, New Delhi April 2000 ISBN 0-7619-9466-1

Some of India's Major Military Conflicts through the Prism of IW Theories

Pathak Ashok, 'India's Geopolitical Posturing and Conflict Termination' 24 September 2018 https://www.vifindia.org/article/2018/september/24/indias-geopolitical-posturing-and-conflict-termination

https://frontline.thehindu.com/static/html/fl1618/16180330.htm 'Army caught napping', Frontline – The Hindu, Volume 16 Aug-Sep 1999 (Accessed 5 August 2019).

https://nuclearweaponarchive.org/India/KargilRCB.html 'Kargil Committee Review Report' (Accessed 5 August 2019)

https://www.thehindu.com/2004/02/06/stories/2004020604461200.htm 'Gen. Padmanabhan mulls over lessons of Operation Parakram' by Praveen Swami, The Hindu 06 Feb 2004 (Accessed 5 August 2019)

https://www.indiatoday.in/india/story/kargil-war-meet-shepherd-warned-army-1572296-2019-07-22. 'How the Indian Army came to know of the Kargil Intrusion.' (Accessed 18 August 2019)

https://www.news18.com/news/india/kargil-vijay-diwas-2019-timeline-of-the-1999-operation-vijay-2246563.html. 'The Sequence of military activities from 03 May to 26 May 1999' (Accessed 18 August 2019) https://nuclearweaponarchive.org/India/KargilRCB.html 'Kargil Committee Review Report' (Accessed 18 August 2019)

Paradigm Shift in Myanmar, Uri and Balakot

https://thediplomat.com/2015/06/the-truth-about-indias-militant-strike-in-myanmar/ (Accessed 18 August 2019)

https://www.indiatoday.in/india/story/indian-army-myanmar-operation-details-indian-air-force-256665-2015-06-10 (Accessed 18 August 2019)

Gokhale Nitin, *Securing India Modi Way*, Bloomsbury India, November 2017 ISBN: 9789389000832

Raj Chengappa, Balakot: 'How India planned IAF Strike in Pakistan | An Inside Story,' India Today 15 March 2019 https://www.indiatoday.in/magazine/cover-story/story/20190325-balakot-airstrikes-pulwama-terror-attack-abhinandan-varthaman-narendra-modi-masood-azhar-1478511-2019-03-15 (Accessed 18 August 2019)

Arjun Subramaniam, 'The Indian Air Force Sub-Conventional Operation and Balakot: A Practitioner's Perspective' ORF Issue Brief Number 294, May 2019 https://www.orfonline.org/wp-content/uploads/2019/05/ORF_Issue_Brief_294_IAF-Balakot.pdf (Accessed 18 August 2019)

India's Political Decision Making and Strategies for IW

http://www.indiandefencereview.com/the-aksai-chin-blunder/ Claude Arpi in IDR dated 02 Feb 2017 (Accessed 18 August 2019)

http://www.indiandefencereview.com/spotlights/where-was-indias-tibet-policy-i/ Claude Arpi Where was India's Tibet policy IDR 22 Sep 2014 (Accessed 18 August 2019)

https://www.thehindu.com/thehindu/2002/01/02/stories/2002010201251000.htm 'Partition Debate' (Mushirul Hasan) The Hindu 02 Jan 2002 (Accessed 18 August 2019) https://economictimes.indiatimes.com/news/politics-and-nation/direct-action-day-the-core-of-pak malignancy/articleshow/9618433.cms C Uday Bhaskar, updated on 16 August 2011, 'Direct Action day the core of Pak Malignancy' (Accessed 18 August 2019)

Political Economy and Fault Line

https://rbidocs.rbi.org.in/rdocs/Bulletin/PDFs/01AR1002188F03B36625C14D11BDF24DBA74C137C6.PDF (Accessed 15 May 2019)

http://re.indiaenvironmentportal.org.in/files/An%20estimate%20of%20poverty%20reductionpdf 'An Estimate of Poverty Reduction between 2004-05 and 2005-06' KL Datta (Accessed 15 May 2019)

https://countryeconomy.com/gdp/india 'India's GDP growth rate 2014 to 2018' (Accessed 3 Feb 2019)

https://www.statista.com/statistics/271322/inflation-rate-in-india/ 'India's Inflation Rates 2014-2018' (Accessed 3 Feb 2019)

http://home.fau.edu/sghosh/web/images/India%20talk.pdf 'The Indian Economy since independence' (Accessed 27 Jan 2019) By IW Freedom

India's Strategies for Information War

Policy guidelines on National Services Scheme. https://mhrd.gov.in/nss-and-ncc-programmes-higher-educational-institutions. https://pib.gov.in/newsite/mbErel.aspx?relid=144920

Kashyap C Subhash, *Our Constitution: An Introduction to India's Constitution and Constitutional Law,* National Book Trust India, Fifth Revised Edition ISBN 978-81-237-0734-1

https://data.worldbank.org/indicator/gb.xpd.rsdv.gd.zs (World Bank Data UNESCO Institute of Statistics) Accessed 5 June 2019.

(https://economictimes.indiatimes.com/news/defence/over-15000-killed-in-naxal-violence-since-1980-mha/articleshow/47664197.cms) (Accessed 5 June 2019).

(https://mdoner.gov.in/contentimages/files/ARC_7thReport_Ch12.pdf) (Accessed 5 June 2019).

(https://mea.gov.in/in-focusarticle.htm?18987/Fact+Sheet+on+Jammu+amp+Kashmir (Accessed 5 June 2019).

Gabriel A Richard, Savage L Paul, *Crisis in Command: Mismanagement in the Army*, Himalayan Books, New Delhi 1981

Dixon Norman, *On the Psychology of Military Incompetence*, Jonathan Cape Ltd, 1976, ISBN 0224011618

Sirohi HS, *Top Brass Critical Appraisal of Indian Military Leadership*, Trishul Publication1993, ISBN 8185384169

Menezes SL, *Fidelity and Honour: The Indian Army from the Seventeenth to Twenty-first Century*, Oxford University Press 1999, ISBN 0195650476.

Sen LP, *Slender was the Thread*, Orient Longman 1986, ISBN 0861316924

Brook Henderson, 1962 Report – Report prepared by Lt Gen T B Henderson Brook and (then) Brig PS Bhagat VC, later Lt Gen (www.indiandefencereview.com/wp-content/uploads/2014/03/Top Secret Documents)

Singh Harbaksh VrC (Lt Gen) *War Dispatches: Indo Pak Conflict, 1965*, Lancer International, New Delhi ISBN 81-7062-117-8

Raghavan Srinath, *1971 A Global History of the Creation of Bangladesh*, Permanent Black Publishers (2013) ISBN 81-7824-380-6.

Jagan Mohan PVS, and Chopra Samir, *Eagles Over Bangladesh: The Indian Air Force in the 1971 Bangladesh Liberation War*, Harper Collins Publishers India (2013). ISBN 978-93-5136-163-3

Malik VP, *Kargil from Surprise to Victory*, HarperCollins Publishers India, The India Today Group 2006, ISBN 8172236352

Puri Mohinder (Lt Gen) *Kargil: Turning the Tide*, Lancer Publisher and Distributors (2016) ISBN 13-978-81-7062-312-0.

Roy Basu Shekhar (Editor), *New Approach: Kargil Misadventure in the Hills*, Paperback 2000 https://www.amazon.com/New-Approach-Kargil-Misadventure-Hills/dp/B002RJPPNO

Indian Army Doctrine
https://www.files.ethz.ch/isn/157030/India%202004.pdf

Joint Doctrine Indian Armed Forces 2017
http://ids.nic.in/dot jointdoctrineindianarmedforces2017.pdf

Rohan Mukherjee, David M Malone https://www.researchgate.net/publication/227734908_Indian_foreign_policy_and_contemporary_security_challenges (January 2011).

'A brief History of India's Foreign Policy' Gateway House Publication 15 August 2016 https://www.gatewayhouse.in/wp-content/uploads/2016/08/GH_History-of-Indias-Foreign-Policy.pdf

CD Sahay, *India's Foreign Policy and National Security Strategy.* https://www.vifindia.org/book/2018/november/19/indias-foreign-policy-and-national-security-strategy

Daniels John D, Radebaugh Lee H, Sullivan Daniel P, Salwan Prashant *International Business: Environment and Operations*, Twelfth Edition, Pearson Fourteenth Impression (2016) ISBN 9788131728772 Printed in India by India Binding House

Glossary

Air superiority operations: Action taken by air power to ensure that enemy's air power is not effective in the theatre of operation or the desired combat zone for a specified period of time. Air superiority can be complete or partial.

Assessment: This defines the level of achievement of the objective in terms of cost benefit ratio and other parameters defined to measure efficacy and efficiency of the operation.

Bandwidth: A range of frequencies transmitted without being strongly resisted by the medium is bandwidth. Higher the bandwidth more is the information that can be sent through the system.

Big Data Analysis: Software assisted analysis of unstructured data—comprising of exceptionally high volume, variety, and being generated at extremely high velocity—is termed as big data analysis.

Bit: The binary voltages are known as bits.

Cellular mobile communication 3G, 4G, and 5G: Depicts the generation of mobile communication. While the first two generations of mobile communications were based on the analog systems (continuous waves), hence were slow, short ranged and had very limited capacity of communications. From third generation onwards the mobile communication system has gone digital (discrete voltages depicting logic zero and one). The 3G cellular architecture provides much higher bandwidth and capability. From the fourth generation network itself, the mobile network was seamlessly integrated with the Internet. Thus, all services of the Internet can be accessed on the mobile network as also on the smart phone. The social media revolution commenced from the 4G mobile network.

Computer network attacks (CNA): These are operations intended to disrupt, prohibit access to deteriorate, destroy, and steal information contained in computers, carried out by computer networks or targeting computers and networks. An electronic attack such as use of electronic magnetic force does not fall under CNA but is part of electronic attack.

Cyberspace: Cyberspace includes Internet and other networks that are not connected to the Internet. It also includes transactional networks, which facilitate flow of money as also networks that form part of control systems that allow machines to speak to each other and with human interface.

Cyber warfare: Involves all activities conducted for thefts of contents, denial, manipulation, disruption, and destruction in the cyberspace.

Data: These are facts, concepts, instructions collected in a formalized manner, which can be transmitted and are suitable for communication, interpretation by humans or automated systems. Data can even be in the form of electronic signals (bits) in particular format as per the protocol of the communication system. Data in itself does not make much sense but data is the most valuable asset. Data is being produced by people, machines, activities, and processes with continuously increasing speed. This results in huge volume, velocity, and variety of data. At the same time new technologies are being developed to make sense of this data. Both these developments have led to emergence of 'data war'.

Data centre: A data centre is a physical facility that organizations use to house their critical applications and data. A data centre's design is based on a network of computing and storage resources that enable the delivery of shared applications and data (CISCO).

Data fusion: Combination of inputs from sensors into various representational forms with the primary intention of restricting the bandwidth for transmission of the fused data from the node where the data fusion takes place.

Data integration: For creating synergistic application of information received from different sensors for accomplishing the task.

Decision: This is the most crucial phase in Information Operations (IO) and IW. It involves selecting a given course of action or decision alternative (and foregoing the opportunity cost of not selecting the other alternatives). It is based on the character of the leader, culture, strength of the organization, and type of objective to be achieved.

Decision cycle: In popular literature, decision cycle is defined as the process of observing (the relevant environment), orienting (with respect to the task at hand or objective to be achieved), deciding (on the course of action), and taking action (on the selected course). It is commonly called as OODA cycle. Observe Orient Decide and Action.

Decision support systems: Includes searching, retrieving, and analysing data (relevant to decision) to enable objective (unbiased), timely decision. This can be done manually or through various computer-assisted means.

Digital Communication: Consists of streaming of very small binary voltages depicting logic 0 or 1 (say plus 5 volts is logic one and 0 volt is logic zero) passing from the transmitter to the receiver through selected media or network.

Econnaissance: This involves broad scanning of the area of interest on ground or in the air from where threat is expected.

Economic war: In this component the target again is the political leadership but the objective is to weaken the national economy or keep the economy of the target nation dependent or supportive of own economy. It can also be the first stage of full scale IW with military aim. The means used here are stealing/ blocking of information through Computer Network Exploitation, infringements in the Intellectual Property Rights (IPR), use tariff and non-tariff methods to influence the international trade of the target nation, blockade, sanctions, and technology theft. This can also be launched by using own international alliances to squeeze out the target nation out of international trade.

Electromagnetic spectrum: Movement of electrons produces electromagnetic waves. The electromagnetic spectrum consists of frequencies ranging from 1 hertz per second to 10 raised to power 16 hertz per second. This entire spectrum ranges from low frequency (1 hertz to 10 raised to power 5 hertz) to tremendously high frequency (10 raised to power 11 to 12 hertz) bands. The frequency of the EM wave affects the information carrying capacity, directional nature, and power. At lower frequencies, these waves are much less capable and are not very directional. But suffer low resistance. At higher frequencies these waves become highly directional, carry much more information and power. Knowledge of EM waves and EM spectrum is important to understand cyberspace, sensors, and Electronic War, which we will discuss in the study.

Electronic warfare: All activities undertaken to control electromagnetic spectrum. It involves any military action using directed electromagnetic energy to control the EM spectrum and to attack the enemy.

Event logging: For effectively monitoring the network for an impending security breach. It automatically logs output from the system error messages and other events to the console terminal.

Execution: This part is in the realm of operations. It involves selection of process or approach, identifying the force structure and weapon mix, plan, contingencies, control measures, reserves etc.

Information: Data collected from the relevant environment so that it makes sense for a given situation.

Information assurance: This involves protection of information and information systems by ensuring their availability, integrity, capacity, confidentiality, and their non-repudiation. Three major stages in the process include protection, detection, and reaction. It includes computer security and information security.

Information operations(IO): These are continuous operations within the military information environment that enable, enhance, and protect friendly forces' ability to collect, process, and act on information to achieve an advantage across the full range of military operations. IO includes interacting with global information environment and exploiting or changing an adversary's information and decision capabilities (US Department of Defence). IO includes actions taken to affect adversary's intelligence and information based systems while defending own information and information systems. The core of all these concepts is information system. In-fact the 'enabling' aspect of information system for decision-making further elaborates the importance of this central resource. (US Joint Force Doctrine).

Information warfare: Includes actions taken to preserve the integrity of one's own information system from exploitation, corruption, or disruption, while at the same time exploiting, corrupting, and destroying an adversary's information system and in the process achieving an information advantage in application of force. (Quoted by Edward Waltz in *Information Warfare Principles and Operations* from Joint Chiefs of Staff Publication 1-02, March 1995).

Integrated control enablers (ICE): These are enablers that ensure control over the enemy. The ICE includes network operations, ISR, predictive battlespace awareness, precision navigation, and precision targeting.

Intelligence: Comparison information in the context of prevalent environment or background knowledge or other pieces of current information and interpretation in the context of problem or objective at hand, which should eliminate deception/ manipulation by the adversary and should generate various decision alternatives/ courses of action.

Interdiction: The process of separating the enemy forces in contact from their follow up and logistic elements. Primarily undertaken by the air force or long-range artillery.

Interoperability: The ability of computer systems or software to exchange and make use of information. The ability of military equipment or groups to operate in conjunction with each other. Just like synergy, the environment of inter-operability also is a cultural aspect. It emanates from the bottom of the organizational hierarchy and is supported from the top hierarchy.
In the 'Joint Doctrine Indian Armed Forces' the SF are tasked to support offensive and defensive operations; these are specially selected troops (perhaps for their mental and physical robustness and commitment to duty). These forces are trained and equipped to operate in territory isolated from the main combat forces. They have deep reach with precision strike capability and are versatile. The impact of Special Forces operations depends on the quality of intelligence and stealth. These forces operate under direct strategic control and mission command.

Knowledge: There is no universally acceptable definition of knowledge. Neither is it our purpose to go into the details of various philosophies where the issue is addressed in different ways. For the purpose of this study, knowledge is created by processing, analysing, and reflecting on the information collected by our sensory systems as also by the sensors deployed for the purpose with a view to support current or future decisions in designated environment. Hence, knowledge will be objective, tacit, and contextual. There will be scope for abstract and conceptual knowledge in relation to situation at hand.

Knowledge management (KM): KM is a discipline that promotes a collaborative and integrated approach to the creation, capture, organization, access, and use of information assets of an organization.

Lock and Key security: Primarily deals with traffic filtering with the ability to allow temporary access through the firewall for certain individuals. The entry is through authentication; after the transaction, the firewall closes the temporary access.

Media: This is part of the physical path (also called physical layer) in between the network machines and components through which the packets move between the transmission and receiver.

Meta propaganda: This in fact is fake news. Also includes biased publications pushing false media which distort public perception for political gain.

Military cyberspace: All networks, communications, and data centres specifically used by the military, weapon platforms (aircraft, tanks, missiles, logistics elements in installation and on the move, networked soldiers in combat). This cyberspace is generally considered in isolation from the non-military users though such an isolation is almost impossible to create and maintain. It should also include social media network in the area of interest and influence; the digitized national media reporting on the military activities must form part of the military cyberspace.

Military deception: These are series of measures designed to deceive the enemy by manipulating, deteriorating, or falsifying evidence to trigger a reaction that is detrimental to his interests. It is meant for the enemy decision makers by affecting their information collection and analysis process. Military deception aims at desired behaviour of the adversary. Hence, for successful deception we need to know the way the enemy thinks and takes decisions, the information collection networks and processes for decision making, information dissemination systems through which the decisions are conveyed for execution, physical activities that are undertaken by the enemy for executing a given decision.

Netwar: Its objective is perception management of target population to bring about desired influence on national behaviour. The targets are society at large, which can include political, military, and political spheres. Primarily exploits the Internet, electronic, print, and social media.

Network-centric warfare: It is about human and organizational behaviour. Focuses on combat power that can be generated by effective linking of warfighting entities. Geographically dispersed forces create a high level of shared battlespace awareness that can be exploited to achieve the commander's intent.

Network address translation (NAT): It can be used to hide internal IP network addresses from the world outside the firewall. NAT can also be configured to advertise only one address for the entire internal network. This provides security by effectively hiding the internal network from the outside world.

Network data encryption: This selectively encrypts IP packets that are transmitted across external network.

Operational level: In the context of our study the operational domain lies at the theatre level. For instance, Western Theatre, Northern Theatre and so on. In India, there are five operational theatres responsible for the Northern, Western, Eastern, Southern, and South Western geographical regions of our territory. Besides, we have Central and Training Commands.

Operations security: All activities and processes that prevent the enemy from accessing critical information, which can help him in discerning our plans and intentions are grouped under OPSEC.

Outcome: This is a measure of impact of the operational success at the strategic level in terms of the overall goal and the vision at the higher defence organization or even at the level of the political leadership. It is strategic in nature.

Output: This is in relation to the immediate objective of the execution plan. It is part of the operational mechanism and hence tactical in nature.

Packet: It consists of a specified number of bits (say 32 bits) which consists of address of the recipient, some information and other signatures such as end of the packet, synchronization etc. Thus in short, message is in the form of logic one and zero. If the receiving machine finds that the packet is meant for it (from the address bits), the packet is processed, else it is allowed to go through.

Packet Switching: This mode is also called store and forward in which an intermediate machine in the network stores the packets until a transmission route to the destination is free. Thus a single message consisting of a large number of packets can travel through different routes in the network and get assembled back into the original message at the destination. The message does contain the start and the end so that the destination machine knows that the entire message has arrived. It is important to understand this to identify the tools and techniques used in cyber war.

Perception management: As per the US Department of Defence, perception management involves actions to convey or/and deny selected information and indicators to target the audience to influence their emotions, motives, and objective reasoning. This is also done to target intelligence systems, leaders. The overall goal is to shape the response as per the originator's objectives. There are several tools used such as atrocity accusation, hyperbolic inflation, demonization, and dehumanization, polarization, claim of divine sanction, and meta-propaganda.

Political war: This component of IW is in the non-military part of the conflict spectrum where the adversary uses diplomacy, institutions of the target nation (judiciary, media, political sympathizer in the target political systems etc.) to subvert the decision making and policies at the political level.

Precision-guided munitions: These are projectiles, bombs, or missiles which are enabled to hit the designated target with designed accuracy say from ten to one meter or even less than one meter. These can be guided in their entire trajectory from the launch to destination or in the immediate vicinity of the target. When the guidance is within the immediate vicinity the guidance is terminal guidance.

Psychological operations: To manipulate desired changes in the behaviour of the target group of people, nation, society, by concerted use of various components of information systems. It would involve engaging with media.

Repeaters, hubs, bridges, switches, routers, and gateways: These are network components that are capable of receiving the packets, reading the relevant parts of the message in each packet, and sending these to the desired destinations or channels. All these components are programmed and can be manipulated by the hackers or cyber criminals. These can also contain embedded cyber weapons.

Sensor network: A collection of networked sensor entities to create battlespace awareness.

Sensors: In the context of our study, these are devices that pick up the target information based on the selected properties of the target. These include thermal signatures (heat emission and distribution around the target), seismic activities (ground vibrations), light signals (even in the night) which are picked up by image intensifiers, Electromagnetic Radiations (active sensors based on the EM radiations pick up the reflected waves – RADAR) whereas the passive sensors pick up the EM radiations emitted by the target. Inputs received by the sensors are amplified to make the observation possible and easy. Besides, inputs coming from a network or series of sensors can be integrated (to make a comprehensive analysis) or diffused to ensure transmission at optimal bandwidth.

Special Forces (SF): For our study, these forces are extremely important hence somewhat detailed description. These forces are generally drawn from some parent organizations (Parachute units of the army, marine units of the navy as also from the air force, police and paramilitary organizations etc.). SF are characterized by exceptionally high level of motivation, mental and physical robustness, commitment to the task, highly sophisticated weapon systems and accompanying skills to optimize the use of these systems. Their operational characteristics include capability to undertake a range of unconventional tasks, operate in small teams away from their traditional support base, survive off the land without major logistic support, create required level of destruction with precision and speed, infiltrate deep behind the enemy lines to undertake tasks of strategic nature and conduct exfiltration using stealth and speed. The tasks these forces perform are generally beyond the capability of their regular parent organizations. Some of the characteristic tasks undertaken by the SF are direct action involving seek and destroy, special reconnaissance of strategic target, undertake coercive and disruptive operations to overthrow the target government, counter-terrorism operations of high strategic value, hostage rescue, military information support, foreign humanitarian assistance, security force assistance, civil affairs operations. Since these are strategic resources, the SF are under direct command of theatre commanders. It is extremely important to employ SF very judiciously to derive maximum benefit from their superior capability. The tendency to employ SF for tasks that can be undertaken by the regular parent organizations must be curbed. As per Katoch, drawing Special Forces from the Parachute Regiment is patently wrong policy. The initial Special Forces personnel were not drawn from the Parachute Regiment [9 and 10 Para (SF)]. In 1990 this anomaly was corrected by delinking Parachute Regiment and the SF but the retired officers' lobby of Parachute Regiment prevailed upon the then Chief of Army Staff (COAS) to group SF with Parachute regiment. Again, Katoch feels that the SF in India have been continuously neglected. (from 'India's Special Forces History and Future of Indian Special Forces' by PC Katoch and Saikat Dutta. See endnotes)

Strategy: The dictionary meaning of strategy is 'a plan for achieving something'. Another definition from the Oxford Advanced Learner's dictionary is 'the art of planning operations in war'. Besides, there are definitions or descriptions of strategies in business studies (Mintzberg, Porter etc.). None of these dictionary meanings or descriptions of strategies will suit us here. Our emphasis here is on 'why' and not on 'what'. Thus for the purpose of this study we will define strategy as a combination of core ideology of the nation comprising of the intrinsic and shared value system defining the purpose of the nation to exist in specified geographical context. From these eternal core values and purpose of existence, emanate the visions, mission, and the goals, and approach to realize the vision and the goals. Except for the core values and the purpose, everything else is flexible.

Supply chain management: For the purpose of this study we will address the issue from two perspectives. First, from the perspective of cyber security and second, from the perspective of indigenization. In the context of cyber security, supply chain involves two or more independent companies entering into partnership to deliver goods or services in an environment of cooperation for exploiting their respective core competencies for enhancing over-all quality of the product or the service. Thus if we are getting IT products or services from a company then we need to realize that the concept of original manufacturer needs to be seen in the context of supply chain since many companies in several countries may be involved in delivering the product or service. In the context of indigenization, the emphasis is on cooperation, commitment, commonality of goals across the supply chain including the customer. For making indigenization a success without diluting quality, inclusion of customer in the supply chain is very critical.

Surveillance: This involves focusing on the specific target or area where some elements of threat have been manifested. When a target or area is under surveillance the follow-up action plans of warning, engaging, or neutralizing the target are completely ready to be activated.

Synergy: In the simplest form, synergy is an environment or system where two or more entities, organizations, forces work together in a manner that the combined output from this system is greater than the sum total of outputs from individual entities had these been working separately. It needs to be noted that in many cases especially in the military environment if the forces act independently their efforts may even neutralize each other's gains. Synergy is generated by organizational culture, inter-operability of communications and systems and willingness to subjugate individual projections for the sake of the organizational goals.

Transmission control protocol (TCP) intercept: It protects TCP servers within the network from TCP SYN flooding attacks—a type of denial of service attack.

User authentication and authorization: This is primarily to protect thenetwork from an unauthorized user.

Wisdom: For our purpose, wisdom is characterized by asking the right question. Wisdom is directed at visualizing the outcome or impact in the long run as against focusing on immediate result or output. It is linked with the core ideology and the vision and not with the operational objectives or even the processes.

★★★

Type I (Internal) Network Weapons

Bacteria: It is a small replicating program independent of the host. Its tendency to replicate/eat up memory storage cripples the terminal.

Logic bomb: These are hidden program (logic)in a software, which get activated on a trigger(command)to carry out software destruction function.

Trap doors: These are installed in the program, which provides a covert channel to information in the network/host. The logic is known only to the supplier of the software.

Trojan horse: It is a malicious program hidden in any apparently legitimate program that contains a hidden hostile function. These may be inserted directly into the application program or through compilers that transform source to object codes.

Virus: Virus is a small program, which has the property of multiplying. A virus is always attached to a host program. The rate of increase of types of virus is phenomenal. Introducing a new virus and then the antidote to it has become a very profitable commercial activity in the software community. Virus is of three types; the basic virus has a replicating code. Static stealth virus is encrypted. It has a replicating code and encrypts dormant code to hide static signature. Its crypto key changes to dynamically modify program to change signature. Lastly the dynamic stealth virus has replicating code, encryption and decryption viral code and dynamic key mutation engine to change decryption code.

Worm: It is similar to bacteria but has the capability to travel from host to host in a network. Also, worms can carry out useful tasks if suitably introduced by the network maintenance and management staff.

★★★

Type II (External) Weapons

High energy laser (HEL) weapons: LASER-beams can be used to target sensitive photonic devices with hundreds of kilowatts of power to damage LASER seekers, range finders, target designators, surveillance and other electro-optical sensors over a sufficiently long range.

High energy particle weapons: Intensive research is being done to use charged neutral particle beams to directly transmit particle to a target, penetrating into its internal structure. The transfer of energy is sufficient and lethal to both electronic and mechanical components.

- High power microwave (HPM) weapons. The principle of HPM is based on creating a space charge of electron cloud. This space charge is then made to resonate in a cavity thus producing very high microwave power from 170 KV to 40 gigawatts over frequencies spanning the decametric and centimetric bands.
- High voltages of the order of ten to fifty kilovolts in an area of 300 to 400 square meters (based on the height of explosion) produced by flux compression generator (in which explosion of the device is used to produce the magnetic field).
- Low frequency weapons are being designed for damaging or destroying magnetic media including database web sites and so on.
- Magneto hydrodynamic (MHD) generators. Plasma of ionized gas is made to flow in a magnetic field. The resultant back electromotive force generated current is collected at the

electrodes. These are used to generate the initial current for the FCG weapons.

Microbes: These are very small biological weapons, targeted at the vulnerable components of IT equipment such as rubber, sealant, and electrical connection and are external to the system used to carry out destruction.

Nanomachines: Nanomachines are extremely small robotic-equipment which are unseen by human eyes and cause damage to the electronic equipment when stimulated by an external source. These can be self-programmed also.

Non-nuclear EMP: Generated in a number of ways, such as explosively pumped Flux Compression Generator (FCG). An FCG device uses the explosion to compress a magnetic field thus producing an electrical flux. This flux (voltage per meter) can be of the order of 10 to 50 kilo volts per meter. Another device used is magneto hydrodynamic (MHO) generator. The principle of MHO is again based on the Faraday's laws of electromagnetism. The conductor in this case is plasma of ionized gas. This is made to flow in a magnetic field. The resultant back electromotive force generated current is collected at the electrodes. The MHO devices are used to generate the initial current for the FCG weapons. Another method of generating the high voltage in the chosen target area is high power microwave (HPM) weapons. The principle of HPM is based on creating a space charge of electron cloud. This space charge is then made to resonate in a cavity thus producing very high microwave power from 170 KVV to 40 Giga watts over frequencies spanning the decametric and cent metric bands.

Passive conductive measures: The dispersal of conductive materials in filament form can be used as a potential passive weapon that can affect sensitive electronic equipment, exposed power wiring, or transformer grid.

List of Abbreviations

4IR:	Fourth Industrial Revolution (term used by World Economic Forum)
5G:	Fifth Generation Wireless Communication
ACCCS:	Artillery Combat Command and Control System
AI:	Artificial Intelligence
AIS (Data):	Automatic Identification System
ASEAN:	Association of South East Asian Nations
ATC:	Air Traffic Control
AWAC:	Airborne Warning and Control
BSF:	Border Security Force
BSS:	Battlefield Surveillance System
C2:	Command and Control
C2W:	Command and Control Warfare
CAN:	Controller Area Network
CBI:	Central Bureau of Investigation
CCS:	Cabinet Committee on Security

CDMA: Code-Division Multiple Access

CIA: Central Intelligence Agency

CID: Crime Investigation Department

CIDSS: Command Information & Decision Support System

CISF: Central Industrial Security Force

CNE: Computer Network Exploitation

CNN: Cable News Network

CNO: Computer Network Operations

CNP: Comprehensive National Power

COAS: Chief of Army Staff

COTS: Commercial Off-the-Shelf

CRIS: Centre for Railway Information Systems

CRPF: Central Reserve Police Force

DARPA: Defence Advanced Research Projects Agency (a US organization)

DCOG: Defence Cyber Operations Group

DDoS: Distributed Denial of Services

DHS: Department of Homeland Security

DIPP: Department of Industrial Policy and Promotion

DIT: Department of Information Technology

DKNY: Dona Karan New York

DNS: Domain Name System

DRDO: Defence Research and Development Organization

DSS:	Decision Support System
ECCM:	Electronic Counter-Counter Measures
ECM:	Electronic Countermeasure
EDI:	Electronic Data Interchange
EMP:	Electromagnetic Pulse
ESM:	Electronic Support Measures
FBI:	Federal Bureau of Investigation
FDI:	Foreign Direct Investment
FPS:	Frames Per Second
GCI:	Global Competitiveness Index
GDP:	Gross Domestic Product
GHz:	Gigahertz
GOSCC:	Global Operations and Security Control Centre
GPS:	Global Positioning System
GSM:	Global System for Mobile Communications (European systems based on time and frequency division multiplexing)
GST:	Goods and Services Tax
HDI:	Human Development Index
HEL:	High Energy LASER
HERF:	High-Energy Radio Frequency
HPM:	High Power Microwave
Humint:	Human Intelligence (collected by own troops/ agents)

IB:	Intelligence Bureau (Indian organization for internal intelligence)
ICC:	International Cricket Council
ICE:	Integrated Cyber Environment
ICT:	Information and Communications Technology
IDF:	Israeli Defence Forces
IDSA:	Institute of Defence Studies and Analyses
IL:	Industrial License
INA:	Indian National Army
INDONET:	INDONET Data Network engineered by the Computer Maintenance Corporation of India Ltd has an integrated information management distributed data processing facility
INDU:	Indian National Defence University
INEW:	Integrated Network Electronic Warfare
Infosys:	Information Systems
IO:	Information Operations
IoT:	Internet of Things
IPKF:	Indian Peace Keeping Forces (was deployed in Sri Lanka from 1987 to 1990)
IPR:	Intellectual Property Rights
ISIL:	Islamic State of Iraq and The Levant
ISIS:	Islamic State of Iraq and Syria
ISR:	Intelligence, Surveillance, and Reconnaissance
ITBP:	Indo-Tibetan Border Police

ITU:	International Telecommunication Union
IW:	Information War
JNU:	Jawaharlal Nehru University
JSTAR:	Joint Surveillance and Target Attack RADAR
KM:	Knowledge Management
KYKL:	Kanglei Yawol Kanna Lup
LAC:	Line of Actual Control
LASER:	Light Amplification by Stimulated Emission of Electromagnetic Radiation
LL:	Less- Lethal
LoC:	Line of Control
LTE Latency:	Referred to the delay in transmission of signal/ command and its receipt/activation. In 5G this delay is minimal hence the remote controlled systems work much better in 5G networks
MAC:	Multi Agency Centre (for collecting police-related intelligence from multiple agencies of the states and country in India)
MEA:	Ministry of External Affairs
MHA:	Ministry of Home Affairs
MHD:	Magnetohydrodynamics
MIT:	Massachusetts Institute of Technology
MNC:	Multinational Company
MoD:	Ministry of Defence
NAFTA:	North American Free Trade Agreement

NAT:	Network Address Translation
NATO:	North Atlantic Treaty Organization
NFU:	Non Functional Financial Up-gradation
NIC:	National Informatics Centre
NICNET:	A satellite-based network set up by the Planning Commission to provide information to government and state departments for decision making
NIST:	National Institute of Standards and Technology
NL:	Non-Lethal
NSA:	National Security Adviser
NSCN:	National Socialist Council of Nagaland
NSG:	National Security Guard
NTRO:	National Technical Research Organization
OIC:	Organization of Islamic Cooperation
OODA:	Observe Orient Decide and Act
Opsec:	Operational Security
PCA:	Pakistan Cyber Army
PLA:	People's Liberation Army
PNG:	Piped Natural Gas
PoK:	Pakistan Occupied Kashmir
Psyops:	Psychological Operations
R&AW:	Research and Analysis Wing (Indian organization for external intelligence)
R:	A programming language developed by Ross Ihaka and Robert Gentleman in 1993

RADAR: Radio Detection and Ranging

RBI: Reserve Bank of India

RF: Radio Frequency

RMA: Revolution in Military Affairs

SCADA: Supervisory Control and Data Acquisition

SCM: Supply Chain Management

SF: Special Forces

Sigint: Signals Intelligence

SMAC: Subsidiary Multi Agency Centre, to support the MAC

SME: Small and Medium Enterprise

SOP: Standard Operating Procedure

SPSS: Statistical Package for the Social Sciences

SSB: Sashastra Seema Bal

SWOT: Strengths, Weaknesses, Opportunities, and Threats

Sync: Synchronization

TCP/IP: Transport Control Protocol/Internet Protocol

TIP: Turkistan Islamic Party

TRADOC: Training and Doctrine Command

UNEP: United Nations Environment Program

UNSC: United Nations Security Council

USAF: United States Air Force

USI: United Service Institution of India

VSS:	Vessel Selection System (Use of AI by US Navy)
WEF:	World Economic Forum
WTC:	World Trade Center
WTO:	World Trade Organization